Aleksandra Božović

THE HOLY TRINITY OF THE XXI CENTURY

VOLUME II

GUIDE THROUGH EMOTIONAL INTELLIGENCE

FSC
www.fsc.org
MIX
Papier aus verantwortungsvollen Quellen
Paper from responsible sources
FSC® C105338

Editing and proofreading: Aleksandra Božović
Additional contributors:
Tatjana Božović
Alexandra Allemann
Ana Tucović

Illustrations and graphic design:
Created with the help of artificial intelligence, based on the ideas of:
Aleksandra Božović
Graphic design: Ana Tucović, 2025

Publisher: BoD · Books on Demand GmbH, Überseering 33, 22297 Hamburg, bod@bod.de
Printing: Libri Plureos GmbH, Friedensallee 273, 22763 Hamburg

ISBN: 978-3-6963-8191-2

CONTENTS

CONTENTS **5**

INTRODUCTION **12**

EMOTIONAL INTELLIGENCE **14**

The Importance of Practicing Emotional Intelligence *16*

Why Is Emotional Intelligence Important? *17*

KEY ELEMENTS FOR DEVELOPING EMOTIONAL LITERACY 18

Emotional Abilities *18*

Cognitive Abilities *18*

Behavioral Abilities *19*

ELEMENTS OF EMOTIONAL INTELLIGENCE 19

Knowing One`s Own Emotions *20*

Managing Emotions *21*

Motivating Yourself *22*

Recognizing Emotions in Others *23*

Navigating Relationships *24*

How to Recognize People with High Emotional Intelligence? *25*

How to Recognize People with Low Emotional Intelligence? *26*

Emotional Intelligence in Interpersonal Relationships *26*

Why Are Emotionally Intelligent People More Successful in Life? *26*

Developing Emotional Intelligence *27*

AMYGDALA **29**

DRIVERS OF HUMAN BEHAVIOR (IMPRINTS, TRIGGERS, AND DRIVERS)...33

IMPRINT (IMPRINTING)...35

CRITICAL PERIODS IN WHICH IMPRINTS ARE FORMED...36

TYPES OF IMPRINTS IN HUMANS...38

Supportive Imprint...*38*

Limiting Imprint...*38*

Psychological Imprint...*39*

Cultural Imprint...*39*

Traumatic Imprint...*40*

Filial Imprint (Emotional Imprint)...*42*

Sexual Imprint...*43*

Limbic Imprint...*43*

METHODS FOR CLEARING IMPRINTS...44

HOW TO RECOGNIZE YOUR OWN IMPRINT?..46

Ways to recognize imprints...*47*

HOW TO TRANSFORM IMPRINTS?...50

TRIGGER POINTS / TRIGGERS...56

TYPES OF TRIGGERS...65

External Triggers...*65*

Internal Triggers...*66*

Somatic (Bodily) Triggers...*67*

Emotional Triggers...*69*

Anxious Triggers...*70*

Angry Triggers...*70*

Depressive Triggers...*71*

Traumatic Triggers 72
Developmental Triggers 74
Collective Triggers 75
HOW TO RECOGNIZE TRIGGERS? 76
WHAT TO DO WITH TRIGGERS? 79
DRIVERS 88
"Be Perfect!" 91
"Be Strong!" 92
"Please Others!" 93
"Try Hard!" 94
Conclusion: How are imprints, triggers, and drivers connected? 97
INTUITION / THE SIXTH SENSE 100
WHAT IS INTUITION? 100
THE CONCEPT, STUDY, AND INTERPRETATION OF INTUITION THROUGH HISTORY 102
HOW TO AWAKEN YOUR INTUITION? 106
How and when can you use the power of intuition? 109
How to Connect with Your Intuition When You Are in Trouble? 109
INTUITION AND EXTRASENSORY PERCEPTION 111
How to Strengthen Extrasensory Perception? 112
Signs That You Have a Well-Developed Intuition 113
HOW TO DISTINGUISH THE VOICE OF INTUITION FROM THE VOICE OF THE EGO? 116
VISUALIZATION 125
HOW DOES VISUALIZATION WORK? 128

I Principle: Formulate the Desire Correctly *129*

II Principle: Present the Final Result *129*

III Principle: Complete Immersion *130*

IV Principle: Add Dynamics *130*

V Principle: Visualize at the Right Time *131*

What Is the Role and Significance of Visualization in an Individual`s Life? *132*

How do other sciences and disciplines explain the concept and importance of visualization? *134*

What is the difference between visualization and manifestation? .. *138*

MANIFESTATION 141

HOW TO TURN DESIRE INTO EXPERIENCE? 141

THE ART OF MANIFESTATION – CREATE YOUR OWN DESTINY 145

BENEFITS OF THE ART OF MANIFESTATION147

Why is manifestation important? *149*

AKASHA RECORDS 153

WHAT IS IN THE AKASHIC RECORDS? 155

What is the benefit of knowing the Akasha Records method? *156*

Can everyone read the Akasha Record, and how? *157*

FIFTH DIMENSION 163

Key aspects of entering the fifth dimension in a spiritual sense *169*

Thought – forms *171*

Causal plane *172*

Life in the third dimension *174*

Transition through the fourth dimension – 4D *175*

The Fifth Dimension - Coming Home *177*

ASTRAL PROJECTION 193

WHAT IS ASTRAL PROJECTION AND WHAT IS IT FOR? 193

History and origins 195

BENEFITS OF ASTRAL PROJECTION 201

CHARACTERISTICS OF ASTRAL TRAVEL 202

TYPES AND VARIETIES OF OUT-OF-BODY EXPERIENCE 203

ASTRAL PROJECTION PROCEDURE 206

What if astral projection isn't working? 213

LUCID DREAMS 214

BENEFITS OF LUCID DREAMING 216

CHARACTERISTICS & WAYS TO INDUCE LUCID DREAMS 218

TELEPATHY 221

THE BRIDGE BETWEEN MIND AND CONSCIOUSNESS 221

Quantum Entanglement 224

TYPES OF TELEPATHY 230

SEXUAL TRANSMUTATION 235

Sexual Transmutation Is Not Celibacy 236

WHY IS SEXUAL TRANSMUTATION IMPORTANT? 239

BENEFITS OF SEXUAL TRANSMUTATION 240

MEDITATION 244

Meditation Through the Ages 245

What Is Meditation? 245

TYPES OF MEDITATION 246
HOW TO MEDITATE?.. 247
Why Is Meditation Important in the XXI Century? 249
THE POWER OF SILENCE: THE PRACTICE OF STILLNESS (DAYS OF SILENCE) 251
WHAT IS STILLNESS PRACTICE?.......................... 251
Silence Across Traditions... 252
BENEFITS OF PRACTICE OF STILLNESS (DAY OF SILENCE) 254
HOW TO BEGIN YOUR DAY OF SILENCE?....... 258
GRATITUDE JOURNAL............................. 266
Morning Gratitude Practice 266
Evening Reflection Practice.. 267
Inspirational Quotes on Gratitude... 268
Daily Affirmations.. 269
THETA HEALING 272
Touch the Divine Within.. 272
WHAT IS THETA HEALING? 272
HOW DOES THETA HEALING WORK? 277
How can Theta Healing help remove blocks and improve quality of life?.. 280
THE SILVA METHOD — THE SECRET POWER BEHIND YOUR SUCCESS............. 284
KEY TECHNIQUES OF THE SILVA METHOD.. 285
HO'OPONOPONO: THE POWER OF FORGIVENESS AND INNER HEALING...298

WHAT IS HO'OPONOPONO? 298
From Traditional Ritual to a Modern Method *300*
HOW AND WHY DOES HO'OPONOPONO WORK? 302
WHAT IS HO'OPONOPONO USED FOR? 305
HOW TO APPLY HO'OPONOPONO IN DAILY LIFE? 307
VISION AND LIFE PURPOSE 319
A Scientific Perspective on Life Purpose *319*
The Spiritual Dimension of Vision and Purpose *320*
WHEN PURPOSE IS MISSING 323
THE BENEFITS OF A CLEAR PURPOSE 324
My Path to Purpose *329*
CLOSING WORDS OF THIS VOLUME 333
ABOUT THE AUTHOR 337

THE HOLY TRINITY OF THE XXI CENTURY

INTRODUCTION

"Emotional maturity does not mean
that you do not feel everything –
it means that you know how
to move through all your feelings
without losing yourself."
Aleksandra Božović

There comes a moment in the inner journey when we no longer search for answers outside – instead, we begin to listen to the fragile, quiet messages within. This is the place where the mind retreats into silence, and the heart begins to speak.

The first volume of this trilogy was dedicated to mental intelligence – clarity of thought, inner dialogues, patterns, and the structure of conscious creation. It gave us orientation, a language to understand the world, and the power of conscious choice. Yet no thought, no change in belief can be complete without emotional connection – without meeting what we truly feel. This is precisely where the second part of this holy trinity begins.

Emotional intelligence is not an addition to mental development – it is its depth. If the mental level is the architect who builds bridges, the emotional level is the river beneath them. A river that remembers everything that ever happened. A river that carries both beauty and sorrow, wounds and joy. And if we truly want to understand ourselves, we must dare to step into that river.

This volume is an invitation to descend from the head into the heart. Emotions are our inner guides. They tell us what is authentic, what is suppressed, where we are in balance and where we are not. When we ignore them, they shout through the body – as tension, fatigue, anxiety, or blockages. When we embrace them, they guide us back to ourselves.

In this part of the guide, we will step into the world of vulnerability and strength. We will learn how to recognize feelings, how to express them, how to transform them. We will look into our inner child, the one that may still be waiting for an embrace, for recognition, for safety. We will learn how to become parents to ourselves.

We will talk about boundaries, about when emotions are a message and when they become a burden. About how love is not only a feeling but also a skill. About how the deepest freedom is the freedom to be who we are, with everything that exists within us.

And remember: emotional maturity is not about never feeling pain – it is about understanding it, carrying it with awareness, and knowing how to grow from it.

This volume is dedicated to the heart. To the one that remembers, to the one waiting to be set free, and to the one that beats in its own rhythm and leads us toward wholeness.

Welcome to the second part of your holy trinity. To the space where emotion becomes wisdom, and every tear – strength.

EMOTIONAL INTELLIGENCE

"A feeling is the word we invented
to describe our awareness of the vibration we are in –
and our thoughts are the ones that control that vibration."
Aleksandra Božović

In this chapter we will explore emotional intelligence, which forms an essential part of the Holy Trinity of the XXI century.

Throughout evolution and human development, emotions have long been seen as wise guides. However, modern civilizational changes unfold at such speed that evolution struggles to keep pace. The first laws and ethical codes, such as Hammurabi's Code and the Ten Commandments, can be interpreted as early attempts to restrain and domesticate emotional life. In other words, society had to establish rules to regulate the untamed emotions that govern the human being.

Emotions are one of the most important factors influencing the overall functioning of an individual. They are impulses that move us and play a key role in each person's life. At the root of the word **emotion** lies the Latin word **motere**, which means **"to move."** This points to the fact that every emotion carries a driving force and stimulates change. Another interpretation defines emotion as "an electromagnetic impulse in motion" – in other words, energy in motion.

The basic groups of emotions can be divided into:

- **Anger:** resentment, rage, fury, agitation, bitterness, hatred, restlessness, hostility, grudge, irritability, violence.
- **Sadness:** pain, grief, gloom, loneliness, despair, depression, self-pity.
- **Fear:** anxiety, nervousness, worry, caution, dread, tension, fright, chill, horror.
- **Joy:** happiness, pleasure, delight, enthusiasm, sensual enjoyment, relief, bliss, pride, ecstasy, cheerfulness, euphoria.

- **Love:** acceptance, trust, kindness, loyalty, affection, devotion, adoration.
- **Surprise:** shock, astonishment, amazement, bewilderment.
- **Disgust:** disdain, contempt, repulsion, rejection, aversion, loathing.
- **Shame:** discomfort, guilt, humiliation, misery, regret, remorse.

Since the rational part of our mind needs a moment longer to register and respond, the "first impulse" in emotional situations comes from **the heart**, not from the head. Of course, there is another kind of emotional reaction – one that develops through thoughts. This slower process includes evaluating and forming a conclusion about a situation, which then leads to an emotion. For example, the thought "My boss annoys me" or "Today is truly a beautiful sunny day" provokes a corresponding emotional response. In this case, thoughts precede emotions.

On the other hand, in quick and instinctive reactions, emotions come before thoughts – or simultaneously. Such reactions are especially significant when survival needs are at stake – in those moments, emotions take the lead.

The most intense feelings we experience are often unconscious reactions we cannot control. Love, like anger and fear, arises independently of our will. That is why we often hear people say they did something "because of emotions," even though they did not choose them. Imagine the strength of a person who learns to master what cannot be controlled.

The rational mind does not choose which emotions we feel – they simply arise. However, it can influence the flow of those emotions. And this is precisely what we learn in this chapter: how to recognize emotions in ourselves and others, and how to express, channel, and shape them appropriately.

The cooperation between the emotional and rational mind can be imagined as a dialogue between **heart and head**. When we feel in our heart that something is right, that conviction is often stronger than any rational conclusion. Still, the head has an important role – to clarify, analyze, and structure what the heart sends.

The concept of "emotional intelligence" is quite new. It was introduced only in 1990 by professors **Salovey and Mayer**, who defined it as "the ability to monitor one's own and other people's emotions, to distinguish between them, and to use this information to guide one's thinking and actions." But it was not until 1995 that this concept gained wide popularity, not only in psychological circles but also in social and professional fields, when science journalist and psychologist **Daniel Goleman** reintroduced it with the following definition:

"It is the ability to recognize our own feelings and those of others, to motivate ourselves, and to manage emotions well in ourselves and in our relationships."

This kind of intelligence allows us to become aware that emotions can guide human behavior and influence other people, but above all, it enables us to learn how to manage them. It is also defined as a kind of **"bridge" between mind and heart**, which allows us to consciously and intelligently use what we feel and perceive.

According to Goleman, emotional intelligence consists of two different types of skills, each with specific characteristics.

Personal skills:

- **Self-awareness:** understanding one's internal states, limits, and resources, and trusting one's own abilities.
- **Self-regulation:** the ability to manage one's inner states, impulses, and resources, and to know how to adapt and feel "at home" in new and unfamiliar situations.
- **Motivation:** striving toward goals by knowing how to seize opportunities, making an effort, and remaining persistent despite difficulties, obstacles, or failures.
-

Social skills:

- **Empathy:** the ability to understand the feelings, needs, and interests of others, to meet the needs of another person, and to help them express themselves and their own resources.

- **Social skills:** those abilities that elicit desired responses from others, such as persuasion tactics, effective communication, conflict management, and teamwork.

Emotional intelligence, therefore, represents a blend of **empathy, self-control, motivation, logic, adaptability, and the ability to manage one's own emotions.**

Why Is Emotional Intelligence Important?

Goleman also believes that in **personal, social, and professional relationships, it is not so much the intelligence** quotient that matters, but emotional intelligence. Being able to read, write, and perform complex calculations are important skills, but they are not sufficient to succeed in various areas of life.

Let us take a practical example: in order to pass a particularly difficult university exam or perform well on a school test, it is not enough to have an average or high IQ. One also needs strong emotional intelligence to manage the stress and anxiety that such a situation can trigger, without being overwhelmed and without jeopardizing the final result.

And not only that: above all, **higher emotional intelligence enables us to better understand ourselves**, making us capable of making decisions based on both logic and feelings. A high level of emotional intelligence is linked to **higher self-esteem** and, consequently, a greater likelihood of being satisfied with one's life. Moreover, emotional intelligence is a fundamental condition for building good relationships with other people, enabling us to understand how they feel and to express our own emotions clearly and functionally.

This kind of intelligence allows us to reduce anxiety, **overcome the hardest challenges, calm conflicts, communicate effectively, and empathize with others**, accepting those who are different. Thus, we can build better social, family, emotional, and professional relationships. On the other hand, a person with low emotional intelligence may struggle to manage their own emotions and to understand the emotions of others, which results in a less fulfilling life.

Many people wonder whether emotional intelligence is innate or whether it is a form of intelligence that can be learned and trained over time. The good news is that, while it may be true that some people have a natural tendency toward developing this kind of intelligence, it is equally true that it can be trained – just like a muscle.

KEY ELEMENTS FOR DEVELOPING EMOTIONAL LITERACY

Emotional Abilities

- Identifying and labeling feelings
- Expressing feelings
- Assessing the intensity of feelings
- Managing feelings
- Delaying gratification
- Controlling impulses
- Reducing stress
- Awareness of the difference between feelings and actions.

Cognitive Abilities

- Talking to yourself – leading an "inner dialogue" as a way of facing a topic or challenge, or as a way of improving personal behavior.
- Reading and interpreting social signals – for example, recognizing social influences on behavior and one`s own self-image in the context of a wider community.

- Applying steps to problem-solving and decision-making – for example, controlling impulses, setting goals, identifying alternative courses of action, predicting consequences.
- Understanding other people`s perspectives.
- Understanding norms of behavior (what is acceptable and what is not).
- Maintaining a positive attitude toward life.
- Self-awareness – for example, forming realistic expectations of yourself.

Behavioral Abilities

- Nonverbal – communicating through eye contact, facial expressions, tone of voice, gestures.
- Verbal – making clear requests, responding effectively to criticism, resisting negative influences, listening to others, helping others, participating in positive social circles.

ELEMENTS OF EMOTIONAL INTELLIGENCE

Salovey and Mayer proposed, and Goleman later expanded, a **model** that defines emotional intelligence through several **important elements:**

- Knowing one`s own emotions
- Managing emotions
- Motivating oneself
- Recognizing emotions in others (empathy)
- Establishing and maintaining healthy relationships with others

This represents awareness of your own being – recognizing feelings at the moment they occur, which is the key to emotional intelligence. The first step in understanding emotions is to perceive them accurately. In many cases, this may involve understanding nonverbal signals, such as body language and facial expressions.

The ability to consciously observe your feelings from moment to moment is crucial for psychological insights and for understanding your own personality. The inability to notice your emotions leaves you at their mercy. People who have reliable knowledge of their feelings manage their lives better and know more clearly how they feel about personal decisions – from choosing a partner to choosing a career.

Human beings are emotional by nature, yet many are afraid to embrace and get to know their own emotions. We often run away from our feelings because we don`t know how to express them, master them, or channel them – instead of facing them, whether they are negative or positive. It is very important to know yourself, to face problems and the emotions these problems may evoke. Caring for yourself is essential for good mental health, and it is therefore necessary to enter your inner temple and listen to yourself and your needs.

Many years ago, in the previous XX century, it was not so common or popular to deal with oneself and one`s emotions. Today, however, it is an essential factor in the development process of every individual, without which true success and progress are unimaginable. The ability to recognize negative feelings actually helps a person think more rationally and thus come more easily to their own solutions.

Exercise: Choose a few negative situations or feelings you are currently experiencing. Be as detailed as possible in your description, because the clearer and more specific you are in writing your feelings on paper, the clearer it will become where they come from and what solutions might be available. Truly, without shame or hesitation, describe your situation. Write down why you feel this way, when this feeling first appeared, what caused it, how strongly you feel the discomfort, and in which part of your body you feel it. Include absolutely everything that seems important and that might help you recognize which emotions are alive within you.

Now that you have written your detailed description, put down the pen, close your eyes, place your hand on your heart, and allow yourself to let those emotions pass through you. Give yourself permission – emotions exist precisely to be experienced, and behind every negative emotion there is an unfulfilled desire or request. Be gentle with yourself and know that everyone who works on themselves goes through the same process. Working with emotions has never been easy, but it has always been worth it – I guarantee you that.

Managing Emotions

Managing emotions so that they match the situation is an ability built upon self-awareness. People who lack this skill constantly struggle with feelings of restlessness and suffering, while those who are skilled in it recover much faster from life`s failures and hardships. The truth is that emotions arise as feelings in our bodies, and feelings are influenced by the emotions produced in our mental system.

Listening to our deep emotions helps us connect with the reality of our present experience and distinguish between stories built from potentially negative beliefs or misinterpretations of our mental system. If our mental framework were always perfectly aligned, we would always make the right decisions. But since most people from time to time get stuck in their mental stories, it is desirable to honestly assess and identify their feelings. Managing emotions can have a decisive impact on the quality of our lives and everything that happens to us. Often, the things we fail to raise to a higher level of awareness are what we call "fate." How many hardships could we avoid if we realized that we ourselves are the creators of our destiny – precisely through the choices of our beliefs. Thus, we see that the quality of our life strongly depends on our ability to manage our emotions.

Exercise: In the previous exercise, you learned to recognize your emotions, name them, and allow them to exist. Now we will learn how to manage and master those same emotions you have identified.

Close your eyes, place your hand on your heart, and return to the emotions you previously wrote down. Feel them, allow them to move through your mental system. Let the answer appear to the question: What is it that each of these emotions is trying to tell me? Be joyful in this process of self-discovery, because every negative emotion is actually a friend pointing you to the changes you need to make. What is your emotion trying to communicate? What is it that you need less of, and what do you need more of in yourself so that you don`t feel this way again? What is your inner voice trying to tell you? Listen carefully. What would you like to feel instead?

Spend as much time as needed in dialogue with your emotions, listening patiently and attentively to what they have to say. Once you have your answers, write them down.

You may feel vulnerable at this moment, and that is completely okay. You are not alone in this – everyone goes through it regardless of age or education. Stepping out of your comfort zone has never been comfortable. Continue writing everything you discovered in your conversation with your emotions.

Motivating Yourself

Managing emotions in order to achieve a specific goal is a fundamental ability needed for focused attention, self-motivation, and mastery of your own actions. Emotional self-control – the ability to delay gratification and to master emotional impulses – is an essential element of achieving any success. People who possess this skill are often more productive and effective in whatever they do. The ability to motivate yourself also shows that you have already mastered the technique of recognizing and managing your emotions, which means you are already closer to your solutions. In addition, you now gain the wisdom and realization that there is always a solution and a way out of any situation. This skill will surely help you in your everyday life and in facing challenges. You will discover that happiness is not about always being in a blissful state, but about the ability to turn every situation into a state of grace.

Exercise: Go back to the paper where you wrote down your emotions, the ones you have recognized and mastered. Now we will learn how to channel them and create a key shift that will turn that negative emotion into a positive one. Place your hand on your heart, gently close your eyes, and imagine someone whose opinion you highly respect and value – someone who always has wonderful solutions for every situation. In a few sentences, tell this person about your situation. What would they suggest you do? How would they resolve this problem?

One of the main reasons we remain stuck is our association with the situation itself. To look at the problem rationally and logically, we need to disassociate from it. If we always try to solve a problem in the same way and always look at it from the same perspective, we will keep getting the same solutions – which have not worked so far. It is therefore necessary to step outside of our own framework and think "outside the box." This becomes much easier when we put ourselves in another position.

So, how would the person you admire, who always has solutions, approach this situation? What would they do in your place? What would they increase, and what would they reduce, in order to solve the problem? Be open to the suggestions and ideas that arise, and be aware that if you change nothing, things will remain the same. Allow yourself to step out of your comfort zone – the discomfort of doing so will disappear after the first step, while regret and fear of change could otherwise last forever. Be courageous. Once you have your answers, slowly open your eyes and write them down. The more options you write, the greater your choices for a solution. And do not be afraid – because the only constant in the entire universe is change.

Recognizing Emotions in Others

Empathy, as another ability grounded in emotional self-awareness, is a core skill for relating to people. Those who display empathy are better attuned to subtle social cues that reveal what others need or want. Because of this, such individuals tend to be more successful and well-liked in any community. In themselves and in others, they easily notice emotions and know how to respond appropriately. This is one of the key hallmarks of emotional intelligence and a reliable predictor of success in any communication.

Instead of looking for a culprit in a given situation, people who can easily recognize emotions in others have the ability to step into their counterpart`s role and thus gain insight into their emotional state. This capacity belongs to the craft of great communication masters who, precisely through understanding and compassion, can guide any conversation in the desired direction.

Navigating Relationships

The art of maintaining relationships largely consists of managing emotions in others. These are the abilities that form the basis of popularity, leadership qualities, and interpersonal effectiveness. People who excel in these skills achieve good results in all endeavors that rely on smooth interaction with others; they are social stars. Of course, people differ in their abilities across these areas. Some of us may be very successful at containing, say, personal agitation, yet relatively unable to calm others. Deficits in emotional skills can be improved: to a large extent, each of these areas is actually a set of habits and reactions that can be enhanced with properly directed effort.

Because we are all different, each of us moves through the elements of emotional intelligence in our own way. The very ability to correctly recognize our own and other people`s emotions in the moment, and to establish a healthy relationship with our conversation partner, is a key success factor — both in our relationship with ourselves and others, and in the overall quality of our lives.

In other words, rather than criticizing someone for doing something their own way instead of the way we instructed, it is more appropriate to find what is good in their approach and praise that, while clearly stating that we would still prefer a certain part to be done in a different (desired) way.

It is undesirable and inappropriate to label a person as "bad" or "good." What is correct, acceptable, constructive, and desirable is to comment on their behavior as "good" or "bad." This is a simple example of fostering emotional intelligence in everyday communication and interaction. Generally speaking, a more optimistic outlook on the world will free you from additional stress and many negative emotions, and it will also help you better understand both your own and other people`s emotions.

How to Recognize People with High Emotional Intelligence?

People with high emotional intelligence typically **manage their emotions well, speak about them clearly, and can explain their feelings.**

They are honest with themselves, recognize their weaknesses and emotions, and approach them differently than the average person. They have a developed capacity for self acceptance and self knowledge because they can acknowledge their flaws while also valuing their strengths. They take responsibility and anticipate the consequences of their decisions.

They are empathetic. Aware of their own weaknesses and mistakes, they understand those of others. In the workplace, people with high emotional intelligence understand that employees can have a bad day, and that it is therefore understandable if they make more mistakes. They are perceptive, recognize behavioral patterns, and are highly skilled at positively influencing their environment with their approach.

Moreover, people with high emotional intelligence **never allow themselves to be overrun by negative emotions** (fear, anger, rage, sadness, guilt), because they are able to understand the causes of such emotions and use them for positive action.

People with more developed emotional intelligence tend to be more successful in many areas of life — especially professional ones.

How to Recognize People with Low Emotional Intelligence?

Conversely, people with low emotional intelligence **tend not to talk about or analyze their feelings**; they may carry guilt for a long time after missteps, avoid taking responsibility for their actions, and are often insecure, pessimistic, and inclined to shift blame onto others.

Those who have not developed emotional intelligence are reluctant to analyze their feelings and may long conceal guilt for poor choices. They avoid responsibility for their actions. Alongside setbacks in private life, they also experience failures at work and often change workplaces. Those who manage to enter close relationships or marriage typically end them after a short time due to a lack of mature emotional functioning. They are generally insecure, prone to blaming others, and tend toward pessimism. Overall, people with a low level of emotional intelligence face difficulties across different areas of life. They are usually not successful in the professional world and lack a high-quality social life.

Emotional Intelligence in Interpersonal Relationships

In relationships with others, people with high emotional intelligence do very well. One of the reasons is precisely their ability to interpret — and, even more importantly, to respond appropriately to—other people`s emotions, which is crucial in human interaction.

On the other hand, people with low emotional intelligence often have a very small circle of close friends due to reduced empathy, that is, a lack of sensitivity to other people`s feelings, and difficulty accepting new things and phenomena.

Why Are Emotionally Intelligent People More Successful in Life?

Those with more developed emotional intelligence are more successful in many areas of life, especially in the professional sphere. Their self-motivation tends to be exceptionally strong. They believe in their abilities and are self-confident — though not egocentric.

Because they can detect emotions — both in themselves and in their colleagues, employees, and clients — they can position themselves appropriately. They know how to contain their emotions and do not allow them to take over. With a composed attitude, they bring calm into a heated workplace atmosphere. Emotionally intelligent people are flexible because they are not afraid of change. They have no problem stepping out of their comfort zone. They do not avoid saying no when necessary and know how to say it in a way that does not offend the other side — while also being able to handle negative reactions with poise.

Developing Emotional Intelligence

Emotional intelligence is something that can be developed over the course of life through personal effort and experience. In addition to specialized concepts and programs for cultivating emotional abilities and skills in different groups, there are numerous initiatives to improve the education of professionals about the importance of people`s positive traits.

Moreover, emotional intelligence can be observed **in all aspects of human life,** and its development can be most effectively encouraged through certain psychotherapies whose primary goal is to discover and guide human strengths and virtues. In recent years, interest has grown markedly in programs aimed at **developing social and emotional skills** such as problem-solving, decision-making, emotion regulation, recognizing emotions, behavior management, and more. What scientists particularly emphasize in developing emotional intelligence is persistent self-work and consistent effort in that work to raise one`s level of emotional intelligence.

Psychotherapy and various trainings aimed at developing the abilities listed above are specialized and systematized programs that can truly help those who are ready to work on their emotional competence.

NOTES

AMYGDALA

"Fear does not come to stop you,
but to warn you –
your task is not to obey it blindly,
but to understand it consciously."
Aleksandra Božović

To understand the world of emotions, we cannot overlook the place where our emotions are stored – the place from which they arise. The complete seat and center of our emotions is located in the amygdala.

The word **amygdala** comes from Greek and means **"almond."** In humans, it is a cluster of interconnected formations shaped like almonds, located above the brainstem near the limbic ring. There are two amygdalae, one on each side of the brain, closer to the front part of the head. The human amygdala is relatively large compared to that of our closest evolutionary relatives, the primates.

The hippocampus and the amygdala were two keys to the part of the primitive "nose brain" that, throughout evolution, enabled the development of the cortex and later the neocortex. Today, these limbic structures carry out a large — perhaps the largest — part of learning and memory processes; the amygdala is the cradle of emotions. The hippocampus stores bare facts, while the amygdala retains their emotional framework. If the amygdala is switched off, it can have fatal consequences for the rest of the brain, leading to an astonishing inability to assess the emotional significance of certain events.

It is not only affection and emotions that are linked to the amygdala but also passion as a whole. Animals whose amygdala has been removed or disconnected lose all sense of fear and anger, lose their drive for competition and cooperation, and no longer have any awareness of their personal place within the social structure of their species. Their emotions become dulled or disappear entirely. Tears, an emotional signal unique to humans, are triggered from the amygdala and the structure called **the cingulate gyrus**; when someone holds you, strokes you, or comforts you in another way, they are in fact soothing these very parts of the brain and stopping the sobbing. Without the amygdala, there are no tears of sorrow, no emotions that require comforting — only a flat line.

The connections between the amygdala and the neocortex form the seat where battles are fought or peace treaties are made between head and heart, thought and feeling. This connection explains why emotions are so crucial for constructive thinking—both for making important decisions and for the human ability to think simply and logically.

When people speak of "intelligence," they almost always mean the possession of specific logical and rational cognitive characteristics, such as the ability to learn, to perform complex calculations, to use articulate and refined language, and so on. Only in recent years has knowledge about another kind of intelligence — **emotional intelligence (EI)** — spread more widely. This term, coined in the 1990s, refers to the part of intelligence aimed at **recognizing and managing emotions**, both one`s own and those of others. This was no small innovation, for it gave the emotional realm its deserved integrity and importance: those who possess this quality and know how to apply it have greater chances of success in private, social, emotional, and professional life.

Unlike IQ, which does not change significantly throughout life, **emotional intelligence can be developed and trained**. So let us now learn what emotional intelligence is, why it is so important, and how we can cultivate it.

Exercise: Conscious Reset of the Amygdala – 3-6-9 Calming Technique

Goal: to calm the amygdala and shift focus from the reactive part of the brain to the conscious part (the prefrontal cortex). Steps:

- Pause (3 seconds)
- When you notice your body or mind reacting with strong emotions (fear, anxiety, anger), do nothing — just stop and consciously count to 3.
- This creates a micro-pause and interrupts the amygdala`s automatic reaction.

- Inhale (6 seconds)
- Breathe deeply through your nose—counting to 6 as you inhale. Hold your breath for 2 seconds.
- Breathing activates the parasympathetic nervous system, which calms the body.
- Feel your body (9 seconds)
- Close your eyes and pay attention for 9 seconds to physical sensations: where you are sitting, how your clothes touch your skin, whether your shoulders are tense, how your heart is beating.

This shifts your focus from emotional reaction to physical awareness, reducing the amygdala`s impulse.

Reflection: Ask yourself the following question:

"Is this a real danger—or is an old pattern being activated?"

With this exercise, you train your brain not to react automatically, but consciously—reducing the dominance of the amygdala in everyday situations.

NOTES

DRIVERS OF HUMAN BEHAVIOR (IMPRINTS, TRIGGERS, AND DRIVERS)

"In childhood we receive not only memories, but also imprints that shape the way we love, choose, and react. Only by recognizing them does our liberation begin."
Aleksandra Božović

Although imprints, emotional triggers, and drivers — as well as their consequences — arise from our mental framework and can manifest outwardly in the body and behavior, they nevertheless belong to the realm of emotional intelligence as the true drivers of human behavior, embedded and acquired impressions. This is because the original process that set those triggers and drivers into motion lies deep within our emotional realm.

Every one of our behaviors is actually connected to a specific emotion or instinct that stands behind it. The emotion of love and affection, acceptance and safety, or the emotion of pain, rejection, fear of abandonment... Or perhaps instincts for survival, hunger, thirst, or sexual drive — all of these are drivers of human action. When we look deeper into the motives of human activity, we always encounter the same need: either to experience a certain emotion — or to avoid it.

It is precisely for this reason that this topic belongs to emotional intelligence, since emotions are the fundamental motive and initiator of all human activity. Many people, however, live under the belief that they were born with certain behaviors and a system of values that they call their "personal character." They believe they are simply the way they are and that the character they were born with is difficult to change.

Yet the truth is that we all came into the world as a blank, unwritten page — the so-called **tabula rasa**, as Plato and his student Socrates so vividly described it. They taught that the human soul, in its original form — before the first imprints and the first contact with the outside world — is as pure as white paper, and the mind an unwritten page that life gradually fills for each individual.

In this way, all our experiences and life events draw what will eventually become our character, our lifestyle, our value system, habits, behaviors, and other personality traits. Someone may argue that genetics also plays a role — and that is true. Yet even genetically inherited behaviors, and what we call "character," had to have begun somewhere. They were simply repeated so many times that they became anchored and turned into part of genetic heritage.

We are who we are — because of something that happened to us…or in spite of it.

IMPRINT (IMPRINTING)

"What has once been imprinted into your soul
does not rule you because it is true –
but because it came before
you knew you had a choice."
Aleksandra Božović

Imprints are deeply embedded impressions that are formed in key moments of life — most often in childhood or in states of high emotional intensity. They function as fundamental programs that shape our perception of reality, our beliefs, and our identity.

To better approach this topic, let us first consider the concept of **the imprint**, which provides us with a solid foundation to understand this very important area.

Have you ever wondered why young children imitate their parents — in the way they speak, in their tone, in their attitude toward others, in how they walk, or in everyday activities? Or perhaps you have asked yourself why you keep being drawn to people who resemble your parents in some way? Or maybe you noticed that, at first, you felt awkward and even uncomfortable using a MacBook because your first experiences were with an old PC?

Although these questions may at first seem unrelated, what connects them is — the imprint.

An imprint describes the process in which early experiences or events are permanently etched into consciousness, behavior, or the subconscious mind. This concept is most often associated with early childhood development, but it also applies to behaviors in adulthood. Imprints shape the way we perceive ourselves, other people, and the world around us.

When we speak of an imprint, we refer to childhood or adolescent experiences that affect an individual so strongly that those memories continue to dominate their behavior and identity in adulthood. An imprint is therefore the tendency for certain characteristics of situations from early developmental periods to leave a deep mark on a person — attributes and elements that are later automatically activated in similar circumstances.

CRITICAL PERIODS IN WHICH IMPRINTS ARE FORMED

The critical periods of personality development in which early imprints are most often formed are the first five to seven years of life, when the brain is most receptive to learning. In adolescence, imprints are further shaped through social interactions, authority figures (such as teachers and coaches), and social expectations.

Early childhood (0 – 7 years): During this period the brain functions in wave frequencies (delta and theta) that allow unconscious absorption of information. Everything a child experiences — whether through parental behavior, emotional situations, or repeated messages — becomes the basic model through which they perceive the world.

Strong emotional situations: Sometimes imprints are formed later in life, during moments of highly intense emotions (trauma, sudden success, major life changes).

Transgenerational imprints: In addition to personal experiences, some imprints may be passed down through generations — they are part of family and collective consciousness. Memories of such experiences strongly influence identity development, behavior, and decision-making, as psychological responses to past events.

If we could imagine our mind and soul as a pure, white, unwritten page — tabula rasa — then imprints are the first experiences through which we begin to learn about ourselves and the world. Once an imprint is made in the moment of a powerful experience, it is etched into the subconscious and forms a behavioral pattern that is automatically activated in similar circumstances — with the purpose of protecting us. These behavior models make up our automatic reaction system. Memories of lived experiences can strongly influence our identity, lifestyle, behaviors, and even our daily and major life decisions.

Many beliefs and behaviors we perceive as "our own" are in fact consequences of early imprints. For example, a child bitten by a dog at age three may develop a deeply rooted aversion to dogs that lasts a lifetime. Imprints also shape our perception of love, intimacy, trust, and boundaries. An imprint leaves its mark on the brain during a critical developmental period or at the moment of a powerful emotional event. That imprint, over time, shapes our choices, reactions, and behaviors. A classic example: a child who touches a hot oven learns that pain is danger and acquires an imprint that automatically protects them.

One of my favorite examples, which I often use in my work with clients, is the story of flamingos. Did you know that flamingos are born white, not pink? They turn pink because they consume algae rich in carotenoids. In other words, the environment in which they grow directly shapes their outer appearance. The same applies to us — the environment we grow up in shapes our "color," our patterns, our behaviors, and our worldview. It defines our growth and development.

The famous Austrian zoologist **Konrad Lorenz**, Nobel Prize winner in Medicine, conducted an experiment in 1935 with newly hatched geese, exploring the development of social bonding. He called this process "imprinting." He argued that imprinting occurs during "critical periods" of childhood, when the environment influences physiological control systems that shape an entire life.

In his experiment, he separated goose eggs — half remained with the mother, and the other half he incubated himself. The first half followed the mother, the second followed him. The young geese developed a permanent attachment to the first person or moving object they saw — and this became irreversible. In doing so, he confirmed the existence of biological imprinting: an innate process that shapes bonding.

TYPES OF IMPRINTS IN HUMANS

Supportive Imprint

Supportive imprints are essentially positive programs that strengthen and shape a healthy identity. The way we receive an imprint depends on our experiences, but also on our relationship with the environment.

A positive imprint, for example: a child who regularly receives praise develops a healthy self-image and a belief that they are worthy and capable of success. Positive imprints in early childhood are extremely important. They become the foundation for attitudes toward learning, self-confidence, and the acceptance of mistakes. If mistakes are presented to a child as opportunities for growth, the child develops healthy resilience. If not, patterns of self-criticism and self-punishment take root.

The imprints a child acquires by the age of six or seven often indicate what kind of person they will become — unless these imprints are brought into awareness and transformed. A child who grows up in love and support develops trust in others and a healthy, positive relationship with themselves.

If we take into account that children are your faithful admirers, observers, imitators, and mirrors, then be mindful of what you give them to imitate. In that way, you shape your children into authentic human beings — something you will undoubtedly be proud of. Where there are positive imprints, there are also negative ones, and these play an equally significant role in the formation of an individual`s character.

Limiting Imprint

Limiting imprints are patterns that hinder development, self-confidence, and life freedom. A child who grows up in an environment of constant criticism may develop the belief that they are "never good enough," which can lead to low self-esteem or perfectionism. In such a context, the child`s future becomes oriented toward a constant search for external validation rather than channeling energy toward personal goals.

Children need to be taught from an early age to love and accept themselves exactly as they are, to become their own greatest support, and to form a healthy relationship with themselves — independent of the opinions of others. Research shows that a large percentage of women tend to change partners more often precisely for this reason — to gain confirmation of their value.

If a young girl constantly does everything just to win her father`s love, approval, validation, and attention, it is highly likely that she will continue in adulthood to project her expectations and implanted programs onto her environment. From that deep need for validation, she may move from partner to partner, searching for the missing puzzle piece she never received from her father.

Psychological Imprint

A psychological imprint in humans includes early experiences from childhood, especially during vulnerable and formative periods. Events, environment, and the reactions of parents or caregivers create an "imprint" in the subconscious mind that can shape behavior, beliefs, emotional reactions, and an individual`s relationship with themselves and others.

In other words, a psychological imprint refers to all those patterns of behavior and belief that are formed in childhood. For example, the way a child experiences love, safety, or fear in the family is one of the key factors that indicates the direction in which the child`s personality will develop.

Cultural Imprint

A cultural imprint also plays a significant role in the way imprints are received — leading us to unconsciously label people from different cultural and national backgrounds. The way we were taught about social norms, religions, and values often shapes our attitudes throughout life. Children raised in a culture that values collectivism often develop beliefs about the importance of community, while in individualistic societies the emphasis is placed on personal achievement.

For example, we live with beliefs that Swiss people as a nation are neutral and calculating, while people from the former Yugoslavia are seen as persistent and stubborn. The Chinese are considered hardworking and intelligent, the French warm and passionate, while Russians are perceived as direct and brave. This is why traveling is so important for expanding and developing awareness. Through travel, we learn about one another — about similarities and differences — and gain deeper understanding and respect for the diversity among nations.

The truth is that we are all the same — the same substance flows through all of us: blood. And just as the environment affects the color of flamingos, our environments shape our values, beliefs, destinies, lifestyles, and quality of life. We need to learn from one another through acceptance of differences. This is how we expand our awareness of what we want, what we are aligned with, and what truly fulfills and makes us happy.

I remember one client who was born Christian, yet his inner world never matched the external imprint assigned to him in childhood. His journey was very painful, marked by a deep sense of guilt and fear of God`s punishment. It was not that his connection with God did not exist — on the contrary — but that connection did not fit within the framework of the Christian religion.

After years of searching and self-work, he discovered a deep resonance with Buddhism and finally found peace and his "temple" within himself. The realization that it does not matter which God we pray to, but that we carry the Divine within us in a way that suits us personally — was a turning point in his life.

Traumatic Imprint

One of the most important types of imprint is the traumatic imprint. Negative experiences such as neglect, abuse, or emotional rejection can leave deep marks on emotional and psychological development. The world can sometimes be harsh, and such harshness easily etches itself into our subconscious, significantly influencing personality development and quality of life.

The deepest wounds most often come from those closest to us — family members, partners, and friends. Precisely because we experience our primary environment as a safe haven, we often do not recognize that it can also be the source of pain. We often grant those people the right to treat us however they wish, believing they have that right simply because they are close to us. We do not defend ourselves, we do not set boundaries — because we feel we are not allowed. This is where the words of Carl Jung come into full play:

"Everything that we do not bring into consciousness appears in our lives as fate."

An example from coaching practice was a courageous woman who, after years of postponement, finally decided to seek help. She had been in a bad marriage for more than two decades, convinced that "at least she was married" — no matter the cost. Her husband was in control. Her place was — in the kitchen. When guests arrived, she was allowed only to greet them and immediately return to the kitchen. She had no right to sit with them or take part in the conversation. For years she heard that she was incapable, worthless, stupid, and that without him she could not survive. There was also physical violence. Every attempt to express her opinion was met with insults, threats, control, and pain. Over time, she began to believe it.

Her fear was immense, but her inner longing for freedom was even greater. The process of self-work was long, difficult, and painful. But eventually the moment came when she gathered her courage, packed her things, and spoke her truth — directly to his face. Aware that she was risking her life, she said: "I know he can kill me and that I may never see the Sun again… but I cannot go on like this. I am going all the way." The risk was real. The fear was justified. But the will to finally break free was stronger. And she succeeded.

Today she is a woman who earns her own money, learns languages, has friends, sets boundaries, and does not allow belittlement, abuse, or humiliation. She became aware that she carried deeply embedded traumatic imprints that her husband had systematically pressed into her for year — but also that she had the power to erase them and write her own new story.

Filial Imprint (Emotional Imprint)

The early years are crucial for the development of emotional stability and empathy. Interactions with caregivers leave marks that shape self-confidence, attachment, relationships with others, and the way a child explores the world.

If the experience is positive and attachment is secure, the child develops a healthy relationship with themselves and with others. If the experience is inconsistent or negative, patterns of insecurity and fear are formed, carried into adult life. This emotional imprint often leaves a deep mark on the architecture of the brain and determines the trajectory of further emotional and social development.

In psychology, this concept has been extended to human emotional, cognitive, and social aspects. The idea of imprints has been most developed in fields such as developmental psychology, attachment theory, and neurolinguistic programming (NLP).

John Bowlby and Mary Ainsworth developed attachment theory, which explores how early relationships (especially with parents) shape attachment patterns throughout life. Thus, early emotional reactions become "anchors" for later experiences in an individual`s life. For example, a traumatic event may leave a deep emotional imprint that shapes reactions to similar situations in the future.

Practical example: As a child, Marko constantly sought his father`s love and approval. His father was strict and rarely showed emotion — instead of praise, he often noticed only mistakes. When Marko brought home a drawing from school, his father would say: "You could have done better." Marko then began to believe he was not good enough and took on the role of the "perfect child" who could never make mistakes. Later in life, he still tried to win recognition — working overtime, striving to do everything flawlessly, and fearing abandonment in relationships if he did not please others. He was drawn to authority figures and partners who were cold, distant, and demanding — thus unconsciously repeating the familiar pattern from childhood.

This is a classic example of a filial imprint — how early experiences with parents can shape the life and emotions of an adult.

Sexual Imprint

Sexual imprinting has also been observed in humans, manifesting in the formation of a preference for a certain "type" of partner — most often modeled on parental characteristics such as physical appearance, personality traits, or even mannerisms. However, some individuals who carry negative imprints from their relationship with their parents may choose partners who are the exact opposite of their parents — in which case the preference is for contrast. This principle points to the complex interaction between the familiar and the attractive in shaping sexual preferences, clearly reflected in life and in the choices of partners one makes.

For example, women who grew up in dysfunctional and abusive families often tend to attract similar partners later in life — abusive ones. If a child grew up around alcoholism and destructive behavioral patterns of their parents, it is highly likely that they will choose partners with similar or identical problems. This is not about logic or rational judgment, but about an imprint deeply ingrained in their mental and emotional structure. Since we are creatures of habit, it is natural for us to seek what feels familiar — regardless of whether it is good or bad for us.

These are deeply rooted programs that a person is usually unaware of, believing instead that their choice is guided solely by the feeling of love.

Limbic Imprint

The limbic imprint refers to experiences we have in the mother`s womb, as well as immediately after birth. The time spent in the mother`s womb forms the first and deepest imprints related to our behavior and our basic need for survival.

Any disturbance during the period in the womb can have serious consequences for an individual`s entire life. Hence the scientific findings that when a mother listens to pleasant music, the baby in her womb reacts with joy. Every emotion of the mother directly influences the experiences of her baby. Since the child is part of the mother`s body and connected by the umbilical cord, it also experiences everything the mother feels.

That is why the mother`s mental, emotional, and physical state is extremely important, because these first imprints remain permanently recorded and programmed into the child — and have a tremendous impact on its development, quality of life, and the challenges it will face later on.

METHODS FOR CLEARING IMPRINTS

Methods for clearing limiting imprints are diverse — from NLP techniques, deep emotional and somatic processes, and hypnotherapy to energetic work. Still, the most important step is your readiness to change.

In developmental psychology of social learning, imprinting can lead individuals to make irrational decisions due to the "gosling syndrome" — the human tendency to "imprint" the first idea or concept learned and then judge all subsequent ideas against that initial past model. This implies that people prefer to repeat old, familiar behavior patterns and tend to be closed to the unknown.

Social learning, in psychological theory, is learning influenced by the external environment rather than innate or internal forces. The leading figure of the social learning concept — often called **modeling** — is Canadian psychologist **Albert Bandura**. He conducted numerous studies showing that children learn many behaviors by observing others — such as sharing, aggression, cooperation, social interaction, and the ability to delay immediate gratification.

In Bandura`s classic study of imitation learning, children who saw a model punished for aggressive behavior displayed significantly fewer aggressive responses compared to children who saw the model rewarded or neither rewarded nor punished. This study led many psychologists to ask what kinds of "learning experiences" children receive from watching popular television shows and films, especially those depicting antisocial and violent behaviors.

Later research on the effects of media violence proved controversial, producing two opposing theories: one claimed that observing violence may allow such urges to be sublimated (experienced symbolically and thus reduced), while the other argued that watching violence actually increases the urge to behave violently.

This is precisely how behaviors arise that we later call character, habits, values, and lifestyle. The human (and animal) brain naturally chooses what is familiar — whether it is good or bad for us. Habits that gradually become automatic behavior patterns remain deeply engraved in the subconscious, which is why working with them is challenging.

The good news is that today we can recognize an imprint, which enables more rational thinking and a healthier, more fulfilling life. A person ready for change can, through inner work, acknowledge and uncover the root of their behavior and then decide which areas they want to transform. Changing lifelong identities and behaviors is a deeply emotional process — a kind of metamorphosis — and it is often quite painful.

That is why emotional preparation, openness to change, and strong perseverance are essential. Most importantly — the willingness to do what you fear most: step out of your shadow and your own confines, and face the fears that limit you. You are what you believe you are. And the truth is — you can be anything you choose, if you are ready to change.

Human beings are mental and spiritual beings. Change is natural to us. With evolutionary development comes the need to ask ourselves the right questions and look deeply into the truth of who we are. When we do not change, we stagnate. The need to be "always the same" is an illusion, because the only constant in life is — change.

Evolutionary psychology, which studies behavior, thoughts, and feelings through the lens of evolutionary biology, offers further insight into the design and development of the human mind. Evolutionary psychologists believe that human behaviors are shaped by physical and psychological predispositions that helped our ancestors survive and reproduce. In this context, the human brain and body contain mechanisms designed to function together — so as to enable success in the environments our ancestors once inhabited.

For example, people living in remote regions or harsh mountain areas have minds adapted to survival in extreme conditions. Their reactions, instincts, and behavior patterns differ from those of people living in modern urban environments.

Similarly, a bat could not survive with the brain of a beluga whale — because it needs a brain suited to a body that flies at night and catches insects midair. Every brain is evolutionarily shaped to the role and needs of its species. Hence the question: What is the impact of our evolutionary past on the design of the human mind today, in the XXI century?

Cognitive and language development: Although humans do not experience imprinting in the same way many animals do, early childhood experiences deeply affect the development of language and thinking. In the first years, children quickly absorb nuances of speech and behavior from their environment. These early experiences shape neural pathways and lay the groundwork for future cognitive abilities.

For example, a child who watches a parent assemble furniture or cook from a recipe learns to think in sequences, solve problems, and understand that mistakes are not the end — but part of the process.

HOW TO RECOGNIZE YOUR OWN IMPRINT?

Now that we have explained the concept and types of imprints, it is important to emphasize that every individual can become aware of the imprints they carry — and, based on that awareness, begin to develop healthier behavior patterns.

The fact is that we all carry certain imprints. The question is what we do with them — and whether we are even aware of them. There is no person who has not received any imprints — we have all had to come into contact with the external world, from the mother`s womb, through birth, to the formation of self-awareness and the building of the ego. Those very events, positive or negative, make up our first imprints.

Imprints help us understand ourselves and others at the deepest level of being. They teach us how to recognize our own shadows, to see reflections of our experiences in others, and to find ways to accept, illuminate, and transform them into something useful and healthy.

The most important thing in this process is openness to insight and change. There is no need to be ashamed of your imprints — shame would be recognizing them and doing nothing about it. The remedy lies in truth. Only when we admit, accept, and embrace our imprints are we ready to work on transforming them.

Whether they are traumatic, limbic, sexual, filial, or other types of imprints, what we need to know is that — no matter what happened in the past and what influences we received — today we have the right to choose again. Today we can change those influences in accordance with our own values. No one can take that right from us, nor can we hand it over to others. That is our power — and our responsibility.

For example, if a mother was frequently in conflict with the father during pregnancy, or if as a child we imitated the destructive behaviors of a father who mistreated the mother and later carried that pattern into our own relationships — it is time to change it. The truth is that those imprints left marks, but it is also true that today we have a power we may not have had then — the power of choice. We can choose a new path, a new way. A beginning.

Ways to recognize imprints

One effective way is **self-observation** — identifying recurring behavior patterns and emotional reactions, especially in stressful situations. I regularly teach my clients to create an imagined "inner assistant" — a part of themselves that observes from the side and notes everything they say, do, and repeat. At first this may feel odd, but later it becomes an extremely useful tool, especially in deeper processes.

Most of the time we operate from our conscious mind — but what truly interests us lies in the subconscious. That is where everything happens; where everything begins and ends. This is why it`s important to observe ourselves from the outside and learn to listen. Ask yourself:

- What belief about myself do I keep repeating? (e.g., "I`m not good enough.")
- Are there situations that trigger intense emotions I don`t understand?
- How did my parents behave toward me? What messages did they send me?

As we have already noted, every behavior comes from somewhere and represents a response to a certain emotion we carry deep inside. There is no person without an imprint — whether negative or positive. We are not who we think we are; we became who we are — because of something, or in spite of something that happened to us.

That is why **studying our childhood** is one of the most valuable methods to help us discover what we took from our first and primary environments — what imprints influenced the formation of our self-image. What did we pick up from parents, caregivers, and early teachers? It is said that only about ten years after leaving the parental home does a person truly gain the ability to get to know themselves. During those ten years of independent life, we will encounter many imprints implanted earlier, which we repeat out of habit — because that is what we know.

We are creatures of habit, and this is precisely why it is difficult to distinguish between what is authentically ours and what we adopted from the environment. In this developmental stage, a person reacquaints themselves with who they are and begins to question their behavior in an attempt to discover where it comes from.

You have surely caught yourself doing something exactly the way your parents did — and even though it annoys you, you still repeat it. This is not genetics; it is an imprint deeply embedded in your inner code. You simply don`t know any other way. That is why it takes a great deal of understanding, gentleness, and self-awareness to transform such behaviors into something that is truly yours and that serves you.

A person should continually examine their identity and what they include under that identity. Life is given to us as an opportunity to discover what we have adopted — and to change it in accordance with our own needs. The key to success here is awareness of the imprints within us.

Beyond the way we do certain things, it is also important to ask:

- How did my parents behave toward me?
- What messages did they send me about myself, others, and the world?
- What trace did those messages leave in me?
- Are those beliefs useful to me today?

The reactions we have in **relationships** with others can, through the process of self-observation, bring valuable insights into who truly lives within us and what we are made of. Pay attention to the fears, insecurities, and frustrations that arise in relationships. Many of them may be consequences of early imprints.

Be brave and honest enough to write down all the reactions that keep you from forming harmonious relationships. Talk about them with the people you are in conflict with — or find a friend, coach, or therapist who can help you gain a healthy reflection of your patterns. This can have a profound impact on your further development.

Be aware that postponing these processes achieves nothing — you only pass them on to another date and another person with whom, by default, you will repeat the same pattern. They will not disappear on their own. They will wait for you — until you notice them and decide to bring them to light.

No matter how old you are, excuses that it is “too late” no longer apply. Everything you do not bring into awareness today — you pass on to future generations, leaving them the same burden they will also have to fight. The sooner you start, the faster you will reach inner freedom — for yourself and for those who come after you. If you cannot do it for yourself, do it for them. Close the circle. Save yourself and others.

Even one day lived free of imprints is worth more than a hundred years lived under their weight. The choice is yours.

Dreams and intuition are also invaluable in the process of discovering and bringing imprints to awareness. Subconscious messages often surface through dreams or intuition — "a feeling" in certain situations. They clearly show you where to look. Do not ignore those signs; you cannot escape them. You can only postpone them — but they will wait for you.

Because imprints are often very subtle, it is difficult to differentiate between an imprint and our true, authentic self. That is why we can rely on our dreams and intuition, because in that realm we receive messages from the higher levels of consciousness. That field has no need to "pretty up" reality or blur it. Higher awareness is clear and precise in its communication — the question is only whether you are ready to hear it.

So, write down your dreams. Find ways to implement into your reality the messages you receive through dreams and intuition. You will be rewarded — with freedom, clarity, and with yourself.

HOW TO TRANSFORM IMPRINTS?

Awareness and Acceptance - The first step is to recognize that an imprint exists and that you acquired it in a specific context. Every behavior pattern comes from somewhere and was formed at a precise moment in time — and we have repeated and refined it ever since, until it became part of our character. Just as a positive imprint can form, so can a negative one. The fact is that we all carry imprints that strongly influence our personality development and lifestyle. Everything we do, we do either because of something — or in spite of something that happened to us.

Self-observation can lead you to awareness of those imprints, to accepting them — and, ultimately, to transforming them. This process will not "fade" with time — imprints will not disappear on their own; they can, in fact, grow deeper and stronger. Therefore, the earlier we begin to work with them, the more time we will have to live without their negative impact. Be gentle with yourself in this process. Do not judge or blame yourself for what you discover within. The first step toward transformation is acceptance — only then can you come to freedom.

Writing and Introspection - Writing is one of the most powerful tools, and I warmly recommend it to all my clients — no matter what process we are working on. Writing helps you develop the skill of neutral observation and articulate your thoughts and feelings clearly. Half the problem is already solved once it is on paper.
Keep a journal in which you record key memories, emotions, and the beliefs that accompany them — this is how you will trace your imprints and gain new insights into how to deal with them.

Write about childhood memories that often resurface — because they hold messages of great importance. Also, write down situations that trigger fear, sadness, or anger, as well as your beliefs about love, success, and trust. This material is invaluable and can help you understand from whom and when you adopted certain imprints and how they influence your life today. Writing is like a mirror of the soul — it tells you stories you might never dare to say out loud. In that space between your thoughts and the words on paper, the subconscious has a chance to express what the conscious mind might not know how to formulate.

Cognitive Behavioral Therapy (CBT) - Working with a professional is an irreplaceable part of transforming imprints. CBT stands out in particular because it focuses on recognizing and replacing dysfunctional beliefs with healthier patterns of thinking and behavior.

Working with a coach or therapist — especially through CBT or trauma-focused therapies — can help you identify and transform deep imprints. With a structured approach and expert support, you can achieve profoundly positive change over time.

Neuro-Linguistic Programming (NLP) - One of the most powerful tools I use with clients is NLP — Neuro-Linguistic

Programming. NLP brings exceptional results, especially when it comes to imprints.

Different NLP techniques — such as reframing or anchoring — can help you change the emotional perception of your imprints, gain clear insight into what you carry from the past, and view it from a neutral, empowered perspective. NLP coaching is highly effective for quickly recognizing and reprogramming unconscious beliefs.

For example: if you have carried the imprint since childhood that "you will never be successful," NLP can help transform that imprint — by changing the way you interpret the experience and creating a new belief framework. Another powerful NLP approach is assigning constructive meaning to your imprints. In this way, you can understand how those imprints were formed — and how to release them.

Exercise: Identify a negative imprint: "I always had to try hard just to be noticed." Then ask yourself: How can I reshape this experience into a source of strength? Perhaps that very struggle helped you become persistent, creative, and empathetic — and now you can consciously choose new patterns that serve you better. Ask: "What can I learn from this?" Change the meaning: "It taught me the value of effort, but I no longer need to seek validation all the time."

Mindfulness Techniques - Meditation and present-moment awareness help release the automatic reactions that arise from imprints. In meditation you give yourself space and time to listen to your inner, subconscious world — the one the waking mind often overlooks.

Focus on the present moment and observe your thoughts and emotions without judgment. Let thoughts pass through like they`re moving through a mental doorway — remember they are only thoughts. As they came, so they will go. Pay attention to what remains behind those "mental curtains," patiently waiting to be noticed. That very part of your subconscious is key in transforming imprints. Insights will arise about behaviors and the moments when the imprints were formed. When a negative pattern appears, allow it to exist — and accept it. Over time, you will begin to hear the message behind the pattern and release what holds you back.

Choose a helpful belief about yourself that you want to install in your awareness, and release the old, negative belief with an exhale. Repeat an affirmation such as: "I am free from the past" … until it becomes part of your subconscious.

Inner-Child Therapy - Working with the "inner child" allows you to give yourself the support and love you may not have received in the past. Many people experienced something in the early period of forming self-awareness that left traces and consequences we may still feel today. The way we give and receive love as adults, and the way we process primary emotions, can be answers to how we were loved when we were small. Even though we are grown, the traces of those early patterns are still visible; they are simply veiled by the more complex expressions typical of adulthood.

In some cases, even that complexity is absent, and a person reacts exactly as they did as a child — perhaps using the same words and gestures. Working with the inner child is an inevitable moment in everyone`s process. It is very important to find your inner child — who lives within you at every moment — and to pay attention to it. The wisdom of the inner child should not be underestimated. It watches our life with a keen eye and answers whether we are where we dreamed of being, doing the work we once imagined, surrounded by the people we wished to attract, and whether we are happy and fulfilled as we longed to be.

Moreover, inner-child work points precisely to the parts of us and our inner programs that need more attention — where our imprints are hidden and how to transform them.

When you feel ready for this journey, close your eyes and imagine a childhood situation that left an imprint. Bring that event to life as if it were happening before you now. Add the colors, sounds, and scents you remember. Allow this process to lead you to your inner child. Find them and observe — in what posture or position do you find the child? Notice their activity as you approach, their facial expression, movements, surroundings, and the tone of their voice. Come closer and sit beside them. Greet and touch them, and begin a conversation.

Discover what hurts, which memories remain bitter, and give the comfort they did not receive then. Listen, soothe, embrace, and promise to take care of them. Repeat affirmations such as: "You are safe and you are loved," until you are sure the child believes you. Hug them tightly and thank them for the precious insights they shared with you.

Example of imprint transformation:

Imprint: A child who was often ignored develops the belief that they are not worthy of attention.

Awareness: You recognize that, as an adult, you avoid conflict out of fear of rejection.

Action: Through introspective work and strengthening self-confidence, you begin to express your opinions even when there is a risk of not being accepted.

In the same way, you can map all of your imprints and discover:

- How did they arise?
- What impact do they have on you?
- What concrete actions can you take to transform them into behaviors that are helpful, healthy, and truly yours?

Do not forget — every behavior began at some point, from some emotion. Within every problem lies its solution; likewise, every imprint carries a message, a task, and a potential for growth. See imprints as friends. They do not come to hurt you — but to illuminate what needs your attention.

Nothing in your life is accidental. Imprints are not here to break you, but to awaken you. They invite you to become the best version of yourself — if you are ready to see and hear them. Imprints have a profound impact on our lives — but they are not immutable. Through introspective methods, therapeutic tools, and personal work, it is possible to transform negative imprints and create new, empowering patterns of thought and behavior. Imprinting is a powerful process that shapes our lives, but it is not final. Awareness of imprints, understanding them, and applying the right techniques enable you to take charge of your life — and live freely, consciously, and fulfilled.

NOTES

TRIGGER POINTS / TRIGGERS

"There are moments that move you far more powerfully than they 'should.' It isn't the moment — it's something long within you, waiting to be healed."
Aleksandra Božović

Trigger points are specific stimuli that automatically activate subconscious emotional reactions and behavior patterns. They are linked to earlier experiences and imprints that remain recorded in the subconscious mind.

Trigger points oder triggers, (Eng. trigger points) denote specific places in the body or psyche where suppressed tension, trauma, or emotional wounds are stored. When activated, they cause pain, discomfort, or unconscious reactions. These points can be both **physical (muscular) and psychological.**

Triggers are psychological, emotional, and neurobiological phenomena that activate automatic reactions in a person. They are unconscious mechanisms set in motion by certain external or internal stimuli, eliciting strong emotions, bodily sensations, or thought patterns. They are most often connected to past experiences — especially trauma — but can also arise from deeper unconscious programs that shape how we respond to the world.

Basic types of triggers:

- **Emotional triggers** – Certain people, situations, or words can evoke strong emotional reactions. *Example:* If someone had highly critical parents, they may react strongly to criticism — even when it is constructive.
- **Sensory triggers** – Sounds, smells, visual cues can evoke memories and emotions. *Example:* A perfume may stir longing because it recalls someone from the past.
- **Social triggers** – Specific social contexts or interactions can awaken unconscious patterns. *Example:* A person may struggle with authority figures due to strict parents in childhood.

The site of a trigger`s activation can be an **external or internal stimulus**. It may appear on the bodily level as intense pain when pressing a specific spot, or on the emotional level as inner pain and a sense of hurt.

In essence, these are the specific situations, words, images, sounds, smells, or sensations that provoke an intense emotional reaction — often linking a person back to a prior experience, trauma, or subconscious belief.

Reactions to triggers can be **automatic and unconscious**, often producing stress, anxiety, anger, or sadness. They are automatic responses to specific cues — people, places, things, smells, words, or colors. The reaction that emerges is not merely a fleeting emotion; it frequently reactivates deeply rooted patterns connected to unresolved trauma.

A trigger is any stimulus that unconsciously activates an emotional, mental, or physiological response. These responses can be **mild** (discomfort, irritation) or very **intense** (panic attacks, dissociation, uncontrolled aggression). Triggers function as reminders of past events — even when a person is unaware of the connection between the trigger and the original experience. The brain unconsciously "recognizes" similar situations and launches automatic responses.

When a person encounters a situation that subconsciously resembles a previous experience, the brain automatically interprets it as danger — or as an opportunity — depending on the prior emotion associated with it. These reactions are quick, instinctive, and often unconscious.

They may manifest as:

- **Bodily reactions** – tension, rapid heartbeat.
- **Emotional reactions** – anger, fear, sadness.
- **Behavior** – avoidance, defensiveness, withdrawal.

Modern neurological research has shown that triggers can be traced to the brain`s limbic system — especially the amygdala, which is responsible for emotional reactions and for our emotional memories.

When the brain registers a threat, the amygdala retrieves memory and initiates a fight, flight, or freeze response. If a person has experienced trauma, their amygdala may overreact to similar stimuli

— turning them into triggers. The amygdala governs our **"fight / flight / play dead"** response.

The fight-or-flight response has an important evolutionary function. When danger is perceived, the amygdala signals the body to release stress hormones. Heart rate increases, blood pressure rises, muscles tense, blood is redirected to the limbs, and the body prepares for action. These are those moments when a person seems to gain "superhuman strength" — for instance, to lift a car and save a child. The body sweats more to prevent overheating, and the muscles tense to enable rapid response. Because speed can be life-saving, the amygdala reacts in a fraction of a second — before the prefrontal cortex (the rational mind) even grasps what is happening.

Although these responses are useful in life-threatening situations, they can hinder us in modern life. Our nervous system does not distinguish between emotional threats and actual physical danger. When someone says something that touches our emotional wounds, the body reacts as if it were in danger. The amygdala "recognizes" the similarity of feelings we already carry and signals the body to prepare.

The hippocampus, responsible for memory, may misinterpret the present moment as a repetition of an old trauma. The prefrontal cortex — the region responsible for rational thinking — is often "switched off" at such times. This is why a person can feel "trapped" in their reaction.

Beyond mental responses, triggers can also provoke bodily memories — a person may physically feel tension, pain, or discomfort. This is especially present in people who have survived violence or emotional injury — the body remembers what the mind has suppressed.

Every human being has emotional triggers — positive or negative — and they look different for everyone. Life moves quickly and dynamically. Something happened at work. Someone said something that struck us. We read an email. A child ran into the street after a ball. We got our dream job. We broke up with a loved one. A child was born. We heard a song on the radio. One word took us back to childhood. A scent that reminds us of home. The taste of coffee from the past. The loss of a dear person. All of these are emotional triggers

— engraved deeply into the subconscious, shaped by how we experienced and remembered them.

It would be nice if we could box up all our feelings and deal with them when convenient. Unfortunately, people — and feelings — don`t work that way. At any moment we can experience a full spectrum of emotions, regardless of whether we feel ready to handle them. We are not designed to suppress our emotional reactions. Our emotions provide vital information about what is happening — inside and out. They are like our personal alarm system. But sometimes (or more often than we`d like) we notice we have an emotional reaction that is out of proportion to the actual event. This is precisely what mental health professionals call a trigger. Triggers have a deep impact on our lives, often determining our reactions in ways we do not fully understand. Recognizing and managing triggers is key to better mental health, emotional well-being, and deeper self-understanding.

In the realm of mental health and emotional balance, the term "trigger" has become common. It is also used casually in everyday speech — sometimes too lightly — ignoring its weight and complexity. To truly understand what it means to be "triggered," we must delve into the layers of emotional reactions, past trauma, and the effects triggers can have on a person`s mental state.

Everything that exists — began somewhere. If we view the body as a kind of memory card, as a clean white page — a **tabula rasa** — we can see that everything the body has experienced leaves a mark. From birth to this day — every feeling, every emotion, every event, positive or negative — leaves a record in the body.

The single factor that determines the quality of our lives is how we have stored and programmed those experiences within. Many people are unaware that we all have our own trigger points that "speak" to us through pain. If we ignore the signals these points send, they grow stronger and louder. In the long run, such neglect can have serious consequences for our physical and mental health.

Everything has a beginning — so do pain and illness. If we were to "rewind the tape" of a trigger point`s emergence, we would see it began as a mild pain at a specific spot in the body because a certain emotion left a trace on our inner memory. The good news is that these traces can be changed, modified, or completely erased and replaced with new ones.

Trigger points indicate the places that need our attention. They are our body`s calls to free ourselves from pain and restore balance — both physically and emotionally. Each time we re-experience a triggering emotion, the body automatically launches the same physiological response and activates the same point. Today it may be a subtle ache; tomorrow it can develop into illness. Therefore, to truly release pain, it is not enough to work only at the physical level using massage, physical therapy, or other methods. That only temporarily relieves surface pain, while the trace of the trigger remains in our mental map.

The real intervention must occur in our mental and emotional systems. When we release a trigger point from within, the body naturally reflects that change. If we consider our "holy trinity" — mind, spirit, and body — it becomes clear that true change requires work on all three levels. Although trigger points manifest physically, their true source lies deep in the emotional level of our being. Working only at the outer level can free us from visible consequences, but not from causes. To truly uproot deeply embedded patterns, we need to dive into the unseen parts of ourselves. When we change deep programs, change happens spontaneously in mind, spirit, and body. It`s a whole system. Every change weaves through all levels of our existence. Every part of us must receive the message that something is changing. And the body — as the last link in the chain — often finds out at the end.

That is why alignment across all levels matters. Otherwise, imbalance appears as discomfort, blocks, or physical symptoms.

The first level to recognize change is our emotional part. We often hear the phrase: **"Listen to your heart."** Even though the heart does not literally think, we instinctively place a hand on our chest when we want to express truth. There, in the center of the chest, we feel our deepest emotions. The role of emotions is linked to the amygdala—the brain region responsible for emotional reactions. It is precisely what "fires" when you make a decision "from the heart."

When a decision is made at the emotional level, it is then passed to the mental part of our being. There it is analyzed, planned, evaluated; strategies and ways of implementation are sought. This process depends on the type of person and their neurological patterns. It is precisely there — within the mental system — that trigger points begin to form. The time it takes for a decision to travel from the emotional and mental levels to the body — and for the body to become aware of that message — is the space in which a trigger arises.

The body is the last to receive the message. This is why trigger points manifest physically — as pain, tension, or illness. If we want to integrate change throughout our whole system, all three levels — mind, spirit, and body — must be aligned. Otherwise, our system will notify us that something is off-balance. This is why it is essential to listen to what the body is telling us. The body never lies — it stores information, emotions, and memories. And it reacts when mind and spirit are out of tune. When we learn to hear those signals and pay attention to our trigger points, we open the door to deeper healing and freedom.

An example: One of my clients had a powerful fear of people — so strong that she avoided them. At first, she felt discomfort in their presence; over time, she spent less and less time with others until she stopped going out altogether to avoid contact. In our work, we discovered that a past emotional injury had led to her need to close up like a shell and isolate herself completely. Every contact with people triggered a choking sensation in the chest, pressure, cramps, and bodily pain she couldn`t explain.

In a further stage of the process, we found that this old wound had created new programs and beliefs, yet the body had not "received" the message, because the decision had not reached the bodily level. The body, therefore, remained in imbalance. She had clearly decided she no longer wanted to spend time with unpleasant people who drained her energy and with whom healthy growth was impossible.

So — **the decision existed**. It had been passed along — to the mental level. But the body knew nothing of it. Because the body does not speak our language but communicates through sensations, every time she encountered people, the body sent messages — tightness in the chest, choking, pain. She did not understand that language. The body first speaks softly — whispering how it feels in certain situations.

But if we do not learn to listen, it becomes louder — until it shouts through pain, tension, and various physical sensations, hoping we will finally hear it.

We often see people whose bodies are "screaming" — but they ignore the signals, attributing them to illnesses they believe appeared out of nowhere. As if a disease just "came out of the blue." **Humans are not designed to be ill.** Every illness is the body`s attempt to orient us — to show where change is needed. Every illness is a once-unnoticed thought. A need we ignored.

Everything that is — began somewhere. Here, too, this applies. The body constantly communicates with us — giving signs and signals about how it feels in every life situation. The body itself cannot think or decide — but it can feel. And through the feelings it sends, we know whether something is good for us or not.

Only when my client found a healthy way to protect herself from negative people and their influence did the body receive the message of what had actually changed — and it found a way to align with her emotional and mental parts. The choking, chest tightness, and bodily pain disappeared the very moment she became aware of a new pattern that replaced her old one — the one where she fled from people and withdrew.

The body finally received the message about what the heart had decided and the mind had accepted. It adopted the adjustments that helped it adapt to the decision and synchronize with the new behavior. Until that moment, the body had "kept the brakes on," sending signals of its unwillingness to proceed under the current conditions.

What matters to understand is that these three levels — **mind, spirit, and body — are inseparable**. Though each is responsible for its part, the functioning of the human system is possible only through their unity, shared work, and mutual cooperation. While the concept of triggers is commonly discussed today in the context of trauma, emotional regulation, and behavior, its history reaches far back — from philosophical reflections on unconscious reactions, through pioneering psychological research, to modern neurological and therapeutic approaches.

Ancient philosophers did not use the term "trigger," but they reflected on the idea that external stimuli can provoke unconscious, automatic human reactions.

The Stoics, for example, argued that emotions are not caused by events themselves, but by our interpretations of them — suggesting that our responses to triggers result from **inner interpretations** rather than the external event.

Plato spoke of deeply embedded ideas in the mind that shape our perception and understanding of the world. **Aristotle** described principles of association, claiming that certain behaviors can be activated by recalling earlier experiences — a concept key to understanding how triggers form through experience and repetition.

In **Buddhist teaching**, the term **sankara** denotes unconscious mental formations that influence perception and behavior. Sankara represents karmically active volition or intention, influencing rebirth and shaping the course of life. In this sense, sankara parallels karma and encompasses actions of body, speech, and mind.

In other words, sankara describes mental tendencies formed as a result of past experiences that influence future drives and behaviors. Its purpose is not elimination but **purification** — much like today`s approach to triggers: not to suppress or erase them, but to make them conscious, understand them, and integrate them. Just like modern approaches, Buddhists divide sankara into three levels:

- Bodily
- Verbal
- Mental

This ancient division still reminds us that inner work is a holistic process — and that every form of inner transformation must occur simultaneously on all levels of our being.

As early as the XVII century, French philosopher and mathematician **René Descartes** claimed that the human body functions like a complex machine in which certain stimuli can elicit reflex reactions — independent of conscious thought. This idea laid the groundwork for later neurological studies of automatic reactions and triggers.

A century later, Scottish philosopher and economist **David Hume**, in his theory of associative learning, emphasized that the mind relies on associations between ideas and feelings — crucial for understanding how triggers emerge through experience and repetition. Through repeating the same behavior patterns, a lasting program is created and implemented in the subconscious — and this is what we call a trigger.

In the XIX century, Russian physician, psychologist, and Nobel laureate **Ivan Pavlov** demonstrated with dogs that a neutral stimulus (a bell) can become a trigger for an automatic physiological response (salivation) when repeatedly paired with a significant stimulus (food). This experiment laid the foundations for understanding classical conditioning, which explains how emotional and bodily triggers are formed through association.

Beyond these thinkers, many others have contributed to the development of trigger theory. The renowned **Sigmund Freud**, father of psychoanalysis, argued that repressed memories and traumas remain in the unconscious and can be activated by certain stimuli. According to his theory, triggers are symbolically linked to repressed experiences and can evoke strong emotional reactions — even when the person does not know their true source.

After World War I, psychologists observed that many soldiers had strong emotional and physiological reactions to sounds reminiscent of combat (explosions, screams). This phenomenon was later recognized as **post-traumatic stress disorder (PTSD)**, with war sounds identified as key triggers.

Swiss psychiatrist and founder of analytical psychology **Carl Gustav Jung** spoke of archetypal triggers — which activate deep unconscious patterns associated with the collective unconscious — profoundly influencing modern theories of triggers.

Canadian psychologist Albert Bandura showed that triggers need not be directly experienced — they can be learned through observation. For example, a child can develop a fear of dogs after seeing a parent react fearfully to a dog.

The evolution of trigger theory shows how various disciplines — philosophy, psychology, neurology, and therapy — have, over time, built upon one another to explain how unconscious stimuli shape human behavior. Today, understanding triggers is crucial not only for healing trauma but also for personal development, emotional regulation, and improved mental health.

TYPES OF TRIGGERS

Triggers can be divided into different categories depending on their source and how they operate. These categories often overlap, because the human psyche is a complex system in which bodily, emotional, and mental reactions interweave. For that reason, many triggers appear in combination — with others we experience both from the outside and from within.

BY TYPE OF STIMULUS

External Triggers

These are stimuli from our environment that activate unconscious reactions. In other words, any situation that comes from outside and negatively affects us can be considered a trigger.

The world unfolds around us, whether we want it to or not. Perhaps our greatest challenge lies in finding a way to accept what we cannot change. Because the only thing we can truly influence is our response, our attitude and the way we react to what befalls us.

Each of us has surely experienced something frightening or painful that left a mark, a mark that later appears as a trigger. Today, those triggers influence where we are, how we feel, and how we`re doing.

The outer world often feels like a vast jungle where challenges and dangers lurk from all sides. It is natural that many people bear inner traces and scars that shaped them — and some, marked them for life. The way we "stored" those experiences — the way they became part of our being, our code, and our system — determines the course of our fate and the quality of our life.

So, **the way we remember external events creates our inner reality and the path we walk.**

Examples:

- The sound of a siren can trigger panic in someone who has lived through war.

- A perfume`s scent can evoke memories of a past love and set off a wave of sadness.
- The sight of a certain object can create discomfort if it resembles a traumatic experience.

Internal Triggers

These are inner mental, emotional, or bodily stimuli that activate a reaction. That is, whatever happens within us — regardless of the outside world — our negative thoughts, beliefs, and feelings are internal triggers.

Like all others, these internal triggers arose long ago. Because of them — or in spite of them — we became who we are today. The first internal triggers left a kind of scratch on the heart. With each repetition, a new layer sticks to the previous one. Over time those layers become so intense and firm that they grow into a part of our character.

For example, if a child once faced an unpleasant or dangerous situation in which no one present helped, they may adopt an inner trigger: the belief that in life they must think only of themselves — because that`s what others did then. That first trigger becomes a new program in the child`s system, where they "record" that in similar situations they must act differently to avoid the pain they once felt. Over time they learn to look out only for themselves — to stay safe. Later, seeing another child in a similar situation, they may respond as those did who once failed to help them — coldly, indifferently, self-focused.

Examples:

- **A thought like "I`m not good enough"** can provoke anxiety. This is one of the most common triggers we carry through much of life — an inner replica of messages once spoken by parents or other authorities, which we continue to repeat to ourselves automatically.
- **An inner sense of tension** can unconsciously prompt self-harming behavior. If, as children, we didn`t learn healthy

ways to handle tension, the same pattern will follow us into adulthood — regardless of status, wealth, or whether we have children of our own. The trigger will still be there — faithfully waiting to be noticed, acknowledged, and transformed.

- **A dream** can set off a bodily reaction to a repressed trauma. As Sigmund Freud suggested, dreams are a conversation with our unconscious. If we learn to listen to inner messages, dreams can bring valuable insights and show which traumas still quietly shape us — waiting to be seen.

Somatic (Bodily) Triggers

Any negative situation that sparks bodily reactions — skin flushing, rapid breathing, trembling, stiffness or paralysis in certain areas, difficulty breathing, inability to speak, or pain in a specific body part — constitutes a somatic trigger. You may know the phrase: **"That harsh word killed me."** This expression can be linked to the body`s response to certain situations.

Words are powerful — they can lift a person from bed or knock them into it. When the body isn`t ready to receive a certain message, somatic triggers activate — choking, chest pain, facial flushing, elevated blood pressure. These are expected reactions of a body trying to defend itself from the message it`s receiving.

What`s especially interesting about bodily triggers is that they contain **their own film reel**. Like a strip of film recording every detail — from the trigger`s origin to the present — they store the full story of how they formed and what they hold.

When the first trigger is engraved on our white page — our tabula rasa — we feel a faint sting, a vague, hard-to-name ache at that spot in the body. Each subsequent layer, each new "episode," sticks over the previous one, and with time the faint sensation becomes tension, then a kind of muscle paralysis — for which we stop using a body part in the usual way.

Our body parts don`t have their own brain to "think," nor a heart to "feel." **The body communicates through sensations — not in words, but in feelings.** That`s how we know when something is pleasant — or not. If we ignore the signs the body keeps sending, eventually it will "scream" in the language of sensation. The pain becomes unbearable and we wonder, "Where did this come from?" The usual answer: visit a doctor. We expect them to know better than we do what`s wrong. The doctor will, of course, do their best — recognize symptoms, give a diagnosis, prescribe medications. But what a doctor often cannot tell us is — **where the pain truly began.**

The question isn`t always:

"What hurts?"

but:

"Who hurts you?"

Some answers don`t come from medicine — they come from within. As long as we try to treat the problem from the outside while neglecting the inside, we cut at the body without touching what`s actually wounded. Many try to heal for years with pills and surgeries without ever stopping to ask, **"Where did this really start?"** And when there`s nothing left to "cut," we often return — to ourselves. To where it all began.

No doctor can know better than you what your body is trying to say. You need to **rewind the tape** to the trigger`s origin. Analyze the content and press **pause** at the right moment. **Zoom in**. See the critical point where the pain was born. **Accept the wisdom of that experience**, learn to revise the memory — and free your body.

Only then can we release illness and restore well-being. Only then can we close **generational loops** and free not only ourselves, but those who come after us.

If not for yourself — then for them. This is your temple. It is within you. From you everything begins — and with you it ends.

Unlike bodily triggers that play out externally, emotional triggers activate from within. Like somatic ones, emotional triggers can be **extremely strong and, at times, feel almost fatal** for the person experiencing them.

The sensation can resemble unbearable pain — an inner shutdown, as if the person is "dying" inside and losing contact with their own existence. In that moment, a trigger reel forms within — a kind of mental - emotional film on which **absolutely every detail** of its origin is recorded. That reel remains permanently stored in us and influences all future situations in which any element resembles something from the original experience.

If, in some later situation, we encounter even one element that echoes the first event — a specific word, tone of voice, or a look — that can be enough to reactivate the trigger and provoke a strong emotional response.

Examples:

- A person who felt **abandoned** by a parent in childhood may experience a powerful emotional collapse when facing a similar situation as an adult. The old feeling activates because the brain recognizes similarity and — failing to distinguish past from present — automatically launches **the same reaction pattern.**
- Emotional triggers can be **extremely painful**; many describe them as **feeling like "dying inside."**
- Being ignored by a partner can activate memories of a parent`s behavior, triggering anger, rage, or a craving for validation and acceptance. Almost all of us have been in such a situation at some point — and we know how emotionally draining and difficult it is.
- We all have a **need to be seen and affirmed** in our existence. Yet the way we seek that reveals **the level of our emotional maturity and inner intelligence.**

BY EMOTIONAL REACTION

Anxious Triggers

These triggers evoke fear, tension, and panic. **Any negative memory** of events related to failure, shame, or disappointment can act as a trigger - causing a person to experience intense negative emotions when facing similar situations again.

Phobias and fears are often emotional triggers. For example, a person who has a fear of heights may experience anxiety or panic when faced with the prospect of climbing to a high place.

High-pressure situations, as well as everyday challenges, can provoke **stress and anxiety**. This includes work deadlines, public speaking, important conversations, and other demanding circumstances. Major life changes - even positive ones - can trigger a mix of emotions. For example, starting a new job or moving to an unfamiliar place may bring both excitement and anxiety, and sometimes stress.

Examples:

- Loud noise can trigger a panic attack in someone with post-traumatic stress disorder (PTSD).
- Looking at a bank statement may cause intense anxiety in someone struggling with financial pressure.
- A mother who sees her child under a car may experience a sudden wave of panic that activates an incredible surge of energy - strong enough to lift the vehicle with her hands and save the child.

Angry Triggers

These triggers activate feelings of anger, frustration, and aggression. All of our past experiences of such emotions can be reactivated by new situations that resemble those from the past.

Examples:

- Injustice can spark a strong reaction of anger in a person who once felt powerless. These are the situations where, for example, in a legal case, at work, or during a family conflict, you experienced injustice but lacked the resources or strength to stand up for your rights.
- A partner's tone of voice can trigger an unconscious aggressive reaction if it resembles that of a parent who used a similar tone, body posture, or expressions in childhood. If you grew up with strict parents, any communication today that echoes those methods can become your emotional trigger.
- A colleague raising their voice during a meeting can provoke intense anxiety in someone who associates it with a parent who often yelled. The triggered response may manifest as a rapid heartbeat, withdrawal, feelings of insecurity, or sudden anger.
- Such reactions indicate that there is still a time or situation the person has not yet processed emotionally. In this case, the colleague is not the "culprit" but rather **the trigger** - the activator of a memory still waiting to be resolved.

Depressive Triggers

These triggers are linked to feelings of sadness, emptiness, and hopelessness. All situations that once activated such emotions leave traces we may carry through life - until we bring them into awareness.

Interactions with certain people or reminders of past problems can provoke strong feelings such as sadness, anger, or frustration. This can also explain why certain issues arise in our relationships today. What we have not healed with former partners, we unconsciously transfer into future ones. That is why it is best to enter a relationship only when **emotionally healed** - to protect yourself from repeating old patterns and to protect your partner from carrying the weight of your unprocessed wounds. A partner is not responsible for enduring the consequences of unresolved emotions from your past, nor obliged to carry the burden of defenses that were once triggered by someone else. A partner should be someone you grow and evolve with - which is why it is so important to **consciously face the "loose ends" you carry from the past.**

Just as in romantic relationships, the loss of a loved one leaves deep marks we may consciously or unconsciously carry into our environment and onto new people in our lives. Events or anniversaries tied to grief, such as the death of a loved one, are often emotional triggers that awaken intense feelings. It is natural for pain to demand its own time - time for mourning, quiet processing, and acceptance. But it is important that this time does not turn into a lifelong lens through which you see everything that follows. Life goes on - and it needs you, just as you are, ready for new connections and new experiences.

This trigger - loss - may be one of the hardest. But it also teaches us about **impermanence, about letting go**, and about the truth that nothing - not even our own life - is eternal. Within that realization lies wisdom.

Examples:

- The sight of the place where a loss occurred can evoke deep melancholy.
- A song that recalls a former love can trigger an emotional downturn.
- Being in the hospital where someone close passed away can provoke sadness, anxiety, or a sense of emptiness.

BY ORIGIN

Traumatic Triggers

These triggers are connected with past traumas and can provoke strong emotional and physical reactions. They include all events that remind a person of traumatic experiences from the past - such as abuse, accidents, losses, assaults, or any other events that left a deep imprint. They are often activated through sensory stimuli - a smell, tone of voice, touch, place, word, or image. The brain does not distinguish time - what happened once is relived as if it is happening **now**.

Traumas leave scars that influence future choices and the quality of our lives. Almost all of us have experienced some form of trauma - whether it was a physical injury, a car accident, psychological or physical abuse, the loss of a loved one, the destruction of a home, or violence.

The most intense triggers come from the outside, often suddenly, leaving no space for preparation. They sometimes leave us speechless - frozen in the moment. At times, it takes a long time to face them and gather enough strength to move forward.

I once had a client who, as a fourteen-year-old girl, experienced sexual assault. She never spoke about it - not to her parents, nor to her friends. For years, she carried that experience silently and heavily within herself. That evening when she came home, she was beside herself. She remembers nothing of the path she walked or the streets she passed. Her father was watching television and didn`t notice her entering. Her mother greeted her with disapproval, scolding her for coming home late. Without a word, she went to the bathroom, took off her clothes, and curled up under the stream of cold water, trying to wash away the traces. She cried as quietly as possible, so as not to draw attention. In her hand she held a brush, scrubbing harshly at her skin in an attempt to "clean" the memory from her body - until her skin turned red and nearly bled.

Years later, during our work together, she discovered that she still, unconsciously, repeated the same behavior - harshly scrubbing her skin - every time she experienced discomfort or a touch that reminded her of that moment. That was her trigger. It had lived in her for a long time - until she chose to bring it into awareness and transform it. No matter what we have lived through - it is important to know: **triggers can be transformed**.

Sometimes, the strongest triggers become our greatest drivers - the force that leads us toward freedom, strength, and purpose.

Examples:

- A person who survived a car accident may panic every time they see a similar car.

- A loud tone of voice can trigger fear in someone who has lived through domestic violence.
- A person who was abused may have a strong reaction to certain phrases or touches.
- A person who survived war may experience anxiety or panic when hearing an explosion or seeing a uniform - leading to "war flashbacks," rapid heartbeat, and a feeling of suffocation.

Developmental Triggers

Developmental triggers are connected to childhood experiences and unconscious beliefs formed during early development. They are mostly tied to the period of our formation, when we adopt behavioral patterns and build our personality. We can say that this type of trigger is closely related to the first three years of a child`s life. It is then that the child gains their first experiences and beliefs, learns about the world, and discovers themselves in it. This is considered one of the most significant periods in a child`s development, as during this time they adopt their first - and often lasting - inner programs and patterns of behavior.

Example: A person whose parents told them "You must be perfect" may experience intense anxiety when making a mistake. Such a trigger can have a profoundly strong impact on the quality of life. Every time that person makes an error, the old pattern is activated - the inner voice of the parents - repeating the very same sentences once spoken in childhood. Over time, this inner voice becomes so present that the person perceives it as part of their character, not recognizing that it is something adopted - not innate.

What is especially important to emphasize is that such triggers are often **passed on to the next generations**. For example, a person may unconsciously place the same pressure of "you must be perfect" on their own child, believing it to be normal and correct. This is how generational cycles are created, shaping entire family destinies.

As Carl Jung said: **"Until the unconscious becomes conscious, it will direct your life and you will call it fate."** It takes **only one awakened member of the family** to put an end to such patterns - to close the vicious circle and allow freedom for all future generations. A person who was emotionally neglected in childhood may, in adulthood, have a strong emotional reaction when their partner ignores them. In that moment, the old pattern is activated - the same sadness and need for attention the child once didn`t receive. The person may react with raised voice, withdrawal, aggression, passivity, self-harm, or some other behavior that once brought results.

Even though they are no longer a child, the person automatically reaches for patterns that once worked - because their body remembers them as survival mechanisms.

Collective Triggers

Collective triggers are linked to archetypal and social themes that can evoke strong emotional reactions - even when the individual did not personally experience the event. They have the power to awaken collective empathy, sadness, anger, compassion, and solidarity toward events affecting other people or social groups. This century provides us with countless examples of collective awakenings of consciousness that push boundaries, change laws, influence life rules, and provoke global reactions.

We are witnesses to dramatic social changes: wars, destruction of cities, ecological disasters, rapid technological development, geopolitical and economic crises, and pandemics that have shaken the entire planet. All of these bring about collective movements, initiatives, and sensitivities that impact the emotional state of the individual, regardless of whether they are directly affected or not.

On the other hand, the media often use such content to manipulate collective consciousness - steering the masses in directions that serve particular interests. Surely, each of us has at least once experienced a surge of energy, a desire to "save humanity," precisely as a result of an emotional reaction to a specific piece of content. What we see, hear, and feel through our visual, auditory, and kinesthetic channels has a strong impact on our inner state, our way of thinking, and our life decisions.

Examples:

- Images of war can provoke fear and helplessness in people who never directly participated in conflict, yet carry collective unconscious trauma from past generations.
- Social injustices - such as violence against the vulnerable, injustices toward minorities, or disadvantaged groups - can trigger strong emotional reactions in individuals who are naturally sensitive to the suffering of others.

HOW TO RECOGNIZE TRIGGERS?

We all have our specific triggers. Their appearance differs from person to person. Being " triggered " means having a strong, unpleasant emotional reaction to a stimulus that, on the surface, doesn`t seem significant enough to cause such distress. This is the moment when the **fight / flight** mechanism activates, and the body reacts as if life were in danger - before the rational mind even realizes what is happening. In such moments people may panic, feel emotionally overwhelmed, withdraw, cry, or respond defensively.

Symptoms of being triggered include:

- a sense of fear, agitation, or insecurity,
- rapid heartbeat, sweating, trembling,
- difficulty breathing, chest tightness,
- an urge to flee or an aggressive reaction,
- unpredictable mood swings,
- bodily tension (clenched fists, jaw),
- emotional flashbacks,
- delayed outbursts of anger or sadness.

Any of these symptoms can arise in response to a provoking stimulus. What makes triggers so hard to identify is their highly individualized nature. Although it`s impossible to compile an exhaustive list of triggers - or even to say definitively where they come from - we can still notice the relationship between cause and effect in how triggers form.

Often, once a trigger is identified, it becomes much easier to see what it is linked to. For example, if someone was left by a partner in the autumn, they may subconsciously feel an unexplained sadness every subsequent autumn, without being aware of why or how that sadness relates to their present reality. Only when they connect the symptoms of sadness with their current experience can they gain insight into which external and internal stimuli are activating the trigger - and then unpack and analyze them.

We do not choose to have the reactions we have. Triggers happen too quickly for our rational mind, which in that instant lacks the power and choice to notice the amygdala`s command that activates fight / flight. But we do have a choice about what happens next. Even when we are triggered, we can practice the discipline of learning how to manage our state of being.

Understanding the phenomenon of being triggered and knowing your own triggers is the first step. Without that awareness, we are at the mercy of our triggers. With awareness, we give ourselves the possibility to make different choices about what we can do when triggers activate.

Most importantly, we need to direct our attention the right way. In the moment we are triggered, our attention is locked on the apparent cause. We think we know what the problem is and what activated our trigger, yet it usually has to do with a different person who is the true trigger - or a different event responsible for activating it. In fact, the trigger was already within us, and the current event or person only activated its presence. We must train ourselves to recognize that the intensity and quality of our reaction are not caused by the current event, but by something that happened in the past. Those feelings, that core wounding, that conditioning - all of it has been within us from before.

A trigger is a response waiting to be stimulated, like an accident primed to happen. In reality, we might not otherwise feel the need to do something or respond in a certain way, but when we are triggered we are unable to assess what is needed in that moment - and even less able to act effectively.

The good news is that we can learn to manage our reactions in ways that are appropriate and acceptable to us and our environment. This is a critical discipline for leaders and for anyone who wants to contribute to a better world.

Our reactions to triggers can vary:

- **Anger** - when you feel manipulated, disrespected, or betrayed.
- **Pity or sadness** - when you feel the other person is weak or defeated.
- **Shame or guilt** - when you feel their emotion is somehow your fault.
- **Defensiveness or hostility** - when you feel you are being blamed.
- **Frustration or overwhelm** - when you feel pressured to handle others' emotions.
- **Fear** - when you expect the situation to escalate into something worse.

In short, a reaction to a trigger can be any intense emotion or sensation within us. When you identify your most common emotional triggers and explore the thoughts or memories attached to them, you are ready to choose a new response. Instead of surrendering to the trigger, realize that you can steer your thoughts and memories.

Then you can look at the current situation objectively and choose a healthier or more fitting response. This doesn`t mean you will never be triggered again - it means you can avoid letting the trigger dictate your behavior and words. The next time you feel any emotional reaction, ask yourself whether it is actually your trigger. Identify the thoughts and memories that influenced your reaction in that moment and consider how you can respond appropriately to the present situation.

There are different types of triggers, but they share one thing in common: they are unexpected. The event that triggers you can be anything from a stressful encounter with a colleague to an argument with a partner. Sometimes it can be something as small as a change in routine. Whatever it is, it matters that you can spot it and know what to do with it.

- **Awareness** - The first step is recognizing when the trigger activates and which feeling comes with it.
- **Linking to the past** - Understanding where that trigger comes from and which imprint created it.
- **Reprogramming** - Through NLP techniques, hypnosis, mindfulness, or other methods you can change how you respond to the trigger.

WHAT TO DO WITH TRIGGERS?

Listen to your mind and body - A key step in learning to recognize your triggers is paying attention when situations bring a strong emotional response. Beyond sudden emotions, you might notice physical signs of anxiety such as pounding heart, upset stomach, trembling or dizziness, sweaty palms, and so on.

Notice your reactions - Every emotion has a corresponding physical sensation. When you are upset, you will likely feel it in your stomach, chest, or neck. Your mind might go blank, or you might have any of the symptoms above. Chances are it will feel mostly the same each time. Once you recognize that feeling, it becomes easier to identify it as a trigger. That knowledge empowers you to step out of "automatic reaction mode" and step into self-care.

Take a pause - When you notice these signs, stop to reflect on what just happened and what reaction it activated. Say you spent the afternoon deep-cleaning and rearranging the living room. When your partner gets home, you wait excitedly for a comment. Instead, they head to the kitchen for food and then settle on the sofa without a word. You feel disappointed your effort went unacknowledged and you start getting angry and frustrated. You notice your heart racing and your jaw clenching. It takes everything not to snap and say, "Do you notice anything different?" or "I can`t believe you`re so unaware!"

It is rarely a good idea to respond immediately when you`re stirred up. Take time away from the situation to process your emotional response. Once you practice recognizing when you`re triggered, you can begin developing coping mechanisms. Even if you can`t fully step away, there are many helpful practices. Deep breathing can be done anytime, anywhere. If you`re in a stressful conversation, try reframing and repeating back what you heard. This buys you time to slow down and begin thinking about your response.

Trace the roots - Try to trace the feelings back to their origin by recalling other situations that made you feel the same. Maybe you suddenly felt like a teenager again, trying to make the house look perfect to earn approval from an indifferent parent who traveled often. When the emotional trigger (your partner`s indifference) activated, you were transported back to that time when nothing you did felt good enough.

Be curious - Sometimes the link between you and your triggers isn`t obvious, so you may need to dig deeper. When strong emotions arise, don`t ignore or suppress them. Approach them with curiosity to gain insight into what might have triggered them. Do you notice certain patterns that stand out and repeat?

Pay attention to how you feel - Do you feel agitated and overwhelmed or have trouble settling? Notice these symptoms when they show up, especially if they appear suddenly or seem unrelated to your circumstances. If you feel this way and don`t know why, there is a good chance you are triggered.

Something is bugging you - Is there something that suddenly weighs on you? If it`s a major issue with high stakes, your concern may be understandable. But if it`s a routine occurrence that stresses you out, there may be more to it than meets the eye.

Listen inward - We all have those situations we can`t stop thinking about. We think we`ve let it go, but when we talk about it, we feel exhausted again. If you find you can`t stop thinking about a particular situation, something about it may have triggered you.

Accept your feelings - Trigger reactions are known for being explosive. If you notice you`re overreacting (or doing so often), pay attention. You may not be reacting to the current situation but to the underlying source of the trigger. Acknowledging your feelings is essential. Take time to listen to them without judging yourself for having them. Allow yourself to feel whatever emotion arises without trying to push it away. Certain events may trigger some people, while a particular type of person or situation may trigger others. If you`re not sure what your triggers are, keeping a journal to identify patterns can help.

Trigger warnings - A trigger warning is a statement at the start of a text, video, or other content that alerts the audience to sensitive material. This is usually because the content contains references, depictions, or discussions that could trigger trauma. Trigger warnings can help people with anxiety, PTSD, or other mental health conditions.

They can also help people who haven`t experienced trauma but are sensitive to graphic content. It is wise to include these warnings when content is potentially distressing and publicly available. It can be jarring to encounter an unexpected trigger while relaxing, watching a movie, or scrolling social media. Trigger warnings help a viewer prepare for content that might upset them - or opt out. Pay attention to such signals.

Own your feelings - First, remind yourself it is perfectly okay to feel whatever you feel in that moment. Sad, angry, scared, furious - triggers can stir many emotions, and that is normal. Before you work with those emotions, you need to accept them. Denying or ignoring what you feel usually makes things worse over time. It may help to remind yourself of the differences between past and present, but do this with self-compassion, not self-judgment.

Say a coworker takes your book and asks, "What are you reading?" If that reminds you of classmates who teased you and hid your books, you may feel upset and irritated and want to snatch the book back. Instead, acknowledge that while past circumstances may have caused pain and made you feel that way, those circumstances are not repeating now. This reminder can help you regain control and actively choose a different response, like offering a brief summary of the book or a light follow-up about what you`re reading.

Give yourself space - Physically stepping away can help you avoid emotional overload. If you can, excuse yourself for a short break. This can help you avoid an impulsive reaction you might regret. When you are alone, try breathing or grounding exercises to calm down. The goal isn`t to avoid the triggering circumstances entirely. You are simply giving yourself a moment to cool down so you can handle the situation more productively. When you feel steadier, you can return with a clearer head.

Keep an open mind - Generally, most people in your life aren`t trying to make you feel bad. Some of the words or actions that upset you may be byproducts of their own triggers or factors you aren`t aware of. Your partner walked in and didn`t notice you completely rearranged the living room? Maybe they received bad news or had a tough day and needed to decompress before talking. Everyone has unique emotions running beneath the surface at any given time, and you may not know what`s going on unless they tell you. It`s also easier to misread behavior or intent when you don`t know someone well. All the more reason to consider their perspective.

Communicate - When someone`s actions trigger your emotions, opening up can help you avoid a repeat. Take a minute to calm down if needed, then use I-statements and healthy communication skills to address it. Instead of slamming a drawer and yelling, "Where did you put my tape?" try calmly saying, "I feel frustrated when you take my things without asking and don`t put them back." In some cases, invite the other person to practice better communication. If the silent treatment, passive-aggressive behavior, or unkind or sarcastic remarks are emotional triggers for you, try gently asking, "What`s on your mind?" or "I`m sorry, I`m not sure what you mean by that."

Take care of yourself - Being triggered is not a pleasant experience and can be emotionally draining. Since this kind of stress can involve intense physical reactions, tending to your basic needs is crucial. Hunger, dehydration, and physical exhaustion can trigger - or worsen - trauma responses. Make sure you take good care of yourself and give your body what it needs to recover.

Practice mindfulness and meditation - Engaging in mindfulness and meditation helps you develop self-awareness so you can better understand your thoughts and emotions without judgment. Mindfulness allows you to observe your triggers and emotional responses without being overwhelmed by them. Regular meditation can improve overall emotional resilience and your ability to remain present.

Observe others - When we understand that all human behavior is an attempt to meet a perceived or real need, we can choose to look beyond behavior and get curious about the need driving it. Behavior is like the tip of an iceberg - the larger submerged part is the need underneath.

Keep a mood journal - Regularly tracking your emotions can help you recognize specific patterns, such as emotional triggers and periods of greater vulnerability. You may find it easy to stay composed when your boss critiques your work, but not when you feel your partner doesn`t want to spend time with you. This information can lead to positive change. If your usual response to that trigger shuts you down inside and makes you feel worse, decide instead to start a conversation with your partner the next time those feelings arise.

Talk to a professional - Trauma responses are complex. If you notice you are routinely triggered - or if it feels impossible to manage your triggers - consider speaking with a counselor, coach, or mental health professional. Even if you feel you have your triggers under control, discussing them with a therapist or coach can help you refine your coping strategies.

Emotion regulation is a difficult skill for most people, and it`s not always easy to identify triggers on your own. Your instinctive reactions may be so deeply rooted that you don`t realize how they are causing harm. If you are too close to your triggers to recognize and address their impact, therapy can help.

Coaching provides a safe, nonjudgmental space to identify provoking situations and explore potential reasons behind your triggers. A coach can also help you practice more productive communication strategies to express emotions and offer guidance and support while you work on revising the sources of your triggers.

Develop a grounding routine - A grounding routine can help bring your focus back to the present. Parasympathetic breathing or progressive muscle relaxation are simple practices you can use to reconnect with your body and regulate emotions. For example, if you feel overwhelmed, try slow deep breaths while counting to five on each inhale and exhale. This technique can help you relax and observe your emotional triggers without being caught up in them.

Set healthy boundaries - Identify and communicate your boundaries with others. Clear boundaries can prevent situations that provoke negative emotions. Learning to say no when needed, to state your needs, and to communicate assertively contributes to healthier relationships and reduces the likelihood of triggering situations.

Build a support system - Nurture a strong network of supportive friends, family, coaches, or support groups. Having people with whom you can talk about your experiences and emotions can provide validation and perspective. Sharing your feelings and receiving empathy can be crucial for processing and coping with emotional triggers. Remember that these strategies work differently for everyone, and it is essential to find what suits you best.

Combining multiple approaches and seeking professional guidance when needed can improve the effectiveness of managing emotional triggers. If trauma is a significant factor, consulting a mental health professional is especially important for personalized support and direction. It can help to have a set of self-help practices you can use to calm yourself. If you feel comfortable, share them with a friend, family member, or coach so they can help you decompress.

Exercises for recognizing and transforming triggers

Self-awareness and introspection: keep a reaction journal:

- Write down situations when you experienced an intense emotion.
- Ask yourself: What happened? How did I react? What does it remind me of?

Pattern identification: look for recurring themes in your reactions.

- Which situations or people frequently trigger reactions?
- Is there a connection to past experiences?

Working with the body (somatic therapy): pay attention to physical reactions to triggers (rapid pulse, sweating, tension). Breathing exercises or meditation can help you calm down and recognize the cause of the reaction.

Reframing (NLP technique): reshape the meaning of the trigger: Instead of seeing your reaction as a weakness, view it as a signal of an unresolved issue.

Example: Instead of "I am angry because they are ignoring me," consider: "This is an opportunity to face my fear of rejection."

Mindfulness exercises: focus on the present moment and observe emotions without judgment. Use affirmations such as: "I am safe and secure."

Visualization and imagery: imagine a situation that upsets you, but picture a different outcome.
Example: If your trigger is a loud argument, imagine yourself responding calmly and resolving the conflict.

Exercise for releasing a trigger

To understand how to work with triggers, I want to guide you through a brief practice. Choose something that is a trigger for you. It should not be overly traumatic - choose something you can easily recall. Because triggers take over very quickly, we will try to slow everything down and bring awareness to what is happening while you are in a safe environment, where you can get to know these signals and rehearse a new response. This can help you respond more skillfully next time and prevent escalation.

Let`s take a few breaths and settle. Close your eyes if that feels comfortable. Focus on the inhale and exhale, even on the pause in between. Feel your body relaxing with each breath as you rest comfortably in your chair. Now bring your trigger to mind. Return to the moment when it happened. Really return fully to that point in time. Where were you? Who or what was involved? What exactly happened? Try to bring back the feeling you had then. What do you feel in your body? Notice physical sensations and the reactions of your face. How do your neck, your jaw, your chest feel? What is the sensation in your stomach?

Notice all the emotions appearing in many places in your body. How deep is the sensation? How would you describe it? Warm, cold, soft, hard? Simply notice what is here, right now. Which emotions go with it? Is there hurt? Does anger arise? Frustration? Fear?

Stay here for a moment and experience this moment. What is present? Now reflect briefly on thoughts about the situation. As an observer, without following memory trails, simply note the thoughts that appear. Is it anger showing up as a feeling? Hopelessness? Are there victim thoughts? Blame? Whatever the thoughts are, just note them and let them go. You may notice that thoughts link to the emotion and amplify it. If you find yourself caught in a thought, let it go and return to observing.

Breathe in and out naturally, noticing your thoughts, emotions, and awareness. Now that you realize you can let them go, you can also see that you do not have to react to them at all. You have a choice. Return to your breath, feeling your body breathe. The breath moves in and out, restoring a sense of calm in your body. If any emotions remain, try this: make a tight ball with your fists, squeeze your muscles firmly, hold, spread your hand, and release. Shake out your fingers.

Now take a good deep breath in - and let go.

How was that for you?

NOTES

DRIVERS

"Sometimes we're not driven by a true desire,
but by an old voice that whispers:
you have to be... to be loved."
Aleksandra Božović

Drivers are unconscious inner propellers that govern behavior, motivation, and the way a person proves themselves to the world. They are often the result of early imprints and learned patterns that have become the "rules" a person unconsciously follows.

As unconscious patterns of behavior, thoughts, and feelings, they arise in early childhood as a response to the expectations and demands of the environment, primarily parents, authorities, or society. They act like "programs" that push us toward certain behaviors and influence our decisions, emotions, and relationships with others, and are often linked to basic human needs: acceptance, success, love, or safety.

Drivers are, therefore, unconscious inner mechanisms, beliefs, or behavior patterns that "drive" us and motivate us to act in certain ways. In the context of psychology and Neuro-Linguistic Programming (NLP), drivers are often seen as "compulsions" that shape our reactions in various situations, often unconsciously. These are all those moments when it feels like something was stronger than us and we had to act a certain way.

The messages we carry from childhood - formed under the influence of parents and/or significant others about how we should be and how we should behave, as well as early child perceptions and conclusions - function as compulsory motivation and strongly affect us later, during growing up and the formation of our personality.

On an unconscious level, a person feels compelled to constantly fulfill certain conditioned "instructions for life" (most often originating from parents) through specific behaviors in order to feel OK and/or experience themselves as important (worthy) or accepted, and to defend against the consequences of ingrained psychological prohibitions.

Why do people do this? Why does something "unconsciously push" them to behave a certain way in a given situation, even when they themselves notice it may not be best for them? Why do we feel frustrated if we can`t do something exactly as we "set our minds to"? These are questions we can answer by recognizing our own drivers.

The concept of drivers comes from Transactional Analysis (TA), developed by **Eric Berne**, and was expanded by psychologists such as **Taibi Kahler and Claude Steiner**. According to their research, drivers are formed as responses to messages we received in childhood and become part of our inner belief system - "inner voices" that push us toward certain behaviors. Drivers can be motivating, but they often lead to stress, exhaustion, or dissatisfaction.

According to psychologist and transactional analyst Taibi Kahler, drivers are ways we learned to adapt to our environment when we were young. They develop in the years when we can understand what the adults around us approve of or disapprove of, and we try to adapt to them so we can feel good about ourselves. Some messages we pick up from verbal responses, others from nonverbal reactions to us.

So, as we can see, drivers develop in early childhood as a child tries to meet the expectations of parents and other authorities to gain love, attention, and acceptance. They can have both positive and negative aspects - on one hand, they help us be successful and socially adapted; on the other, they can limit us and lead to stress, perfectionism, and burnout.

In work with clients, we often touch on this very important topic related to a psychological phenomenon that is universal and visible in most people through their behaviors - the phenomenon of psychological drivers or "pushers" that compel a person to behave in certain ways. We are often unaware of this influence and follow it blindly throughout life, without questioning the usefulness of such behaviors. Especially during childhood, and later as we grow, we adopt certain behavior templates from important figures (primarily parents and other authorities), considering them correct. Very often these patterns are part of upbringing, and sometimes they appear within certain religions. These behaviors often get embedded so deeply that we pass them on to future generations.

When we say "psychological driver," we mean a kind of inner compulsive behavior that, in a way, defines our identity. If we try not to act according to the driver, we feel bad, uncomfortable, and insecure. So we keep acting in line with the driver even when negative consequences are obvious. Although these are generally "OK" behaviors - behaviors that present us as good and worthy people - if they are overly present, compulsive, and if we expect others to practice them, they can seriously hinder our personal and social functioning. If drivers are used to achieve a goal, they can be effective; if used to avoid something, they take on the function of self-limitation and/or self-sabotage.

Today, drivers are especially pronounced due to high social expectations, the fast pace of life, and the need for constant proving. People unconsciously follow their drivers, which can lead to burnout, anxiety, and dissatisfaction. We can notice people`s drivers through many aspects of behavior: words, tone, speech patterns, gestures, posture, facial expressions, the way people dress, and how they keep their home or office. We usually have two main drivers, and understanding them can help us understand ourselves and others.

Taibi Kahler identified five basic drivers that children inherit from their parents. These drivers push us to behave in certain ways regardless of whether that is an adequate "here and now" response or not. They are compulsive and we feel we cannot choose our reaction - as if a higher, stronger force is directing us. We then believe we are OK only if we are strong, perfect, or if we rush through life trying to please and make others happy.

The five basic psychological drivers are:

- Be Perfect!
- Be Strong!
- Please Others!
- Hurry Up!
- Try Hard!

Characteristics that indicate a person carries this driver are: striving for perfectionism, having high expectations of oneself and others, fear of mistakes and failure, constant need for validation from others.
Positive side of this driver: Precision, attention to detail, professionalism.
Negative side of this driver: Stress, procrastination, inability to enjoy achievements. This driver often develops when parents force the child to obey their commands without question. People with this driver have an obsessive need to do things so perfectly that no one can find fault with them. They often struggle with tasks they cannot do "perfectly," feeling completely blocked, which can lead to not completing the task at all. A simple example: if their closets are not perfectly functional, they may not even try to organize their clothes, leaving them scattered across the room. For these children, the main parental message was: "You can always do better."

Individuals with developed perfectionism hold high standards of what is good and perfect, standards that constantly grow, leaving them never satisfied with the current state, because "it can always be better." They have high expectations of themselves and others in many areas of life. Avoiding mistakes is crucial to them, because when they make one, they question their own worth. They also need to be seen as perfect in the eyes of others. These individuals often suffer from anxiety throughout life due to their immense desire for control — and life cannot always be controlled. We must accept uncertainty and unpredictability as essential parts of life.

Example: a person with this driver may work on a project for hours, endlessly refining it, and never feeling it is good enough. They may also have trouble delegating tasks, believing no one else can do the job as well as they can.

Characteristics that indicate a person carries this driver are: suppressing emotions, independence, and avoidance of asking for help. This is a person who never seeks support and carries the entire burden alone, feeling responsible for everything, undervaluing the need for rest and support.
Positive side of this driver: Independence, resilience, ability to remain composed in crisis situations.
Negative side of this driver: Emotional distance, difficulty connecting with others, exhaustion.

This driver develops from parental messages to the child not to show emotions. Verbal commands such as: "Crying won't solve anything," "Don't cry like a baby/girl," "It's not good to show feelings, people could use them against you," "Feelings are for weak people," "Only the strong succeed," influence the formation of this driver.

"If I want mom and dad to be proud, I must be strong." A person with this driver seemingly never shows stress. They will do everything alone, always reliable and firm, never showing weakness — and often not looking kindly on weakness in others either.

This driver is usually developed by people with strong parents who belittled signs of weakness and emotion in themselves and others. For these individuals, it is extremely important to always feel strong and comfortable, never showing weakness (tears, sadness, helplessness). Problems usually arise when exhaustion or physical symptoms appear because suppressed emotions have had no outlet. These individuals also tend to label others as "weak" if they show vulnerability in life situations.

Example: a person with this driver doesn't show emotions even in the most difficult situations. They may be going through a stressful period but will never ask for help because they believe showing vulnerability is a sign of weakness.

Characteristics that indicate a person carries this driver are: putting other people's needs before their own, fear of rejection and conflict, striving to make everyone happy, difficulty setting boundaries.
Positive side of this driver: Empathy, support, kindness.
Negative side of this driver: Loss of identity, feeling of being used, passive aggression.

This driver often develops when parents constantly encourage the child to be "nice" and "sweet," giving them attention only when everyone around them is happy — otherwise ignoring them. A person with this driver depends heavily on others' opinions and will do anything to keep people around them satisfied. They struggle with criticism, even if it comes from someone completely unqualified. They are always oriented toward others, trying to "read" their thoughts in order to know how to please them. For example, they may buy the best gifts, because they find ways to discover what the other person wants. In relationships, this person may ignore their own needs to fulfill the wishes of friends or family.

Someone who has developed this driver was taught throughout life that it's important to always be there for others, never say "NO," and constantly make others happy. The mere thought of refusing to help or not being available makes them feel like a bad or less valuable person. The problem arises when they expect the same from others, and when those expectations are not met, they may react strongly, quickly labeling others as selfish — even when they're not.

Example: a person with this driver will accept extra work even when already overwhelmed, just to avoid disappointing others. They may feel exhausted but will continue helping everyone around them.

"Hurry Up!"

Characteristics that indicate a person carries this driver are: constant sense of urgency, impatience, working under pressure, quick thinking and decision-making.
Positive side of this driver: Efficiency, resourcefulness, ability to get things done quickly.
Negative side of this driver: Mistakes, stress, inability to slow down and enjoy the moment.

The reason this driver develops is one simple message: "Hurry up." Since parents often tell children to hurry, it is no wonder many people carry this driver. People with this driver try in every way possible to save time and complete as many tasks as possible. It should be noted that a person can have more than one driver, and the intensity is not always the same. Some people are heavily influenced by their drivers all the time, while others fall under their influence only in crises or unpredictable situations.

The "Hurry Up" driver can create panic even at the smallest obstacle, because the person feels there's never enough time. This driver pushes people to do everything fast. They rush around constantly and rarely take a minute to relax. They often eat quickly and speak quickly, not giving themselves time to enjoy what they are doing. They may achieve a lot (though not always), but often feel tired and unable to sit calmly and "smell the roses."

Example: a person with this driver constantly hurries themselves and others. They may complete tasks quickly but will often make mistakes due to excessive speed.

"Try Hard!"

Characteristics that indicate a person carries this driver are: belief that nothing comes easily, focus on effort rather than results, feeling they always have to "try a little harder," often engaging in many activities at once.
Positive side of this driver: Persistence, work ethic, energy.
Negative side of this driver: Lack of results, frustration, exhaustion.

This driver develops when parents insist that the child must keep working regardless of the meaningfulness of the task or the results (a common message being: "I don't care about your grades, it's important that you study"). Such individuals are constantly working, always feeling life is hard, endlessly fighting for something, unconsciously seeking validation from parents that they are good — because they are working. They are characterized by incredible enthusiasm at the start of a project, but often struggle to finish it. Once the enthusiasm fades, they move on to something new.

A person with this driver grew up learning that it is important to always be busy, to constantly pursue goals, to succeed in many areas at any cost. Therefore, someone who rests, or has a slower-paced job or profession, is seen as lazy or not valuable enough.

Example: a person with this driver may take on too many commitments without finishing any. They always feel they haven't done enough, no matter how much effort they put in.

Exercises for Working with Drivers

Awareness of drivers – Make a list of your drivers and become aware of the situations in which you use them most. Reflect on how they support you, but also how they limit you. Ask yourself:

- What messages did I often hear in childhood?
- How do I react in stressful situations?
- Are there patterns in my behavior that harm me?

Questioning beliefs – Ask yourself:

- Is it really necessary to be perfect/strong/fast?
- Do I strive for perfectionism?
- Do I constantly put others' needs before my own?

Test the opposite behavior – for example, consciously make a small mistake and observe how you feel.

Working with affirmations – Affirmations for each driver:

- "I can be successful even if I don`t do everything perfectly."
- "My strength lies in expressing my emotions."
- "I am worthy of love without constantly pleasing others."
- "I am good enough just the way I am."
- "I can ask for help, and that doesn`t make me weak."
- "I don`t need to please everyone – my needs matter too."

Relaxation techniques – Focus on the present moment and recognize when your driver is taking over.

Breathing exercise:

- Close your eyes, breathe deeply, and imagine releasing inner pressure.
- Mindfulness and conscious breathing for those with the "Hurry Up!" driver.
- Setting boundaries and practicing saying "no" for "Please Others!"
- Working with bodily sensations to release suppressed emotions for "Be Strong!"

NLP techniques – Reframe inner messages:

- Instead of "I must do everything perfectly," say: "It`s enough to do the best I can."
- Instead of "I must please others," say: "I can help others, but my needs are important too."
- Reframing – changing the meaning of beliefs (e.g., "I don`t have to be perfect to be valuable").
- Visualization – creating an image of yourself with more balanced behavior.
- Anchoring – using positive emotions to overcome destructive patterns.

Journaling – Keep a diary and write down situations when you felt stress or pressure.

- Which childhood message reappeared?
- How did you react?

Setting boundaries – Learn to say "NO" and clearly express your needs, especially if you have the "Please Others!" driver.

This is perhaps one of the most important lessons you will ever learn. Out of the need to please others, we often forget that we matter too, which makes setting healthy boundaries essential.

Working with a therapist or NLP coach – Professional help can assist in identifying and transforming deeper beliefs.

Anchoring techniques – an NLP method that creates a positive emotional response to situations that normally activate drivers.

Drivers are powerful motivators of our behavior, but they often come with an emotional cost. Understanding your drivers allows you to recognize them, break negative patterns, and create a healthier, more balanced lifestyle. Through introspection, NLP techniques, and boundary setting, it is possible to transform drivers from compulsive patterns into conscious choices. This shift brings greater freedom, satisfaction, and emotional stability.

Understanding drivers is crucial for personal development, relationships, and professional success. Once we become aware of them, we can use them as tools for growth instead of being unconsciously controlled by them. Working with drivers leads to greater freedom, balance, and a fulfilling life.

Conclusion: How are imprints, triggers, and drivers connected?

- **Imprints** are fundamental, unconscious programs that shape how we see the world.
- **Triggers** are activators that spark specific reactions based on those imprints.

- **Drivers** are unconscious inner directives that govern our behavior and motivation.

Understanding these three elements gives us deeper insight into ourselves and others, as well as the opportunity to consciously change patterns that no longer serve our well-being. By working with these aspects, you can profoundly transform your life, freeing yourself from unconscious limitations and creating your authentic self.

Now that you know all about the drivers of human behavior, I encourage you to work with them. The truth is, the process may be painful, but it is healing and necessary. Only when you become aware of the points that block and drive you will you be able to live the life you have always dreamed of. Let these words guide you toward your goals and free you from everything that holds you back. As your faithful companion on this path of personal transformation, I want to remind you that you truly can. All the strength you need is already within you. All it takes is your decision. Let it be this very moment. Good luck!

NOTES

INTUITION / THE SIXTH SENSE

"When the mind doubts and the heart is silent,
intuition already knows.
Intuition is truth without proof."
Aleksandra Božović

Intuition, in other words, represents our sixth sense, a strong instinct, our Higher Self, divine guidance, inner voice, spiritual antenna, flash of insight, gut feeling, spiritual compass. Intuition is that feeling we can never escape – and it is almost always right. It is something that exists deep within us and helps us make decisions that can, at times, even save our lives.

In its developed form, intuition offers a wide range of abilities and powers, and at its highest level it represents transcendental knowledge and a state of overall connectedness with Truth. When we become aware that, in every moment, we are guided by our Higher Self and protected by the Universe, by God, we will begin to understand the importance and meaning of intuition itself.

When we learn to listen to our inner voice – which is constantly in contact with us and communicates in various ways at every moment – when we allow that voice to speak and lead us, we realize the great truth: the wisest teacher lives within us. So let us together step into the secrets of intuition.

WHAT IS INTUITION?

We have all, at some point, found ourselves in situations where we acted in a certain way without any logical explanation, often without much reflection. We simply knew, we felt it was right – and sometimes we even say it was a "higher force." What is it that happens in that inexplicable moment?

Intuition, the sixth sense, instinct, the Higher Self, divine guidance, inner voice, a feeling... It is something intangible, non-concrete, non-empirical, and yet relentlessly present and strong enough to guide us in very concrete ways in our actions, decisions, and situations. That inner voice, that spiritual antenna, spiritual compass – or, as the English like to say, **"the gut feeling"** – this is precisely our intuition. The term itself comes from the **Latin word intuitio, meaning looking, observing**. Intuition is that feeling you cannot get rid of, which is almost always unfailingly right. A good or bad feeling in the stomach is also linked to intuition.

We have all, at least once in our lives, experienced the sense of knowing exactly what would happen in advance and acting accordingly. Such experiences are named – and explained – as intuition. The sixth sense does not carry this name by accident.

We know we possess five primary senses, and without them our lives would be without meaning. Yet the sixth sense, often underdeveloped and unnoticed – since most people walk this planet without conscious awareness of the intuition they inherently possess – plays such an important role in our lives that anyone who has experienced the full capacity of intuition would never again want to let go of what it can offer. And that is exactly it – a matter of renouncing a power we have always carried within us, which we dim by failing to awaken to it and by not maintaining its presence in our lives.

Intuition is our innate gift, our sense, and a part of our being that is capable of leading us through life with radiant light, teaching us all we need to learn – if only we are open and surrender to the guidance of this part of ourselves. In its lowest, undeveloped form, intuition appears as an insight, that is, a brief glimpse of truth that directs us where we need to go. For many people, this is an inexplicable phenomenon, and they are often left astonished when retelling such remarkable experiences. However, in its developed form, intuition offers a wide arsenal of abilities and powers that transform the life of an ordinary person into something entirely different and more beautiful.

Some of these abilities include various forms of foresight – clear and undeniable insights that offer a broader picture of truth, as well as the sense of being guided by a higher understanding. Intuition also gives us the ability to communicate with the living world around us

– with plants, animals, and to empathically sense other people completely.

The feeling of sensing a person, a situation, an event, or even the future – registering it and catching it in our energetic radar or scan – speaks of our connectedness with intuition, the Higher Self, the force of the Universe. The language of symbols through which the Universe communicates with us becomes increasingly clear; the messages arriving through the most unusual messengers are easily interpreted, and the feeling of being guided becomes ever stronger.

In its highest form, intuition represents transcendental Knowledge, a state of overall connectedness with Truth, where there is no room for fear or doubt. A person who has developed their sixth sense becomes creative and capable of taking control of their own life. They know they are a co-creator of their reality and joyfully play the earthly game of creating and learning, while freeing themselves from fear and barriers. This is why the knowledge of chakras also deals with these questions – including the activation of intuition through practices of opening the crown chakra.

THE CONCEPT, STUDY, AND INTERPRETATION OF INTUITION THROUGH HISTORY

Although only recently a subject of experiential study, the phenomenon of intuition has been strongly present throughout human history in philosophy, art, and even science.

The idea of intuition has long fascinated philosophers, who interpreted and understood it in various ways. The founder of intuitionism as a philosophical school is considered to be **Plato**, who used the term **noesis – or intuitio** – viewing intuition as a perfect source of knowledge and true Truth, through which reality is recognized without intermediaries.

It is a very specific type of perception, not carried out with the eyes and, according to some interpretations, not even with the rational part of our being. In different cultures and regions, intuition is identified and defined differently: in Eastern cultures it is connected with religiosity and spirituality, while in Western cultures it is linked to the subconscious part of the mind.

Swiss psychologist **Carl Jung** described intuition as one of the four primary psychological functions of humans, alongside perception, thinking, and feeling. According to his theory, intuition is an irrational psychological function that represents unconscious perception – a type of unconscious understanding of certain contents we call experiences. It is not sense perception, nor feeling, nor rational reasoning (although it may appear in these forms), but rather a complete and entire knowing, without us knowing where it comes from. It is instinctive knowledge, a perception that most likely arises from the subconscious – from our Higher Self.

As later researchers concluded, intuition is a process that gives a person the ability to acquire knowledge directly, without prior analytical thinking – serving as the bridge between the conscious and unconscious parts of the human mind. This is why intuition is said to appear in many different forms.

History gives us many examples of the **"Eureka!" moment**, especially in times of relaxation, sleep, or states of not consciously thinking about a subject of interest. It is said that **Archimedes** discovered his laws entirely by accident – through intuition.

Centuries later, in some of Mozart`s letters, we learn that his greatest inspirations came not when he was working, but while walking, riding in a carriage, or at night, when he couldn`t fall asleep.

These are the voices from within that do not leave us in peace. Voices about our path, our choices, our feelings, everything that unfolds within and above us. It is the frequency through which we establish connection with the Universe and receive messages from the Universe, from the Higher Self. Everyone receives messages in their own way – and there will be more to say about that.

We know similar stories about other artists such as **Gogh and Da Vinci**, famous musicians like **Mozart**, scientists like **Tesla** and **Einstein**, philosophers of both ancient and modern times, writers and poets. For example, various sources state that **Mendeleev,** who was working on the classification of elements by their chemical properties, saw the entire periodic system in a dream and simply wrote it down the next morning. Beyond all this, intuition is also understood as so-called absolute knowledge – knowledge that comes from our past lives and guides us in the present and future – as a kind of providence, a gift from higher forces granted to mortals.

Osho described it beautifully in one of his books with the words: " Intuition cannot be scientifically explained, because the phenomenon itself has nothing to do with science and is irrational."

The most famous and perhaps most often mentioned form of intuition is the one warning a mother of danger to her child. There are countless fantastic, unbelievable, even amusing stories of how a mother, without any visible sign of warning, and even across great physical distances, prevented an accident, tragedy, or simple mischief. It is often said that women have more developed intuition than men. The question is whether this idea is based on fact and reality – and, if so, what gives women this stronger gift for intuitive understanding of the world?

Interesting statistical data from various studies on this topic show that, when it comes to nonverbal communication, women generally have more developed skills in facial expressions than men, which makes it easier for them to sense hidden emotional messages people send. In addition, they have stronger empathy, hide their emotions less than men, and express their feelings more clearly through mimicry, gestures, and tone of voice.

One explanation lies in the historical social position of women. For centuries, women were placed on a lower rung of the social ladder compared to men, and as such, they were in a better position to observe and study the behavior of those who held more power. Moreover, in the role of mothers, caring for children and following their development, women had to learn to recognize the nonverbal signals through which a child expresses its needs. This became another factor that strengthened their intuitive capacity. Of course, this does not mean that men lack intuition, nor that both genders cannot further develop it throughout life.

Looking at these conclusions, we can say that possessing intuitive abilities is based on a number of intertwined factors – not only personality traits and gender but also a kind of evolution shaped by one`s position in society and family.

It has been scientifically proven that the sixth sense truly exists in the part of the brain responsible for conflict resolution. This area of the brain – the anterior cingulate cortex – raises an alarm about dangers that have not yet reached the conscious mind. The cingulate cortex is located at the top of the frontal lobes and along the walls separating the left from the right hemisphere. This brain area alerts us when it recognizes danger or a mistake. It teaches us and warns us in advance of behaviors that could lead us to negative consequences.

One of the most beautiful definitions of intuition is that it is **a flash of insight**. How else could we explain those inner visions and realizations that saved people`s lives, connected them with soulmates, brought them countless blessings, or helped them avoid negative events?

Intuition is that inner compass that always knows what is best for us. It is the ability to discover what is hidden within and to feel connected with everything around us. It is the direct perception and experience of the primary Truth – which lies beyond mind and intellect, beyond the possibility of explanation. Without reasoning, without evidence, without justification – pure, raw instinctive knowing. As if, in a second, someone removed the veil from your eyes, opened a window, and expanded your perception – bringing you closer to all answers and to the path ahead.

This is the voice that, through all our senses, awareness, and feelings, delivers messages about certain things. It is the collection of all information we receive through various sensory, electromagnetic, and external channels.

We often think we are in a strange mood when we are actually in the process of receiving information. We believe some thoughts just "came" into our mind, that we "just" made a decision about something that had not yet happened, or that we "just knew" we had to leave a place at that exact moment. These very states – the ones we doubt most and marvel at most – are in fact the moments when we are connected to our intuition, to our Higher Self.

Intuition allows us access to inner guidance that comes from the depths of our being. It allows us to remove illusion and draw closer to the inner primal Truth – to see further, to go deeper. Beyond the Mind, beyond words, beyond the known. Living from the soul means listening to intuition. It is the voice of the inner Teacher, leading us from the darkness of unconsciousness into the Light of expanded awareness.

That feeling in the stomach is intuition, or inner wisdom, which people often ignore. It can appear as a hunch, an impression, inspiration, telepathy, a pleasant or unpleasant gut feeling, a dream, a coincidence, a smell, a taste, an inner voice. By ignoring this voice, we distance ourselves from its guidance. And we do so because, in truth, we do not trust ourselves – our inner, essential Self.

As humans, we are very inclined to dismiss this guidance, misinterpreting it as mere coincidence, whim, or even madness. And yet, this is not surprising – surrendering to the inner voice requires great courage. Sometimes it can even feel frightening, which is why a certain degree of what could be called "madness" is desirable. That madness could be defined as the ability to connect with the unseen, the beyond.

Since intuition is a gift we have received from our Creator, it would be ungrateful of us not to accept this gift, not to awaken it, not to activate its power, and not to allow it to guide and lead us. What matters is that we open ourselves to our inner light, knowing that we always carry the answers to all questions within us – and that we are, in truth, always in contact with our intuition, our map, and our soul.

HOW TO AWAKEN YOUR INTUITION?

Listening in silence, meditation, solitude – Journaling or spending time alone is the best way to begin awakening your intuition. Spend at least 30 minutes each day in solitude and contemplation. This way you learn to listen to what is happening within you and directly strengthen your intuition.

To begin, find a comfortable place where you can be completely relaxed and undisturbed. Sit comfortably, breathe deeply, and quiet every rush of irrelevant thoughts that try to fill the space of your inner window. Simply focus on your breathing, and when you feel complete calm, ask: "How can this help me solve this situation?" Allow your emotions to flow freely. Then listen to what your intuition has to "say." Do not immediately dismiss its solution as illogical. Silence the inner critic. Instead of trying to rationalize your inner voice, listen to it without criticism, ridicule, fear, or rejection.

It is also important to pay attention to what your body has to tell you in everyday life situations. For example, when you feel a stomach ache connected to a strange sensation, a lump in your throat, pain in your stomach, tension in your shoulders, shallow breathing, sweaty palms - all of these are signals that your body wants to tell you something about the situation you are in. Do not underestimate the value of these signals. They are what protect you. They are what save your life.

Become aware of the energy of the people around you - Intuition will help you surround yourself with quality energies. Connect with your Higher Self and recognize who gives you energy and who drains it. When you receive a message from your inner voice, do not overanalyze it or question its intent. Usually, the first feeling you get is the right one. They say the first impression is crucial. Pay attention to what exactly happens in your body after meeting new people. What exactly is that feeling? Is it pleasant or not? Do you feel disinterest or sympathy? Whatever it is, know that your intuition is almost always right. During conversations, besides listening to your interlocutor, try to recognize their emotions. Do they feel bad, happy, angry, full of hope, or sad?

Name the emotions you notice in yourself while listening. The better you can read others' emotions, the easier it will be to cooperate with your intuition. Notice the tone of voice, the volume of your interlocutor`s voice. Allow all five senses to absorb all necessary information so that your sixth sense can do its job better. After gathering the information, your intuition will always find a way to let you know everything you need to know about that situation or person.

Connect your intuition with your dreams - Before going to bed, ask a specific question, e.g., "Is this the right job for me?" In the morning, stay in bed for a few more minutes and recall the dream that carries the answer to your question. If you do not succeed, try to fully connect with your Higher Self and patiently wait for the answer to appear, or you can try again the next night.

Research confirms that the brain, especially the prefrontal cortex, is most active and ready for creativity right after sleep, when we are in Theta or Alpha brainwave states. Your subconscious mind has wandered freely while you were sleeping, creating contextual and temporal connections. Creativity, after all, is about linking different parts of the brain.

Unlike the 80% of people between the ages of 18 and 44 who check their phones within 15 minutes of waking, you can choose to go to a quiet place, meditate, connect with your Higher Self, write down the thoughts you bring from your dreams into waking life, and keep a journal - because this will make your connection with your intuition even stronger. **Intuition first whispers, and then it shouts louder and louder.**

Each time we ignore our inner voice, it becomes louder and louder - not to punish us, but to reach us. That voice does not necessarily have to speak the same language as you. Nor does it necessarily need to be in the form of a voice. It can be an image or vision that enters your mental field, or a feeling that carries a specific message for you. That voice may also appear through dreams or through immediate signs such as emails, clock hands aligning, people who bring you certain messages, instinctive feelings, symbols you notice, numbers, or words repeating in your head - anything that will grab your attention. In this way, your intuition tries to get in touch with you.

Your inner voice is always trying to guide you, and when you constantly ignore it, it becomes inventive and clever. The guidance of your inner voice can also occur in your dream while you sleep. But if you persistently ignore it, it can reach out through painful interventions such as illness or material loss, or even the loss of a loved one. The inner voice always tries to wake you up and will use every available means to help you face the truth about who you are and how to align with yourself.

How and when can you use the power of intuition?

Choose a situation in which you feel indecisive and keep circling between two possibilities. This time, give the feeling from the depths of your soul a chance to lead you to the right path. Sit in a quiet place where no one will disturb you, calm yourself, inhale and exhale slowly, and gently enter a peaceful state where you can reflect on the problem of making a decision. Then simply choose one option.

For example, you are not sure whether you should move to a new location because of a new job. Imagine the scenario in which you decided to move and observe what inner feelings it awakens in you. Do you feel restricted and anxious, or free and warm? Are the feelings pleasant or not?

Then imagine the scenario in which you decided not to move for the new job. Again, carefully observe your thoughts and discover whether the feelings awakened are generally positive or negative. Of course, take as much time as you need. At the beginning, you may not get clearly defined answers, but if you continue to listen to your body with the same attention repeatedly, you will develop a fairly reliable sense of the right decision for you.

Allow your mind to send you a message through the visual channel in the form of an image, a flash, a vision, or a sign that will hold meaning for you. Also, allow your auditory channel to deliver the message in the form of a sentence that appears in your head out of nowhere. Finally, allow your kinesthetic world to give you the answer to a specific question through an inner feeling. Be completely certain and full of trust that you can always and without doubt rely on your Higher Self. It always knows better than you what your path is and what is truly good for you.

How to Connect with Your Intuition When You Are in Trouble?

Your intuition can very quickly and clearly reveal whether a person or a certain situation is good for you or not. Of course, in order to achieve this, it is necessary to sharpen, refine, and train your senses. Recall a situation when you returned from a meeting of any kind and didn`t feel good for no particular reason. Notice what happens in your body as you recall that experience. First, check in with your stomach, then with your shoulders, arms, and legs, and concentrate on what these parts of your body are telling you about a person or situation. Are you tense or relaxed? Do you feel comfortable or not? Take enough time to become aware of all those physical reactions that help you connect with your intuition and receive the answers you are looking for.

It is very important to emphasize that the sixth sense works perfectly when the other five senses have done their part well. So, allow your five senses to gather all the information they need. This information is sent to the sense of intuition, which then makes a general decision about what it has found in those inputs. It summarizes, filters, and examines everything the other senses have brought in and offers its contribution in the form of everything within you that needs to protect you, warn you, and continue guiding you along the path that is good for you.

For example, you may feel tightness in your stomach, or some other reaction in the abdomen toward a certain situation or person, tightness in your throat, blockage of the throat chakra, or simply a general discomfort in the body. There are situations in which your body screams that something is wrong. However, this can also just be a reaction to some trauma or stressful situation from the past. In such a case, the present moment acts as a trigger. In this way, intuition recognizes a behavioral pattern or situation and sends signals to the body, which you then receive in the form of pain in a specific part of the body. This is a sign from your inner self that you need to pay attention to the very moment that causes this physical reaction. That feeling urges you to be aware of the danger and do something about it.

If we ignore that sign, voice, or perhaps pain in the body that is trying to tell us something, it can lead to dramatic consequences. That is why it is very important to know how to communicate with your body and how to keep open the portals through which we receive messages of great significance for our growth. Otherwise, it could be fatal for us. Therefore, it is desirable to be as aware of your body as possible, to establish daily contact with it, and to carefully observe how it reacts to certain people and events. Whether you feel comfortable or not, every piece of information is very important and useful for you.

Your body is tuned in such a way that it instinctively knows when something is wrong or out of balance, and these warning signs can mean the difference between life and death in certain situations.

Exercise: Personal Stress Detector

Our body, especially the stomach, can be a good indicator of stress levels. The exercise is very simple: deeply focus on your stomach. Is it calm or active? Is it tight or relaxed? Tense or soft? What feeling do you have in your stomach? Fear or excitement? If you are tense and tight, you are most likely under the influence of some form of stress. Ask yourself what would ease or remove that feeling.

Visualize walking through beautiful nature — or even better, go for a walk — or meditate, pray. Sometimes it is enough to just sit quietly and breathe slowly for a few minutes. Whatever comes to your mind, take enough time and dedicate yourself to those positive and pleasant thoughts. While doing so, become aware of as many colors as possible, intensify them, add cheerful tones, shapes, textures that you like, different scents and other sensory details that engage your senses. Literally bring that scene, that imagination fully to life. Allow it to overwhelm you completely. You will know you have succeeded once your stomach becomes relaxed and at ease, and that good feeling begins to spread within it.

INTUITION AND EXTRASENSORY PERCEPTION

The sixth sense, or extrasensory perception, is the ability to perceive the subtle dimension, the invisible world. It also includes the ability to understand the subtle cause-and-effect relationships of many events that are beyond intellectual comprehension.

Knowledge from the subtle dimension is received from the following sources:

- Automatically, thanks to a person`s ability to access the Universal Mind and Intellect.
- As a response to questions posed by the person to an entity from the subtle world. This happens through the sixth sense, mediated by the subtle mind and intellect of that person.

There are various factors that determine who will receive knowledge through the subtle intellect. The spiritual level of the person is one of the key factors in determining who can access knowledge from the subtle world. Depending on the degree of development of the sixth sense, a person can access lower or higher levels of the Universal Mind and Intellect. The sixth sense should be used solely for spiritual growth, which leads to awareness of our Creator, fulfilling the higher tasks of our soul with which each of us came to this planet.

How to Strengthen Extrasensory Perception?

With the help of simple but very powerful exercises, intuition can be enhanced in a fun way, opening the path to abilities that can raise our lives to a higher level.

One such exercise is **object reading**. It is done by having several people put one personal item each into an opaque bag. Then all the items are poured onto the floor in front of the person who will read them. The important thing is that no one knows who placed which item in the bag. Then each participant picks an item from the pile and holds it in their hands. Holding the object, the person tries to connect with it and sense what it has to say about its owner. Messages may appear in the form of images, visions, feelings, or thoughts. At the end, everyone shares what they have learned from the object they chose, and only then is the true owner revealed. It is astonishing how many significant and accurate messages can be received in this way, and all without much effort. Each of us has the ability to sense reality around us — we only need to refine this ability in order for miracles to start happening.

Another important exercise is learning to **see the aura**, which will quickly and easily allow anyone to confirm their abilities. Place your hand on a sheet of A4 paper with your fingers slightly apart. Between the index and middle finger, draw a small dot, about the size of a pea, preferably black. Focus your gaze on that dot and look continuously for a few minutes. After some time, which varies for everyone, you will begin to see an energetic layer — the aura — around the edges of your fingers. At first, it may appear whitish, but with closer attention, you will notice specific shades of other colors. With regular practice, the ability to see the aura of other people can develop quickly. And anyone engaged in any form of spiritual work knows just how important this ability is.

Signs That You Have a Well-Developed Intuition

Intuitive people have the ability to observe a person`s interactions for just a few minutes and conclude what kind of character they have, what lifestyle they live, whether they speak and live their truth, whether they tend toward manipulation or have hidden intentions, whether they are sad, or if they carry some major problems in their life, etc.

They sense what kind of energy someone is radiating - positive or negative. People with well-developed intuition strongly feel when something bad happens to someone close to them, they often have dreams that later come true in real life, and they frequently predict unusual things that someone close to them will only experience later. They are capable of seeing what most people overlook. They also understand their own feelings well and can sense what is good for them and what is not.

Here are just some of the signs that you possess strong intuition:

The feeling that someone will call you - Has it ever happened that you thought of someone and at that exact moment the phone rang? This happens to people with a very well-developed intuition. Similarly, you may think of someone while walking through the city and then run into that very person.

There are also deeper levels of awakened intuition, such as when you feel the energies that are within your energetic radar. In this way, you gain insight into who you are energetically connected with and whether all your loved ones are well. If you notice that someone is missing from the radar in your intuitive world, you will receive a message from the beyond about what that person is occupied with and what exactly is happening with them.

Moreover, you can also send a message, just as you receive one. By simply becoming aware that you are knocking on someone`s mental door, if the vision is truly strong and rich in visualization, the person will receive a message from you or, at that very moment, you will briefly appear in their thoughts out of nowhere. Therefore, go within, become aware of your intuitive field, and try to communicate with the world and your Higher Self in this way.

A premonition that someone close to you is in trouble - For example, suddenly you receive a visual message, a flash, a sequence of an event that hasn`t happened in your reality, along with the image of someone dear to you. You are overtaken by a sense of discomfort, your heart starts racing, your palms sweat, and a thought appears in your mind that something bad has happened to your loved one. Intuitive people can feel at the exact second when something is happening to their loved ones. More complex forms of heightened intuition can, in those moments, send an intuitive message to their loved one, warning them of danger and even influencing the outcome of the event.

Unfamiliar places feel familiar to you - People with strong intuition feel familiar in places where they have never been before. For example, they may enter someone`s house for the first time and somehow know where certain things are located without the host ever mentioning it. This does not refer to ordinary things like finding a spoon in the drawer, but to something less obvious.

People with exceptionally strong intuition also have the ability to read the energy of a place they are visiting for the first time. When they find themselves in places where concentrated thoughts have remained imprinted on a location or object, intuitive people can sense the energy of those who stayed there many years ago, to the point of hearing their thoughts. This is usually accompanied by sudden, strong heartbeats, sweaty palms, dry mouth, and eyes wide open. This is a sign that the person, at that moment and in that place, is in the very process of exchanging energy through the intuitive field.

Surely, you also know those moments when you pass through a space for the first time and suddenly get goosebumps or feel the energy of the place and whether it is pleasant or not. All of these are signs that your intuition is speaking to you.

You dream something and it comes true – Such dreams feel more real, and when you wake up, you feel different than after ordinary dreams. Individuals with a well-developed intuition sometimes dream something that later happens in waking life. More complex forms of strong intuition also receive messages in dreams in the form of clear guidelines, signposts, or sentences. Although, at that moment, they may not know what to do with that information, they feel the need for the message to be transmitted, understood, and carried into the world of waking reality. That is why it is very important to write down the thoughts you find in your mind immediately after waking up. This is a direct conversation with your Higher Self.

You sense something about a person through touch – For instance, you shake hands with someone, look them in the eyes, and already know more about them than they could imagine. You may sense what kind of person they are, perhaps even what they do. People with very strong intuition have the ability to touch an object and sense who it belongs to or what kind of life its owner has lived. There are also advanced forms of intuition in which, within a few seconds, you can even know the zodiac sign of that person.

You know what will happen to others – Intuitive people can sense when something significant is about to happen in the lives of those close to them. This is not about knowing someone so well that they can easily draw logical conclusions – but rather about completely unexpected events. They are able to predict what no one else expected to happen.

Intuition is, therefore, the most powerful tool we have, we just need to learn how to use it. Although there are many exercises to strengthen intuition, sometimes the hardest part is distinguishing the voice of intuition from the voice of the ego.

HOW TO DISTINGUISH THE VOICE OF INTUITION FROM THE VOICE OF THE EGO?

Most people have a very strong mind that constantly offers opinions and tells stories, but it can sometimes stand in the way of connecting with intuition. To better hear the voice of intuition, here are four common signs that appear when the ego is blocking the path to the voice of intuition.

If you notice any of these signs, the message is always the same – stop and listen. Here are the signs to pay attention to:

Indecisiveness – If you feel like you are spinning in circles of indecision about a certain matter, you should trust that it is intuition speaking to you. When it is hard for you to decide or you feel resistance toward something, it is often a warning sign from intuition telling you that you do not yet know all the necessary facts, or that something about your choice is not right. When you are indecisive, it is best to pause and wait. Likewise, you can ask for a sign or meditate to receive a clearer message.

Seeking approval – When you are asking for confirmation or approval from others more than you usually do, it is very likely that deep down you already know the answer. When intuition sends us a message that is difficult to accept, we often feel the need to keep seeking other people`s opinions in order to either dismiss or validate what we already know. If you notice this happening, stop and pay attention to the feeling inside. Connect with your inner voice and do not be afraid of the truth. Remember, this is your life and only you know what is best for you.

You feel exhausted – Feeling drained is another warning sign that intuition is sending you. This most often happens when you are surrounded by people who are not good for you. If you suddenly feel depleted, it is a clear sign that you should seek intuitive guidance. The challenge is that it is hard to hear intuition when you are exhausted. So, call upon your angels and visualize protective white or purple light surrounding you. When you leave a certain room or distance yourself from a certain person, your energy level will soon return to normal.

When something simply feels wrong – The most common warning sign that intuition sends us is the feeling that something is not right. In such a situation, take a deep breath and ask your intuition to show you what you need to do. Sometimes stress and anxiety can also convince us that things are worse than they really are, but the feeling that something is off deserves your full attention. You can take a few deep breaths or meditate to clear your mind and reflect on what needs to be done. Never forget, intuition always guides and protects us.

It is up to us only to remain curious, open, and ready, because the amount of one`s knowledge depends solely on the level of their curiosity, openness, and willingness to apply it. Full of curiosity and childlike joy, we can all dive into the depths of our being and awaken the power waiting to be discovered and spread throughout the world. It is the power of the highest Truth and Knowledge, wrapped in the most beautiful gift the Universe has given to humankind – intuition.

As the great Nikola Tesla once said: **"Intuition is something that surpasses Knowledge. We undoubtedly have finer fibers that enable us to sense Truth even when logical deduction or any other deliberate effort of the brain is powerless. In our conclusions we cannot go beyond certain limits, but with intuition we can go to great distances!"** When we were children, we lived this way, we followed our instincts and joyfully created each day. As we grew up, we lost the connection with the state of Truth and accepted the Matrix that the adult world placed over our eyes. However, many have opened their eyes again and regained the childlike view. Fortunately, there are more and more such people on this planet. Let us become aware that at every moment of our lives we are guided by our Higher Self and protected by the Universe. Let us listen to our inner voice, always and everywhere. Allow your intuition to guide you and bring awareness to everything that lives within you. Have the courage to follow your heart and your intuition. In a way, they always know what you truly want to be.
The wisest teacher lives within us.

Exercises for Strengthening Intuition

Meditative Exercise: Connecting with the Inner Voice

This meditative exercise calms the mind and allows you to "hear" the subtle messages of your intuition. Regular practice of meditation and mindfulness creates the inner silence necessary to perceive that quiet inner voice.

- Find a quiet place and time. Sit or lie down comfortably, with your spine straight, and close your eyes. It is important that nothing disturbs you for the next few minutes.
- Focus on your breathing. Breathe slowly and deeply. Notice how your stomach and chest expand on the inhale and relax on the exhale. Focusing on the breath will help you quiet the "noise" of thoughts.
- Set the intention to connect with yourself. Silently say an affirmation or a question that calls forth your inner insight. For example: "I want to connect with my inner voice" or "What does my intuition want me to know right now?"
- Listen without expectations. Stay for a few minutes in a state of quiet observation. Pay attention to whatever arises in your awareness – a thought, a feeling, an image, or a bodily sensation. Intuitive messages are often very subtle – more like a quiet whisper or a gentle sense than a loud thought. You may notice a faint impulse or a vivid idea; accept it without judgment.
- Bring back your focus when it wanders. It is completely normal for your thoughts to drift. If that happens (for example, you start thinking about daily tasks), gently return your focus to the breath or repeat your question/intention. Open yourself again to the feelings and impulses that arise.
- Closing and journaling. After 5 – 10 minutes (or longer, if you wish), deepen your breathing and slowly open your eyes. Briefly write down in a notebook or on paper any impressions you received. Even if you did not notice

anything specific, write down how you felt – relaxed, calm, or distracted.

How this exercise strengthens intuition: Meditation helps to quiet the mind and remove everyday distractions, making us more receptive to inner signals. It is precisely this "quieting of the mind" that allows us to hear intuition more clearly, which is always present within us. By regularly connecting with your inner voice in this way, over time you will build deeper trust in those quiet signals and recognize them more easily, even when you are not in a meditative state.

Exercise with Everyday Choices: Following Your Inner Feeling

This exercise teaches you to listen to your gut feeling in small, everyday situations and to act on it. Through this practical routine, you will strengthen your trust in your first impressions and intuition in real-life conditions.

- Start with small decisions. Choose a few unimportant decisions during the day to practice on. These can be everyday things such as: what clothes to wear, what to order for lunch, which route to take to work, etc. Pick one such situation and pause for a moment before deciding.
- Pause and calm the mind. Before making a decision, take a moment to settle (inhale and exhale a few times). Set aside overthinking about the options for a moment. Instead of analyzing, ask yourself: "What does my inner feeling say about this?"
- Notice the bodily reaction. Pay attention to the first reaction that arises. It can be a mental impulse, but it is often a physical sensation or a gut feeling. For example, one option might create a slight feeling of tension or discomfort, while another awakens a sense of ease or excitement. Our body often gives us subtle hints – if you feel unexplained tension or tightness, your intuition may be warning you, while a feeling of warmth or joy may mean you are on the right path.
- Choose the option according to that feeling. Make your decision based on that initial inner impulse, even if logic tells you otherwise at first. For example, if you spontaneously felt

like wearing the blue shirt instead of the red one – do it, as long as the choice is safe and reasonable. (Intuition will not suggest anything that endangers you or others – such messages are products of fear or ego, not true intuition.)

- Observe the outcome without judgment. After following your feeling, watch how the situation unfolds. Are you satisfied with your choice? How do you feel about the decision you made? Even if the outcome is not spectacular, it is important to notice your relationship to the decision guided by intuition.
- Repeat and record the lessons learned. During the week, try to repeat this exercise daily in different situations. You can keep short notes: write down which decision you made intuitively and what the result was. Over time, you will begin to notice patterns – for example, you may realize that the first feeling was often the right direction. As you notice successful intuitions, your trust in your own instinct will grow.

How this exercise strengthens intuition: By practicing trust in your first impulse, you are actually training the "muscle" of intuition. Many of us tend to immediately turn on logic after the first instinct and start questioning the decision, which suppresses intuition.

This exercise reverses that pattern: you learn to recognize and follow intuition before the rational mind drowns it out. With regular practice, intuition becomes clearer – your "inner compass" becomes more reliable because you use it constantly. Over time, this builds self-confidence in making decisions guided by intuition, even when it comes to bigger life dilemmas.

Exercise with Symbols and Dreams: The Intuition Journal

The Intuition Journal (working with dreams and symbols). This exercise combines journaling with the analysis of dreams and symbols to help you develop deeper insight into your intuition. Often our subconscious sends us messages through dreams or through symbols that catch our attention during the day. By recording these experiences and interpreting them, we learn the "language" of inner wisdom and strengthen our connection with intuition. Regularly keeping a personal "intuition journal" also helps us track our feelings and premonitions over time, allowing us to notice patterns and messages that repeat. (Such practice can be extremely useful even in daily life – it often clarifies emotions and thoughts we were not fully aware of.)

Preparation before sleep: Keep a notebook or journal by your bed every night, along with a pen. Before falling asleep, set the intention that you will write down everything you remember from your dreams in the morning.

- Record dreams as soon as you wake up. As soon as you open your eyes, try to stay still for a few minutes without looking at your phone or getting up. Recall the dream (or fragments of dreams) as much as possible. Then write down in your journal all the details you remember: the place, the characters, symbolic objects, the feelings you had in the dream, etc. Even the smallest detail can be significant. (For example: "I dreamed of a snake in the garden; I felt fear while looking at it.") This habit of recording dreams right after waking up improves your ability to remember them and captures important messages before they fade.
- Record intuitions during the day. Use the same journal for intuitive impressions while awake. If during the day you feel a strong premonition about something or a situation presents itself symbolically, write it down immediately without much analysis. For example, you may have had the "feeling" to call a certain friend – note what you felt and the reason. Or, if a symbol keeps catching your attention (for instance, you repeatedly see the image of a heart or a certain number), write it down in the journal. The key is to record the intuition as soon as it appears, before your rational mind suppresses or explains it, because this way you capture its original form.
- Periodically review your notes. Once a week, set aside time to review everything you have written down. Read through your dreams and see if any symbol or theme repeats. Also, look over the daily notes of premonitions: did a certain feeling occur often? Connect these insights with your real life

– do the symbols or messages make sense in relation to your current challenges or emotions? (For example, frequent dreams about water may reflect emotions; a recurring heart symbol may point to a focus on relationships, etc.)

- Work with symbols through creativity. As an additional exercise, choose one symbol from your dreams or an inner motif that stood out to you that week. Spend a few minutes drawing it, painting it, or describing it in words on a blank page of your journal. Do not worry about artistic quality – the point is to express yourself intuitively. Then reflect on what you have drawn or written: What message does that symbol or image convey to you? This creative approach can help translate unconscious messages into conscious insights.
- Notice the connection between intuition and reality. Over time, your journal will become a true treasure chest of intuitive hints. Occasionally look back at older entries after events have unfolded. Check how often your feelings or dreams corresponded to later outcomes. You may be surprised at how often your inner voice was right. This retrospective linking of notes with real outcomes will further strengthen your trust in intuition, because you will see proof of its accuracy.

How this exercise strengthens intuition: By keeping a dream and intuition journal, you train yourself to recognize and understand the symbols and signals of your subconscious – in practice, you are learning the language through which your intuition communicates with you. Dream journaling has been proven to be useful because it helps you connect with your intuition and "learn" the language of your subconscious mind, which brings great benefits in waking life.

Also, by writing down your premonitions and intuitive thoughts, you give them physical form and acknowledgment. Recording intuition before your analytical mind dismisses it allows you to later evaluate it and realize its value, gradually building greater trust in your inner feelings. In this way, the exercise unites the spiritual and the practical – it encourages you to pay attention to subtle inner signals, while also documenting and reflecting on them. The result is stronger, more conscious intuition that can serve you in everyday life. Good luck!

NOTES

VISUALIZATION

"A vision is not a dream - it is your soul's memory of what is yet to happen."
Aleksandra Božović

In psychological terms, visualization is the process of creating mental images, scenes, or details by using your imagination and capacity to visualize. This technique involves forming clear, detailed pictures in the mind related to specific situations, goals, or desires, and focusing on the feelings and sensations that image evokes.

Visualization is a practice through which a person consciously focuses **material energy** on a specific idea, image, or desired goal over a defined period of time. It is done with the **intention** of sending **energy** into the quantum field, from which it can then harmoniously **manifest** in the **life** of the one who visualizes. Visualization is the creation of a mental image of the desired outcome and charging it with energy so it can translate into reality. This is the work of your imagination. On your inner mental screen you draw bright, detailed images. At the same time, you know exactly what you want. And you are certain of the truth of your desires.

Visualization can serve as a tool for meditation and contemplation, allowing us to focus on specific thoughts, feelings, or ideas, and to deepen our spiritual experience and connection with the universe. Through visualization, we can envision our goals, desires, and intentions, and attract positive energies and changes into our lives. The emotional aspect of visualization plays a crucial role in the process of healing, releasing negative emotional blocks, and transforming emotional traumas. Through visualization, we can release our emotions, express our deepest feelings, and overcome emotional challenges that hinder our spiritual growth.

By creating visual representations of our inner experiences, we can connect with our deeper self, our intuition, and our wisdom. Visualization helps us recognize deep emotional patterns, integrate our sensitive sides, and strengthen our spiritual bond with the world and all living beings. In essence, visualization is an exceptionally powerful tool that can support our emotional, spiritual, and soulful development by connecting us with our inner truth, intuition, and heart, guiding us toward a deeper understanding of ourselves, the world, and the universe as a whole. Through visualization, we can strengthen our spiritual identity, deepen our emotional connectedness with others and animals, and integrate our emotional, mental, physical, and spiritual aspects into a harmonious whole.

The American neuropsychologist **Roger Sperry**, Nobel Prize laureate in Physiology or Medicine, once wrote that the educational system and science in modern society neglect the right cerebral hemisphere. Sperry and his associates observed that these patients could not read a word presented in the left visual field, and that with the right hand they failed to arrange multicolored blocks to form a given visual pattern. On the other hand, patients successfully solved verbal tasks when using the right eye, and nonverbal tasks when using the left hand. From this, Sperry concluded that the brain hemispheres process information differently, that is, they are responsible for two different forms of thinking - verbal and nonverbal. The left hemisphere specializes in language functions and arithmetic operations, while centers in the right hemisphere are responsible for performing nonverbal tasks such as drawing, perceiving spatial relations, recognizing faces, and forming visual models of objects.

Thus, for example, typologies have emerged according to which people differ depending on whether their brain is predominantly "male and rational" or "female and intuitive", or whether they are more inclined toward a "Western analytical" or an "Eastern synthetic" mode of reasoning.

The need to explore this topic more deeply is becoming ever more evident in a time when young people are described as "digital natives" who, from the earliest age, encounter visual forms of communication and therefore learn, think, and process information in ways quite different from older generations who, in that sense, become "digital immigrants". Given that today`s children of the XXI century rely much more on visual modes of thinking and processing, the need to master the technique of visualization is greater and greater.

To enter a deeper understanding of the concept of visualization, it is necessary to realize that visualization is connected with the thinking process taking place within us. Let us begin with an explanation of **thought**. A thought is electromagnetic information that has its **energy, frequency, and vibration**. It is later shaped and manifests into a particular structure or form. The term thinking usually evokes inner speech as a form of soundless communication with oneself. That inner speech makes it easier for us to plan activities, solve problems, and recall events. The only reason an ordinary person cannot "see" a thought is the fineness of its frequency and the limits of our visual range. Our eyes do not have the capacity to perceive that **frequency**. It is a process that unfolds within.

Scientific research using functional magnetic resonance imaging (fMRI) shows that inner speech is almost always accompanied by visual representations of the objects and events we are thinking about. It is therefore easy to see that visualization is grounded in imagination. The more developed it is, the better. A person can completely imagine what they desire. Here, details that convey the desired image become important, as well as the felt sense of desire through all organs and senses. One must smell and hear, feel on the skin what is desired, and even touch and sense the surface of the target. Desire is realized when a person experiences strong positive emotions regarding what they imagine. The mind, heart, and body need to be clear about what they want and align their energy in the quantum field.

The renowned physicist **Albert Einstein**, for example, was known for his ability to visualize complex concepts in physics. Before doing any mathematical calculations, Einstein would first create mental images to visualize problems and experiments. His visualization often helped him arrive at revolutionary discoveries.

The legendary boxer **Muhammad Ali** often spoke about using visualization to envision his fights before stepping into the ring. By visualizing himself winning and claiming championship belts, Ali developed the mental toughness and confidence needed to achieve his athletic goals.

The two-time Nobel Prize winner **Marie Curie** used visualization as part of her scientific process. She visualized atoms and molecules in her experiments to better understand their structure and behavior.

This capacity for visualization helped her make significant discoveries in the fields of radiation and nuclear physics.

The legendary swimmer **Michael Phelps** is known for using visualization as part of his competition preparation. Before diving into the pool, Phelps would visualize every stroke and turn to pre-experience his race. This practice helped him fulfill his athletic ambitions and become one of the most successful swimmers in history.

The well-known host and media figure **Oprah Winfrey** has also acknowledged using visualization to achieve success. Before she became famous, Oprah visualized her future as a successful host and media mogul, creating a mental image of her success.

The legendary bodybuilder and actor **Arnold Schwarzenegger** used visualization to achieve both his athletic and film successes. Before bodybuilding competitions, Schwarzenegger visualized his body becoming stronger and more defined. He also used visualization when he moved into the film industry and became one of the most famous action heroes.

Even the celebrated inventor **Nikola Tesla** used visualization in his scientific work. Tesla would often create detailed mental images of his inventions before physically constructing them, which helped him advance his revolutionary breakthroughs in electrical engineering and mechanics.

These examples show how various well-known figures have used visualization as a powerful tool for achieving their goals, developing creativity, and enhancing their abilities.

HOW DOES VISUALIZATION WORK?

Visualization is one of the most effective techniques for fulfilling desires. However, this method has specific rules, and following them increases its effectiveness and helps you achieve desired outcomes in the shortest possible time.

It is no coincidence that both psychologists and bioenergy experts often mention the power of thought. Constant thinking about any situation truly contributes to the embodiment of that event, precisely because the "obsessive" thought settles in our subconscious. And if you learn how to manage this process, you can get what you want as quickly as possible. This is where knowledge of the five basic principles of visualization will help.

I Principle: Formulate the Desire Correctly

Thoughts should have a verbal form. Before expressing a desire, it must be formulated correctly. There are three important rules regarding the formulation of a desire:

- the desire should be positively formulated;
- use the present tense in the formulation of the desire;
- be precise in your choice of words and sentence structure.

A desire such as "I do not want money problems" is unlikely to be heard by the Universe. The frequency and vibration of the word "not" create a corresponding impulse that reduces your chances of success. The same goes for vague formulations. Remember: the more concrete the image your imagination draws in the process of visualization, the faster you will get what you want. And how can you attract something specific if the desire is formulated vaguely and approximately? Therefore, it is necessary to be very precise in your expression, because what you "order" is exactly what will be "delivered."

So, let us say you want to find a better-paying and more promising job. In that case, you would formulate the desire as follows: "I have a new job, along with a high income and good career prospects."

II Principle: Present the Final Result

The path to every goal is often thorny and difficult, and every person encounters obstacles. Our goal is to present our dream as if it has already come true. If you want to become wealthier, imagine yourself holding a large sum of money in your hands or making a long-awaited purchase.

The surge of positive emotions that arises at the same time achieves two good outcomes at once: it activates your subconscious to guide you toward that goal, and it gives you a strong energetic impulse for action. Surely you have noticed that work is far more productive when you are in a good mood?

III Principle: Complete Immersion

During visualization, be in the role of a direct participant in the depicted events. In other words, be inside the situation and the main actor of your imagined movie. In this case, you increase the effectiveness of visualization.

Imagine the picture of your success in as much detail as possible. Visualize even the smallest details. If there are other people in the situation you imagined, "draw" the elements of their clothing in detail - down to the bracelet on a woman`s wrist. The more realistic your imagined situation looks, the greater the likelihood it will actually come true. Engage all the senses, imagine not only the "image" but also smells, tastes, weather conditions. This will allow you to immerse yourself in the situation as much as possible, and visualization will be far more effective.

IV Principle: Add Dynamics

The more dynamic and intense the idea, the better. In this context, an imagined movie unfolding before your eyes can have a much stronger effect than static images in your mind. Play with it, use your imagination, create a film you can watch in your head again and again with as much detail as possible. In this way, you give your brain the space and conditions to find exactly the solutions you imagined. The brain`s role is to find solutions you ask of it, and it cannot distinguish between real and imagined.

For example, if I were to tell you right now that I am holding a juicy, yellow, large lemon in my hand and cutting it in half with a knife, with lemon juice spraying everywhere, and you even hear how juicy it is as I cut it, you would probably already "start salivating" as a physical reaction of your brain to the idea of cutting a juicy, yellow, large lemon. As you can see, the brain cannot tell the difference between real and imagined.

Suppose your desire is connected to a romantic relationship. Create two visualizations: first, imagine a static situation, like a photograph - you are in the embrace of your loved one. Now imagine something more dynamic - for example, your supposed soulmate confessing their love to you. This second one will surely evoke a stronger emotional reaction in your being. **Visualization is a preliminary version of reality**; as you imagine it, so it will be presented to you. Thus, the intensity and dynamism of your vision greatly influence the effect of visualization.

V Principle: Visualize at the Right Time

Many practitioners and spiritual teachers claim that the most productive time for visualization is right before going to bed and right after waking up. Before falling asleep and during the transition from sleep to wakefulness, the line between the conscious and subconscious becomes thin, making it easiest to "program" yourself to receive what you want at that moment.

What you must be aware of is that a single visualization will not bring any effect. It is like going to the gym once and expecting to have a sculpted and lean figure. Just as we need to exercise muscles regularly to achieve the desired figure, we also need to regularly exercise brain muscles and neurons to achieve desired results. To make a desire come true, it is necessary to systematically visualize, again and again moving closer to the goal. For some, the desire is fulfilled within 21 days after starting a cycle of various exercises - that is precisely how long it takes to develop a habit and for the body to adapt to the wave of changes. Thus, as we can see, here the rule is **seed plus time**, so that results will not fail to appear. A person becomes what they do every day.

There are many different ways and techniques of visualization, but what they all have in common is **perseverance, faith, and**

persistence. If you visualize and devote, let us say, 15 minutes of focus to one thought or idea, and also emotionally connect with it through images, sounds, and stories, you are literally building destiny, and the next thing you realize is that you have created a real **thought structure** – a blueprint of reality.

Time is necessary to get used to the process of visualization and to remove all distracting thoughts, fears, and doubts. Sometimes it happens that during the process we encounter various obstacles on our path, overcome by fear and self-doubt, we give up on the desire and decide not to think about it, so as not to recall or face our failures again. Sometimes various thoughts may flash through, pulling in fear and doubt about what we want, but you need to know that it is just a passing thought. It is necessary to remain faithful, persistent, and consistent in your desire, because a dream can only come true if you think about it, imagine it, and stay on the same wavelength with it.

What Is the Role and Significance of Visualization in an Individual`s Life?

Visualization is applied in various fields such as psychology, coaching, technology, business, education, medicine, geography, marketing, sociology, and many others. For example, scientists use visualization to present complex data on climate change, medical experts use visualization to analyze genetic information, and companies use data visualization to track sales and market trends. Visualization plays a crucial role in the development of new technologies such as virtual reality and artificial intelligence, where visual representations are used for user interaction and presenting results.

Visualization has an important role in the spiritual, emotional, and soulful development of a person because it helps us connect different levels of consciousness, develop inner introspection, and strengthen emotional connectedness with ourselves and the world around us.

Through visualization, we can create mental images, symbols, and metaphors that help us better understand ourselves, our emotions, thoughts, and spiritual experiences. Visualization allows us to dive deeper into our inner reality, explore our dreams, fantasies, and spiritual insights, and find meaning and purpose in our life.

Improving mental skills: Visualization can help in developing mental skills such as concentration, creativity, problem-solving, and decision-making. By practicing visualization, you can enhance your cognitive abilities and become more effective in solving various challenges.

Strengthening self-confidence: Visualizing success and goal achievement can increase your confidence and self-assurance. Creating mental images where you successfully overcome obstacles and achieve your desires can help you believe in yourself and your abilities.

Reducing stress and anxiety: Practicing visualization of relaxation and peace can help reduce levels of stress, tension, and anxiety. Creating mental images that calm and relax you can have a beneficial effect on your emotional well-being.

Achieving goals: Visualization can be useful in setting and achieving goals, whether in business, personal, or athletic fields. Visualizing the achievement of the desired result can help you maintain focus, motivation, and persistence in working toward those goals.

Enhancing performance: Athletes often use the technique of visualization to improve their sports performance. Visualization of smooth execution of movements, competitions, or training can help improve technique, confidence, and concentration.

Overcoming fears and blockages: Visualization can help you face fears, blockages, or negative beliefs. Creating mental images where you overcome your fears can help you gradually surpass them and become more resilient to their influence.

Visualization is an extremely powerful mental skill technique that can positively influence different aspects of an individual`s life. Regular practice of visualization can contribute to improving mental health, achieving goals, and increasing overall well-being.

How do other sciences and disciplines explain the concept and importance of visualization?

Neuro-Linguistic Programming (NLP), as one of the well-known and increasingly present and in-demand disciplines of the XXI century — already discussed in the context of mental intelligence — is an interdisciplinary field that studies mental processes and their impact on behavior and communication. In the context of NLP, visualization plays a significant role as a technique used to reprogram thoughts, emotions, and behaviors in order to achieve desired results and changes, even to the point of healing various illnesses of the body.

The importance of visualization in Neuro-Linguistic Programming can be viewed from several angles:

Reprogramming the subconscious: In NLP, visualization is used to influence the contents of the subconscious and change unwanted patterns of thinking and behavior. By creating mental images that reflect desired goals and changes, you can gradually redirect your thoughts and emotions toward more positive and productive patterns. If we remember the rule that we become what we do through the principle of seed plus time, we will understand that visualization has an exceptionally important role in our lives.

Creating positive beliefs: In NLP, visualization is used to strengthen positive beliefs about yourself and your abilities. Creating mental images of success, confidence, and goal attainment can help build positive beliefs that support desired changes and growth.

Connecting with goals: Visualization is used to connect you with your goals on an emotional level. By creating clear, detailed, and emotionally charged mental images of achieving goals, you can strengthen motivation, focus, and orientation toward realizing those goals. Since emotion is the fuel that moves us to action, only when we create an emotional connection with our own vision do we create and chart our reality.

Removing inner blocks: In NLP, visualization is used to identify and overcome inner blocks, fears, or limiting beliefs. Through the process of visualization, you can explore inner processes, transform negative patterns, and create new, positive ways of thinking and behaving. In this way, we can successfully reprogram all unwanted behaviors and patterns and make deep change at the cellular level.

Exercises for Successful Visualization:

Here are several good and effective visualization exercises you can practice to improve your mental skills:

Meditative visualization: Sit comfortably in a quiet, relaxing atmosphere. Close your eyes and focus on your breathing, trying to relax and calm your mind. Then imagine a peaceful, pleasant place in nature, such as a beach or a forest. Visualize every detail of that place – colors, sounds, scents. Stay in that mental space for a few minutes, focusing on the feelings of peace and calm that the place provides.

Visualization of goal achievement: Visualize yourself achieving your greatest goal. Imagine all the steps needed to accomplish it, as well as the obstacles you might encounter along the way. Visualize yourself successfully overcoming those obstacles and finally achieving your goal. Focus on the feeling of joy, satisfaction, and success you would feel upon achieving it. It is advisable to write down everything you "saw" in the finest detail. In this way, you stimulate the brain`s search for the solutions you seek.

Visualization of self-confidence: Imagine yourself as a person full of self-confidence and faith in your own abilities. Visualize yourself handling challenges and obstacles successfully, solving problems with ease, and achieving your goals. Lean into the feeling of confidence and security that this mental image provides.

Visualization of relaxation: This exercise can help you relax and reduce stress and tension. Imagine yourself in the place that relaxes you most — be it a quiet beach, a peaceful forest, or a cozy home. Visualize every detail of that place – colors, sounds, scents. Focus on the feeling of peace and calm that the place provides, and allow yourself to relax completely.

Visualization of creativity: Use visualization to stimulate your creativity and imagination. Imagine yourself working on a project or task that requires creative thinking. Visualize yourself arriving at new ideas, solutions, and innovations. Lean into the feeling of inspiration and originality that this mental image gives you.

Ask yourself questions like "How would I feel if I were wealthy?" or "What would I do if I could do anything I wanted?" or "Through what can I best express myself? How would I feel and what would I do?" Write it down, tell the story clearly and aloud to someone, record yourself saying it, or share it publicly, inspiring others to do the same.

A Powerful Exercise for Building Faith

It consists of 2 phases:
I phase: For 3 days, practice full breathing for 5 minutes:

- Inhale - 3 seconds
- Breath hold - 9 seconds
- Exhale - 6 seconds
- Breath hold - 9 seconds.
- The breath should be complete: first inhale with the abdomen, as if inflating it forward. Then fill the ribs and the lungs as a whole.
- During exhalation, first exhale with the abdomen inward, as if drawing it in, then release the air from the ribs and lungs.
- After three days of this breathing practice, do the exercise for building faith:

II phase:
At the beginning, perform a simple full inhale for five minutes, and then, bringing it to automatism, mentally say:
"With each breath of cosmic energy, my body is filled with it, and it connects with my faith in achieving my goal. I absolutely know exactly what I want and it is (your desire). And nothing, whether from within or without, will prevent me from achieving what I want." Do this exercise for 21 days.

Exercise to Increase the Dynamics of Visualization

Relax, close your eyes, and imagine yourself with your desire already fulfilled, and watch what happens. What is happening now? Are you happy, are you smiling? Look around — what is the situation there, what is in front of you, behind, to the left and right? What are the colors and shapes of the surrounding objects? Do they even exist? Consider with whom you will share your joy, how you will talk to them or call them, or write on social networks. Simply move through that image mentally, through your imagination, and fully enjoy the fulfilled desire — immerse yourself in this feeling. If, after the visualization, a smile appears from ear to ear and a feeling of warmth in the area of the heart, then everything has gone as it should, and reality will soon materialize this dream.

Exercise for Setting an Anchor in Visualization

To be easily and instantly connected to the sketch of your visualization at any moment, you need to create a single slide as a trigger that immediately connects you to the desired image. This could be a particularly unforgettable moment or something significant for you. You can describe this slide on a piece of paper, find a similar image of what you want or a photograph that reminds you of that moment, and carry it with you or place it where you can see it. It can also be a scent or a melody.

All of this will help not only to return to the visualization more easily, but also during the day, when fears, doubts, and other negativities overtake you, it is enough to remember or look at your slide and your mood will immediately improve, your faith will return, and the desire for realization will appear very quickly. You can create a special vision board in physical form or electronically on your computer. Decorate it with images of everything you have imagined, down to the smallest details. This will be your shortcut to goal attainment.

Releasing the desire during visualization

Release the desire. This does not mean abandoning it or completely forgetting about it, but rather stopping the constant worry about whether it will happen or not, and resisting the urge to check every minute how things are going. When we suffer an accident, break an arm, or are seriously injured, we do not constantly remove the bandage or the cast just to make sure everything is healing properly. At that moment, we have faith that all will go well, and we patiently wait for recovery. In the same way, there is no need here to be fearful or to suffocate ourselves with control, but rather to remain faithful to the process of visualization and to have patience and time for action when the desired outcome begins to materialize in our reality. This means not weighing all the pros and cons, nor calculating the probability of realization, but instead taking steps that lead us toward the dream (learning about possibilities and options, paying attention to life around us, enjoying something new and unfamiliar, rejoicing and giving thanks for our life and the people in it).

Embellishing the vision

Visualization should become a regular habit, preferably a daily one. In order for the feelings and emotions that arise from this process to be sharper, more intense, and fresher each time, you can add new details, colors, shapes, feelings, events, or continue developing the scenario as much and as long as you wish. You can visualize at any time and within any time frame that suits you; the main thing is the final feeling of satisfaction and warmth in the chest or the solar plexus.

For example, if you are given the task to form a sentence in your mind containing the terms concert and audience, you will most likely imagine the image of a concert with many more details than just a few sentences could describe. Moreover, the mental image you create will largely be based on your previous experiences. Use your imagination in all the ways familiar to you, and regularly visit, refine, and embellish your vision with new, appealing details.

These visualization exercises are just some of the ways you can use this powerful mental skill technique to improve your emotional well-being, achieve your goals, and develop creativity. Regular practice of these exercises can help you become more skilled at visualization and harness its potential for success in different aspects of life.

What is the difference between visualization and manifestation?

In one word, visualization represents the ability of a person to effortlessly create images of the future in their mind down to the smallest detail, and in this way create the possibility of pulling that image or vision from the invisible field into the visible field. In other words, visualization represents the ability to map out the future visually. However, in order to truly attract desired outcomes into our reality, visualization is not enough. Knowledge of manifestation is also needed, which serves precisely in that part when we want to "pull" images from the invisible into the visible field. Remember when you wanted to learn how to drive a car? It was the same. You visualized yourself sitting in the car, starting the engine, adjusting the mirrors, shifting into the right gear, ready to go. Since you had already seen it in your mind, it was easy for you to do it in reality. Then you signed up for driving lessons, took enough classes and time to be capable of driving. In fact, your manifestation brought you there, along with all the tasks you completed to achieve it. In the end, you could not believe how easy it actually was.

When you know the difference between visualization and manifestation, you have everything you need. Walt Disney once said: **"If you can see it in your mind, you can hold it in your hands."** So, the first thing that happens in your neural world is **the impulse of an idea.** That idea feeds your neurons so that they activate your brain to find a way to achieve success at that point.

Therefore, visualization gives you a clear vision in the form of scenarios and flashes you want to reach. And the difference between visualization and manifestation lies in the actions you take to get there.

This means that if your vision is not accompanied by **actions** and plans for its realization, it will, in that context, remain only your unfulfilled desire and dream.

NOTES

MANIFESTATION

"Manifestation is not magic –
it is the point where your clarity,
faith, and action speak the same language."
Aleksandra Božović

Imagination creates reality. Therefore, everything you have or don`t have today originates from your imagination and your vision of it. Manifestation is the technique of seeing events in advance. Believing in the unknown means being connected with the Source.

Manifestation does not deal with doubts. In fact, you have not reached the point of manifestation if you are still doubting. That is some level of visualization where doubts still appear in your vision. Manifestation is simply the premiere of the film that is to come, and within it there is no doubt – you simply know it is part of your future.

Manifestation, in one word, can be explained as the art of creating your own destiny. Our thoughts and our beliefs have incredible power and can greatly help us in shaping a reality that is tailor-made for us.

Can you manifest everything you desire? Yes, you can, claim spiritual leaders **Deepak Chopra, Eckhart Tolle, Gabrielle Bernstein, and Oprah Winfrey.** In general, to manifest means to create something or turn something from an idea into reality. This process of creation means using our thoughts, feelings, and beliefs in order to experience something in our physical reality.

When we talk about manifesting the desired (not automatic manifestation), we are talking about consciously creating circumstances for the fulfillment of a desire, consciously turning an idea into reality.

HOW TO TURN DESIRE INTO EXPERIENCE?

Learning how to acquire the knowledge (if you don`t already have it) about how a desire turns into an experience can be demanding, but it can also be quite simple, fun, and rewarding. Although every new knowledge opens new fields for exploration, you still need to start somewhere. Perhaps the best way to begin this creative process of conscious creation is with the ultimate question – "Who am I?"

Who are you, really? – This is one of the most important questions we should first ask ourselves. Why is it so important? Because it is primarily about understanding the true nature of our being, the power we have in creating our lives, and the universal laws that govern this process of creation. When we know who we are, we know we are creators.

Clear knowledge of who we are is the foundation for manifestation. Of course, the question does not refer to – what our name is, what we do, how we look… – but rather to the question – are we something more than this physical body? The answer is – Yes, we are. The world beyond matter is unfathomable and ultimately unknowable, but whoever dares to look into that world knows that we are something beyond the physical body. Who knows what else we don`t know, but we will focus on what we think we do.

To understand who we are, it is important to know:

Everything in life is energy, including ourselves – we are woven of pure energy, the same powerful energy that created this entire Universe. It moves in, through, and around us at every moment. We all have access to this powerful energetic flow that is capable of creating anything imaginable in this world.

Each of us is a powerful creator who directs this energy through the thoughts we think and the emotions we feel daily – we are created in the image and likeness of this Universe, and therefore we are naturally powerful, unlimited, infinite, worthy, abundant, and deeply loved at our very core.

We are the sole creators of our experience, because we are the only thinkers in our minds, we are the ones who feel our emotions – the process of creation, the process of manifestation always begins with us, within us. We are the cause, and the things in our lives are the consequences. The thoughts we continuously think, the beliefs we hold about ourselves and life, and the feelings that arise from within us – all of these determine what kind of experiences we will manifest.

Life will always reflect back to us the dominant energies we emit – we have the freedom to choose what energy we radiate (vibrate) by choosing the thoughts and emotions we hold daily. Therefore, our external reality will always reflect our inner world. We are creators; we manifest the circumstances and experiences we live through.

Applying this knowledge will allow us to become conscious thinkers and deliberate controllers of our daily thoughts and emotions. This requires care for the seeds we allow to grow in our minds and prioritizing the way we feel in each moment. Now we can consciously direct our thinking toward the things we want to attract into our lives and abandon those that do not resonate with who we know we are.

When we know the desires of our hearts, what it is we wish to manifest, the manifestation of the desired will be simpler if we also know and use the divine Truths embedded in the foundation of manifestation and the helpful techniques that accelerate it.

Everything you want has already been achieved, already manifested on some level; what is needed is to bring it into the HERE AND NOW.

Trust in yourself – If we believe in ourselves, we express trust in our creative power, trust that "what you give is what you get," that what we have envisioned will become our experience and will manifest.

Believing in yourself means releasing doubt, judgment, and harmful beliefs that separate us from the desired outcome. For example: "In my life, there is always some obstacle," "I`m doing something wrong." With such beliefs, you direct energy toward the undesired and block the flow and appearance of the desired.

Nurturing trust means being calm, keeping faith, and accepting the present moment, knowing that things are always being prepared to bring us the best, while the invisible forces of the Universe, our Higher Self, work for our good.

When we cultivate trust, we are at peace and in harmony with the situations that occur, and we do not give up the need to judge them based on how they appear on the surface level. We know we are worthy of good things that are coming because we trust the process and ourselves. As a result, our energy will align with our desire, and instead of moving toward doubt, fear, and worry (as perhaps it was until now), we will move toward inner peace, joy, love, and trust.

Trust in the outcome – When we know who we are, what we want, have planted the seed, and have faith that the seed will sprout and grow, then all that remains is to release all control and allow the seed to sprout and grow at its perfect pace.

Surrender is the awareness that everything has its perfect timing and the trust that the harvest is inevitable, as long as we are aligned with the vision of what we desire. Let go of worries about how, when, where, and who. Be relaxed! There is no insistence on a specific outcome or concrete way in which something must manifest. Simply remain in a state of ease, knowing for certain that the desired outcome is on its way – or rather, that we are allowing it to come, since it has already manifested on some level.

Surrendering to the perfect timing allows us to appreciate each step of our journey and release impatience and the thought "it should have happened already," because we recognize that everything is part of success and learning along our path. This brings us lightness because we know the Universe manages the details.

Taking action – Now that we know on what foundations we are "building the house," we can become available, surrender to impulses and inspiration that will guide us toward the things we desire, while moving along the path that leads to the manifestation of the desired. Once we hand over the details to our Higher Self, we become open to taking inspired steps to nurture the seed we have planted.

Thus, we are no longer on the vibration of lack. We give our best and allow the Universe to take care of the rest.

Now is the time to start using techniques and methods for manifesting the desired. Steps for manifestation may include visualization, scripting, creating a plan of steps to take… We can go to a place that inspires us, join a group, participate in events. Since we are all different, it should be noted that everyone should choose the technique that fits their personal needs.

What does it mean to receive the desired? – It means being a conscious witness and a conscious receiver during the journey through the process of manifesting the desired, step by step. It means being in a state of satisfaction and gratitude for each day as it unfolds, and being a joyful creator of what we want. It is the feeling of gratitude for each successfully taken step, the feeling of joy for where we are at this moment.

To receive means to constantly feel good and to let our vibration remain on that frequency, while the things we have asked for gently and easily flow into our experience. For the way we feel now creates the atmosphere of our future experiences. Receiving the desired is deliberate and conscious. We have created the desired in our inner world, and now we allow the world outside us to reflect what we hold within.

Let us always, or as often as possible, be on a high vibration, because this is a game with high stakes.

THE ART OF MANIFESTATION - CREATE YOUR OWN DESTINY

We have already explained how our thoughts and beliefs hold incredible power that can help us shape our reality. Here, we will explore the fascinating art of manifestation - the ability to bring our desires and dreams into the physical world.

The basics of manifestation - Manifestation is based on the fundamental premise that our thoughts and feelings create our reality. By consciously focusing on what we want and imagining it, we can attract the results we desire into our lives. However, this requires clarity, faith, and a deep connection with our desires and goals.

The Law of Attraction - The most well-known principle of manifestation is the Law of Attraction. It states that we attract what we resonate with. By cultivating positive thoughts, feelings, and beliefs, we attract positive experiences, relationships, and opportunities into our lives. The Law of Attraction also explains that our thought energy interacts with the energetic vibrations of the universe, drawing the desired outcomes toward us.

Vision and intention - To manifest our desires, we must have a clear vision and pursue it with strong intention. This requires us to imagine exactly what it feels like to have already achieved our goal, and to connect a powerful emotion to it. By aligning our thoughts and emotions with our vision, we can strengthen our intention and accelerate the process of manifestation.

Faith and trust – Faith and trust are key elements of manifestation. By firmly believing that we are capable of manifesting our desires, we send out powerful energy that amplifies our manifestation power. Doubts and negative beliefs can interfere with the process. It is essential to recognize and replace them with positive and supportive beliefs.

The power of affirmations and visualization – Affirmations and visualizations are powerful tools for strengthening the process of manifestation. By repeating positive statements and vividly imagining ourselves achieving our goals, we shape our subconscious and anchor our manifestation intention deep within. Affirmations and visualizations help us strengthen our belief and align our energy with our desires.

Letting go and trusting – Even when we have a clear vision and intention, it is important to surrender and allow the universal space to manifest our desires in the best and highest way. By releasing the need for control and attachment to specific outcomes, we open ourselves to unexpected possibilities and allow the universe to work in surprising ways.

Gratitudc and apprcciation – Gratitudc and apprcciation arc key aspects of manifestation. By consciously focusing on what is already in our lives and being grateful for it, we send out positive energy and open ourselves to even more abundance and success. By appreciating the present moment and focusing on the good around us, we strengthen our ability to manifest and attract even more positive experiences.

Take action and seize opportunities – To successfully manifest our desires, it is important to take action. The Universe often sends us chances and opportunities to achieve our goals. By recognizing them and acting courageously, we signal to the Universe that we are ready to live our dreams. It is important to be optimistic, to take risks, and to trust our inner guidance system.

Patience and trust in the process – Manifestation is a process, and it is essential to remain patient and hold faith in our manifesting power. Sometimes it takes time for our desires to appear in the physical world. However, with faith and persistence, we can be assured that the Universe is working in its own way to fulfill our intention.

Integration and expansion – When we begin to integrate and successfully practice manifestation in our lives, new horizons open up before us. We realize that we are the creators of our own reality and that we have the power to shape our destiny. We recognize that our thoughts, feelings, and beliefs make us the architects of our lives – and that opens us to a world of possibilities and potential.

BENEFITS OF THE ART OF MANIFESTATION

Positive self-talk – The way we talk to ourselves shapes our thoughts and beliefs. Through positive self-talk, we can influence our mental patterns and develop an inner voice of support. By encouraging ourselves and using positive affirmations, we increase our confidence and strengthen our belief in our ability to manifest.

Emotional awareness – Emotions play a key role in manifestation. By consciously recognizing our emotions and cultivating positive feelings, we strengthen our manifesting energy. Generating joy, excitement, and gratitude for our desires creates a powerful emotional vibration that supports us in manifestation.

Surrounding yourself with positive influences – Our environment has a strong impact on our manifesting power. By distancing ourselves from negative influences and people who do not support us, we create space for positive energy and support. When we surround ourselves with inspiring books, motivating people, and stimulating places, we reinforce our own manifestation efforts.

Physical practice – Our bodies and minds are connected, and physical practices can support manifestation. Through yoga, meditation, breathing exercises, or physical activity, we bring our bodies into a state of harmony and balance. This allows us to calm the mind and strengthen our ability to manifest.

Flexibility and adaptability – It is important to remain flexible and adaptable while pursuing our goals. Sometimes our plans may change, or new opportunities may arise that bring us closer to our desired outcome. By staying open and flexible, we are prepared to walk the path that leads to our results.

Positive actions – Manifestation requires not only thoughts and beliefs but also positive action. By actively taking steps toward our goals, we show the Universe that we are ready to create change and fulfill our dreams. Even small steps can create big shifts and speed up the manifestation process.

Manifestation practices – There are various practices that can enhance manifestation power. Visualization, creating vision boards, keeping a manifestation journal, or practicing gratitude are just some examples. Discover the practices that suit you best and integrate them into your daily routine to strengthen your manifesting ability.

Community and support – It can be helpful to connect with like-minded people and find support in a community that believes in manifestation. By sharing experiences, celebrating successes, and supporting each other, we strengthen our manifesting power and encourage one another on the path to success.

Learning from setbacks – The process of manifestation is not always simple, and obstacles may arise. It is important to learn from them and integrate those lessons into our growth. Challenges should not discourage us but rather be seen as opportunities to grow, redirect, and strengthen our faith in the power of manifestation.

Regular connection with manifestation – Manifestation is a lifelong journey. It is important to regularly invest time in connecting with manifestation and working on our desires. Through daily practices, regular self-reflection, and maintaining a strong bond with our goals, we can continuously strengthen our manifesting power and progress on our creative journey.

As always, it is important to be patient with manifestation and to enjoy the process. The art of manifestation matters because it gives us the opportunity to consciously shape our lives and achieve our dreams and goals. It helps us direct our thoughts and beliefs in order to create positive changes in our reality.

Why is manifestation important?

Fulfilling dreams: Through conscious manifestation, we can turn our deepest desires and dreams into reality. This gives us the tools to actively participate in shaping our own lives instead of passively living within circumstances.

Self-empowerment: Manifestation strengthens our self-confidence and our power of conviction. By believing in and aligning with the ability to create a life from our dreams, we build conviction and confidence.

Clarity and focus: Manifestation helps us gain clarity about our goals and desires. By focusing on what we want to manifest, we can efficiently align our energy and resources, accelerating our path to success.

Improved mental and emotional health: The practice of manifestation requires a positive mindset and emotional stance. By consciously focusing on the positive, we develop a more optimistic and healthier perspective that improves our overall mental and emotional well-being.

Attracting positive experiences: The energy created through manifestation draws positive experiences and opportunities into our lives. By focusing on the positive and directing our awareness toward our goals, we attract a series of events that help us realize our desires.

Exercises and Techniques for Successful Manifestation

There are many practices and techniques you can try to train your manifesting skill. Choose the ones that suit you best and bring you joy and fulfillment. With regular practice and trust in the process, you will learn to strengthen your manifesting power and create positive changes in your life.
Here you will find some techniques that can help you practice manifestation:

Visualization: Sit in a peaceful environment and vividly visualize that you have already achieved what you want to manifest. Feel the emotions connected to it and imagine what it feels like when your goal is already achieved.

Affirmations: Repeat positive affirmations that reflect your goals and desires. Tell yourself positive phrases such as "I attract success and abundance into my life" or "I am capable of achieving my dreams." These affirmations help increase your belief in your ability to manifest.

Visualized lists: Create lists of things you have already achieved as if they have already happened. Write down all your achievements and goals with dates as though they have already become reality. This helps maintain faith in the power of manifestation and align the universe with your goals.

Gratitude journal: Keep a journal in which you write every day about the things you are grateful for. By directing attention to what is positive in your life, you increase manifesting energy and attract even more positivity. Write how you feel, what progress you have made, and which steps you are taking to reach your goal.

Let go: Learn to surrender and trust the manifestation process. Do not try to control the details of "how" and "when," but trust that the Universe will take care of you and provide the right resources at the right time.

Create a vision board: Gather images, quotes, and symbols that represent your goals and dreams and place them on a poster or a board. Hang your vision somewhere you can see it every day to remind yourself why and what you are manifesting.

Meditation: Sit regularly to meditate and calm your thoughts. During meditation, you can focus on your manifestation goals and imagine that they already exist in your life.

Scripting: Write a story or scenario that describes what your life will be like when you achieve your goal. Describe in detail how you feel and what positive changes will appear in your life.

Energy work: Explore different forms of energy work such as Reiki, chakra balancing, or healing practices to release negative blocks or obstacles in your energy field and allow the flow of positive energy for manifestation.

Reframed beliefs: Identify negative beliefs that may prevent you from achieving your goals and replace them with positive affirmations. Actively work to consolidate these new beliefs and embed them in your subconscious.

Creating rituals: Create specific rituals to support your manifestation practice. These can include lighting a candle or using essential oils to create a certain atmosphere and shift into a manifesting state.

Active action: Take practical steps to achieve your manifestation goals. It is not enough to just manifest and wait for things to resolve themselves. Take concrete actions and behave accordingly to advance your goals.

Remember that manifestation is an ongoing process that requires time, patience, and persistence. Every person is unique, and it may be helpful to try different techniques and choose the ones that fit you best. Be open to experimenting and be ready to step onto the path of manifestation. Good luck!

NOTES

AKASHA RECORDS

"There is a space beyond time where all that is,
all that was, and all that will be – already exists as a record.
There we do not ask – there we remember who we are."
Aleksandra Božović

In other words also known as: the Book of Life, Akasha Chronicle, Mind of the Universe, collective unconscious, collective consciousness, the Records of the Soul.

The word Akasha comes from the sacred texts of **Hinduism** and means **space or ether**. Many also call it the field memory, the collective or world memory - or even the energetic record of the soul. **Rudolf Steiner**, the Austrian spiritual teacher, dealt with this topic as early as 1904.

You can imagine the Akasha Record as a multidimensional, universal, vast bank of information or a database in which all information is stored. Within these records lie your past, your present life and all experiences and events so far, as well as your future and all your life tasks. The most common phrase for Akasha is the "book of life." It is not a book in physical form that we can read; rather, the reader energetically tunes in and connects to a specific database. The Chronicle or Record is a dimension of consciousness that contains the vibrational imprint of every soul and its journey. It is infinite knowledge and wisdom, an endless spiritual resource. Akasha can be understood as an energetic vibration that translates into images, forms, symbols, figures, and language that the mind can understand.

All realities we live through arise from this source. The Akasha Chronicle or Record contains the story of every soul that has ever lived on this planet. As **Carl Gustav Jung** explained, it is a spiritual expression for the memory of the collective consciousness. A place where all is one and where infinity begins. Akasha is also a portal to the spiritual world. Every reality that happens already exists there as a possibility or option. It is a manifested world in which pure information prevails.

By extracting the desired information, a path is created to transform it into the desired reality. In this way, we can change our reality by creating it from the information received from Akasha. That information is very subtle and cannot be seen. To receive it, we must first be well prepared on the spiritual level.

To enter Akasha, you must be ready to lose yourself and accept a new Self over and over again. You must be able to let go of your self-image in a second and remain flexible like water, so you can take the shape of whatever you place yourself into. That means being open, in acceptance and understanding with yourself, with the world, and with others.

To enter Akasha, you must be ready to see the truth. The truth about you, the world, and others. Often this realization can be very painful and difficult and there is much to do, but in that moment, be aware of this: the only one who struggles to see the truth is your ego, because it is leaving its comfort zone. Your soul and your essence, on the other hand, seek only truth.

Since you are in the Akasha field, you must be ready to set the body aside while you work on the shadows of your soul. There is no value in having a pretty face, fine clothes, an expensive car, or muscle tone. There is no place for material things. Only you and silence. To read life from Akasha, you must be able to project your soul out of the body so you can easily visit other places from your past or someone else`s, or look at what awaits you, others, and this planet in the future. There, in that moment, you must be able to juggle different perspectives in a single second, with ease.

To live in Akasha means you have reprogrammed your soul from the first page to today. Your language is "belief." Your religion is energy, frequency, and vibration. There is no room for fear, anger, or judgment. To live through Akasha, you must be a master of the elements within you, in nature. To be one with them. Then you will be guided. There, in that moment, even if you close your eyes, you will know where to go. There, you see through time and distance.

Akasha is precisely that higher dimension compared to the one in which we live.

WHAT IS IN THE AKASHIC RECORDS?

Your personal Chronicle is available to you, although practice is needed to separate the messages of the masters from your own thoughts. The Akasha Records lie between the astral and mental levels. From this level the records extend through all dimensions within the Universe.

As already mentioned, all events from your past and even past lives, as well as your present life, are preserved here. When I say "past lives," the condition is that you believe in rebirth. The topic of past lives, reincarnation, or rebirth is a subject in itself, so we will remain within the scope of Akasha. What matters is that aspects of our soul have already lived many incarnations, and certain events from previous lives can influence or interfere with the present life. Of course, it is not necessary to receive messages from previous lives in every reading. Many questions relate to the present life or to the life that is yet to come.

Your Chronicle also contains all your tasks, learnings, and lifetimes, as well as karmic bonds and entanglements with people in your environment. Every one of your thoughts, notions, ideas, actions or inactions from the past, present, or future is here. As are all possibilities and potential realities in your future – every possible scenario that has not yet occurred is stored here. Each reading of information from the Chronicle shows exactly where the problem arose and how to resolve it. The Akasha Records exist so that we can share our individual journeys with one another in this dimension.

Fiat lux – words cited in many sacred texts, meaning **let there be light.** Akasha is beyond time and space. The Fifth Force, an ancient force. It is the quintessence, the essence and substance of the alchemists. It is the all-in-all. The law of cause and effect has its aspect precisely in the principle of Akasha. Every cause produces a corresponding effect. Since the law of evolution and development is subject to the law of cause and effect, karma exists at this level. However, time in the form of past, present, and future does not exist here. There is only one great NOW. Infinity with its cycles. **In the Akasha Records, we are all – One.**

Almost every culture has spoken of the existence of the Akasha Records, just under a different name. The Akasha Chronicle or Record belongs to no religion, although we find references in various sacred texts, including the Christian Bible, the Hebrew Bible Tanakh, the Qur`an, and even in Buddhism there are records of Akasha`s existence. In the Bible it is described as a library on a non-physical level.

Natural laws, gravity, matter, energy, thought-creation, memory – according to Eastern belief, these are different aspects of the one Akasha. Energetic forms arising from human desires, longings, and mental activity, as well as post-mortem experiences of human beings. All life experiences of living beings from the beginning of the world until now arise from the Akasha source. All climatic and geological changes. All events that affect flora and fauna. All activities of the "solar angels," the Starseed children scattered across the world, all nature spirits, all activities of extraterrestrials and beings of subterranean worlds, as well as all visible and invisible earthly and otherworldly forces and energies, are contained in the Akasha Records.

Even the genius **Nikola Tesla** spoke of the "primordial medium" that fills space and compared it to Akasha. Today you can find many meditations on the internet that, using binaural frequencies Tesla himself spoke about, enable access to the Akasha Records.

In his unpublished work "Man`s Greatest Achievements," Tesla wrote that this primordial medium is a kind of force field that becomes matter when Prana or Cosmic energy acts upon it, and when the action ceases, matter disappears and returns to Akasha.

What is the benefit of knowing the Akasha Records method?

At times we have those moments when we feel as if our path is strewn with stones and our life resembles a struggle more than enjoyment. Situations in which we feel stuck and trapped in a vicious circle drain the energy we need for living. Various blocks or unwanted behavioral patterns can also affect our mental health. The feeling that we are living someone else`s life, relationships without joy, or simply the sense that something is missing for life to make sense – these are indicators that something must be done to improve these areas of life.

The Akasha Record can greatly help us in maintaining mental health. Since cleansing the chakras is one of the prerequisites for accessing this database, it keeps our astral body in alignment. This in turn helps us see our life more easily and clearly, to weave visions with ease, and to access their manifestation more readily. All of this is a mark of awakened awareness, in which this technique constantly holds us.

Every answer is already within you, and your heart is the navigation. Often, when we are caught in an emotional whirlwind, we cannot see the whole forest for a single tree. Through information from the Akasha Records we receive clarity and recalibration. Through the answers you receive, you can experience healing and consciously release old patterns.

You can receive information about who you truly are, where you lived in the past, what future experiences await you, the intention of your soul, and many other helpful insights for your personal growth and development. You will experience an expansion of consciousness, make new choices, and be able to understand your life on a deeper level. You will feel peace and truth in and about yourself.

Can everyone read the Akasha Record, and how?

Each of us has had at least one experience in life of accessing this field. In our time, with awareness becoming a central theme, there are many ways that allow any individual to access the Akasha Records. Our bodily senses do not register Akasha, but we can reach it through spiritual practice.

Akasha is a repository of information or a database and contains absolutely all the information that blocks us in life. It is a very powerful field in which all knowledge is stored, including that which concerns us. This field can be available to us at all times. From it, we can see from the perspective of the soul who we are, we can recognize our life purpose, and discover what prevents and limits us from leading a fulfilled life.

The knowledge and energy found in the Akasha Records field will enable our physical, mental, emotional, and spiritual body – and our other subtle parts – to align with the intention of our soul. This is the foundational thing we must achieve in order to realize our highest potentials and improve the segments of life that matter to us.

The aim of working with Akasha is to arrive at one`s own complete truth. From the soul level, you can observe and perceive your life as it is now, the conscious and unconscious decisions, beliefs, and convictions you have made throughout life, and recognize their meaning. In this way you connect with your life purpose and become aware of your task so that you may live peace, love, and fulfillment.

For a long period this knowledge was available only to highly advanced spiritual practitioners, but with the development of today`s level of awareness, these teachings are becoming accessible. Thus, the ancient Yogis reached Akasha through a disciplined spiritual way of living and through Yoga.

Exercises for you:

The most common way to access the Akasha Records is meditation. What is known in religions as prayer can here be used as a form of meditation. Much has already been said about meditation. Each of us has a unique way of approaching prayer or meditation; therefore, all paths that lead us into a deep meditative state are valid. Furthermore, one very well-known method is guided meditation. There are various guided meditations that allow you, with a guide`s help, to access the Akasha Record of your soul with ease.

Visualization during meditation, or in general, can also lead you to the Akasha portal. There are various guided visualizations that take you into that library of preserved data, or visualizations in which you ascend from 3D (the third dimension) to 5D (the fifth dimension), where you also access information from the Akasha Chronicle.

It is very important to honor certain conditions before connecting with Akasha. Here are the most important:

- Do not consume alcohol or intoxicants for 24 hours prior to accessing Akasha.
- Write down all your questions.

- Find a comfortable, quiet place where you can be relaxed and undisturbed.
- Silence your phone so it does not interfere with your work.
- Be ready to surrender completely to the process.
- Bring yourself into a deep meditative state, turn inward.
- Ask the question.
- Be patient – sometimes more time is needed to connect with the Akasha Chronicle.
- Write down the answer.
- Give thanks.

To connect with this powerful source, you need to know your code, your way of connecting, and remove the two biggest blocks that prevent entry into the Akasha field – ego and fear. Entering this field grants you two keys that dramatically accelerate spiritual growth: knowledge and energy.

The knowledge and energy found in the Akasha field allow the physical, mental, emotional, spiritual, and other subtle parts to align with the intention of your soul.

From time to time, we should perform a **cleansing of vows from the past that are stored in the Akasha Records.** This is possible through meditation or prayer by which everything that no longer serves your highest good is cleared from Akasha. You can do it as follows:

We will use a **breathing technique** from Polynesia, called **Kahuna.** This breathing technique enables you to replenish a great amount of life force within you. As you inhale, you can silently count to 4, hold the breath for 4, and then slowly exhale counting to 8. Send this life force to your Self and your Higher Self, so they may carry your request to cleanse your Akasha Record. Then read the following request aloud:

" I renounce all promises, contracts, vows, oaths, pacts, and agreements I have ever made that are not in alignment with my highest good, as well as any vows that negatively affect me in this moment, in all other time zones, in this life and in any other life. I ask that all blockages be removed and eliminated so that I may walk my higher path and purpose. Cancel, nullify, and uproot all promises, agreements, ties, or contracts between me and any entities that cause disruptions, judgments, and condemnations. This includes anything that may be hidden, secret, invisible, masked, unseen, unheard, unknown, unknowable, and undiscovered. Retain all my learnings that will lead me further along my higher path. Cancel all vows, conscious and unconscious, breakable and unbreakable, that have violated Universal Love, Light, and Truth."

Before you access the Akasha Records, write your question at the top of your notes. When you are in a deep meditative state and have completed all necessary preparations, you can begin asking questions or receiving information from the Akasha Chronicle.

It is important to avoid "Yes or No" questions. Formulate questions in the "What, why, how" form. For example:

- What is the purpose of my soul?
- Why am I often ill?
- Who am I?
- What is my true path?
- What is physically wrong with me?
- What are my emotional scars?
- What are my karmic debts?
- Where can I find happiness?
- What is stopping me from finding the job I want?
- How can I find a life partner?
- What is blocking me from finding a life partner?
- What is my life purpose?
- Where is my blockage and how can I overcome it?
- What should I do to attract the right people into my life?
- Finally you may ask, "Is there something I have not asked that you wish to share with me?"

You can ask questions about your current life situation, health, making important decisions, your personal potentials and abilities, questions about your relationships or emotional blocks, as well as questions about your near and distant past and future.

In short, anyone can delve into their own Akasha Chronicle and draw from it all the necessary information for your private life, for the relationships you are in or wish to be in, as well as for your professional life concerning your business, ideas, the work you do or should do.

What we call intuition, a sudden insight, or a feeling that informs us about a situation can be explained as moments of unconscious connection to the Akasha field and accessing information that we cannot explain logically. Plain and simple – we just know. Twins who are emotionally very close often maintain telepathic contact and unconsciously know about each other, especially if the other is in trouble.

Animals in nature can sense and anticipate things that seem unreal or unclear to us. They can, for instance, sense an approaching earthquake. Hours before a real quake, animals begin to react nervously, as if they sense that something terrible will happen. An earthquake is accompanied by a large release of torsion waves produced by friction within the Earth`s crust before the quake itself. Using their sixth sense, animals can feel the oncoming trouble and respond in time and accordingly. Once ridiculed and dismissed, these psychic abilities have now come into the hands of science, where we can find many rational explanations for similar phenomena.

Of course, this is not everything about the Akasha Records. Today there is a large amount of information dedicated to exploring this concept. Here we have included some essential points that will allow anyone to approach this topic with understanding and, with diligent work and effort, to penetrate the records of their soul where all your Truth is contained.

NOTES

FIFTH DIMENSION

"The fifth dimension is not an escape from this world, but a return to the source you come from – your light."
Aleksandra Božović

In my many years of work with clients, this statement took shape and very precisely explains the notion of the fifth dimension, or 5D: **" Telepathy gives us a flash of awareness about someone, manifestation gives us a flash of awareness about something, and 5D is constant awareness of the flash."**

The fifth dimension (5D) represents a deeper understanding of oneself and the world around us - an insight that goes beyond the limits of the visible eye. To understand 5D, we must step into the understanding of quantum physics. The micro-level of everything that exists is the subject of quantum physics. In a word, everything we call " magic " is explainable precisely through the field of quantum physics, and in that way the essence of the fifth dimension is revealed. A deep understanding and knowledge of the laws of nature gives us the key that unlocks the doors of "magic."

Much is said about transitioning into 5D. The foundation of the fifth dimension rests on everything we practiced in 3D. Yesterday we learned how to quiet the mind, how to be present here and now, freed from the past, with refreshed mind programs restored to factory settings. We learned how to meditate, manifest, and visualize, to attract desires easily and quickly, to master the elements within and around us. We learned about the pineal gland, Kundalini energy, and the transmutation of sexual energy. Today, all of that is taken for granted - at least in 5D.

We learned that there is no illness the body cannot heal - if it truly wants to. If the soul and the heart consent, the trinity unites as one, and then there is no stronger medicine than that inner harmony. Today we feel how the body seeks a remedy in various ways - through yoga, meditation, silence, and cleansing. To even grasp the notion of the fifth dimension, it is important first to understand the previous four.

The first dimension represents mere existence. For something to exist, it must have a location or position in space and time. The sum of all positions in the universe constitutes the first dimension. We can imagine it as a line – a path that stretches into infinity.

The second dimension defines size or distance. Between every position of the first object in the Universe there is a certain distance – whether straight or curved. The totality of those distances makes up the second dimension. It can be visualized as a flat plane expanding into infinity.

The third dimension is the dimension of depth – the one most familiar to us because we perceive it with our physical senses. It represents the sum of all dimensions of existence in the physical universe. It operates according to laws such as gravity, attraction, polarity, etc. We will say more about this dimension later in the chapter.

The fourth dimension, according to many physicists, represents time. We will also discuss it in more detail later. Time is an integral part of the fourth dimension, because wherever there is movement, there is time. Movement can be local, across a distance or within a plane – or non-material, in the form of thought. The two main characteristics of the fourth dimension are thought and time. There are two kinds of time:

Physical time is a measure of relative motion between two celestial bodies. If there is no movement – there is no time. On Earth, physical time exists because Earth and the Sun move relative to each other. As the basic unit of time, we have taken one rotation of Earth around its axis. Physical time is variable – which **Einstein** proved with his theory of relativity. As objects approach the speed of light, time slows down. There is even a theory that objects moving faster than light could move backward through time.

Psychological time, as the renowned Indian philosopher **Krishnamurti** called it, is our inner experience of time. It is governed by thought and memory. Psychological time is also variable. You have surely experienced moments when you were completely absorbed in something and time flew by, or the opposite – when every minute felt like an eternity. When there are no thoughts – there is no psychological time. The feeling of the timeless is a key to higher consciousness, because by stepping out of the dimension of thought and time – we open the door to the fifth dimension.

The fourth dimension is much more than physical and psychological time. We can call it the space of creativity. It is the universe created by the mind, a universe in which thoughts materialize. If thought is the ruler of the fourth dimension – then it is vast and inexhaustible. Thoughts do not cease – we create incessantly. There are no empty thoughts. Some thoughts are stronger than others and have a greater capacity to manifest. Still, every thought, every mental image exists somewhere in the fourth dimension.

The mental plane is a sub-dimension of the fourth dimension. All mental life unfolds there. It encompasses each individual`s personal reality, as well as the **collective subconscious** – the term **Jung** used to describe the universal reality of all subconscious minds. The collective creations of the mind shape multiple realities, all of which are part of the fourth dimension. Ideas, concepts, images, symbols, thought-forms – they all exist in the mental spheres. It is not a static warehouse, but a living, active laboratory of Creation, a place where elements meld and rise into a sea of consciousness. This is the source from which the four lower worlds arise, the so-called **"Mayan planes"** in Eastern philosophy.

The key to the uplifted worlds of the fourth dimension is faith. "You will experience what you believe. As you sow, so shall you reap. Here you create your reality," said **Ernest Holmes**, calling this principle the **Law of Mind**.

The fourth dimension is the sphere of metaphysics – the supremacy of consciousness over matter. Here, inner and outer reality meet for the first time. It is a bridge between the worlds of matter and the worlds of spirit, a bridge between linear and eternal time.

In the fourth dimension there also exist so-called **parallel worlds**. These spheres do not have a higher vibration than the usual space and time of the fourth dimension, but they coexist with it – as "parallel realities." The best known among them is the **astral plane**, about which more will be said later.

How do we distinguish a parallel world of the fourth dimension from the reality of the fifth dimension or higher worlds? This is the question that has led many truth-seekers into confusion. Many have mistaken the pleasant aspects of the fourth dimension for the notions of Heaven, Nirvana, or the Divine itself.

First, the fourth dimension is relative. This means that each person experiences it in their own way, in accordance with their own beliefs. If you believe in poverty – that is what you will create. Many religious people see images of their God. Since their faith is so strong, it shapes that reality. In most cases, they do not actually see the true essence of the entity or being. They see a mental or astral image – an entity or thought-form created by their mind. For them, their God is very real. For an atheist, He does not exist.

Second, the fourth dimension is the realm of phenomena. This is the realm of extrasensory perception, intuition, and dreams. It is the creative workshop of imagination, the workbench of the mage. It is also a passage into the astral plane – a vast sphere of indeterminate figures, the "beautiful and the absurd" creations of "apprentice-gods."

The fifth dimension is often described as a space in which time unfolds continuously, where possibilities and realities coexist in a way that surpasses a linear understanding of reality.

It is crucial to understand that the scientific theory of the fifth dimension has its foundations in physics and mathematics, while the spiritual interpretation of this idea has its roots in philosophical and spiritual traditions. These two perspectives are not necessarily in opposition, but they are aimed at different spheres of inquiry. It is important to distinguish properly between scientific and spiritual views of this concept – to avoid misunderstandings and unfounded claims.

When it comes to the fifth dimension, it is important to know that it cannot be grasped mentally or physically if the knowledge from all previous chapters of this book has not first been integrated. The body and the mind can have experiences related to the fifth dimension, but without knowledge in this area, they will not be able to detect, understand, analyze, and extract the wisdom that dwelling in the fifth dimension provides.

Put most simply – it is as if we have a car, a full tank, the keys in hand, but do not know how to drive. It is true that we can experience a ride by letting someone else drive us, but we are not the ones steering the vehicle. The fifth dimension explores the concept of **multidimensionality** beyond our usual perception of space and time.

Physics, metaphysics, spirituality, and quantum mechanics – as well as many other disciplines – engage with the concept of the fifth dimension. Some theorists believe that access to this dimension can provide deeper understanding of the universe and our place in it.

The fifth dimension can offer a perspective that surpasses our limited grasp of reality. When exploring this concept, it is important to keep an open mind, a spirit of inquiry, and a readiness for shifts in perception and understanding of reality – to encourage creativity, intuition, and spiritual growth. Integrating these concepts can expand our sense of the universe and our place within it – more deeply and more inspiringly.

The fifth dimension is a concept we **transcend through consciousness.** It is considered to be present at every moment and in every place, yet it requires a shift in perception to be truly recognized. Imagine being able to see all possibilities and choices at once – and being able to choose the path that best serves your highest good. The theory of the fifth dimension is a complex field that draws the attention of many scientists, philosophers, and researchers. In both scientific and spiritual contexts, this theory offers two entirely different perspectives that should be regarded as **separate domains of thought.**

Theorists such as **Michio Kaku and Rob Bryanton** explore ideas like **"hyperspace"** and "multiple worlds," which point to the existence of a fifth dimension. The **"multiple worlds"** concept suggests that every choice we make creates a new reality in a parallel dimension. In the fifth dimension, we can gain insight into those alternative realities and choices. Here, time is no longer linear – it can be perceived as **all possible times at once**.

The concept of parallel realities suggests the existence of an infinite number of realities that coexist in a multidimensional space. The fifth dimension allows an awareness of their existence. This idea can help us understand that past, present, and future are not necessarily separate entities.

In physics, the fifth dimension is linked to attempts to create a "**theory of everything**" – unifying all known forces and phenomena into a single comprehensive model. In quantum physics, theories such as **quantum superposition and quantum entanglement** open up space for ideas about higher dimensions. Notions like **quantum teleportation or superposition** stimulate thinking about the potentials of the fifth dimension.

Dr. Michio Kaku, one of today`s leading physicists, popularizes concepts like string theory and the possibility of higher dimensions in his works and lectures. In his view, light and gravity may travel through the fifth dimension – which could explain many cosmic phenomena.

Kaku posits that the fifth dimension is "curled up" within our space-time on a microscopic scale – which might have key implications for understanding the nature of the universe.

Rob Bryanton, on the other hand – a musician, writer, and philosopher – approaches the fifth dimension from the standpoint of philosophy and consciousness. In his book "**Imagining the Tenth Dimension,**" he examines multidimensionality through the lens of human consciousness and creative potential. By combining Kaku`s scientific and Bryanton`s philosophical approaches, we gain a comprehensive view of the fifth dimension – as a bridge between classical physics, metaphysics, and spirituality.

In many spiritual traditions, the fifth dimension is associated with **spiritual enlightenment, transcendence, and higher states of consciousness**. It offers a deeper understanding of inner wisdom, compassion, and universal harmony. When we think about human consciousness, we can imagine it as a being that exists in a multidimensional space – where emotions, intuition, ideas, and memories form layered aspects of the fifth dimension.

Great minds have contributed to the exploration of the fifth dimension as well: **Albert Einstein**, although he did not study it directly, opened the door to understanding multidimensional spaces with his theory of relativity. **Theodor Kaluza and Oskar Klein** expanded Einstein`s theory by adding an extra dimension – considered pioneering work on the idea of compact, "hidden" dimensions. **Rudolf Steiner and Carl Gustav Jung** approached the fifth dimension from the perspective of consciousness and psyche. Steiner saw the fifth dimension as a spiritual level beyond space and time – a sphere in which all forms are interconnected through universal consciousness. Jung linked the fifth dimension to the process of individuation, the maturation of the personality, and the attainment of inner wholeness. Both approaches – Steiner`s and Jung`s – suggest that spiritual and psychological development is the key to accessing this higher level of existence and understanding the universe.

All these scientists and great thinkers – and their theories – play a crucial role in shaping our understanding of the fifth dimension and its potential across a wide spectrum of disciplines. Their contributions are essential for deepening our knowledge of multidimensionality and its implications for the nature of reality. The fifth dimension represents a level of consciousness characterized by deeper spiritual knowing, connection with the higher principles of the universe, and subtle energy fields. Scientific achievements in exploring the fifth dimension should certainly not be confused with spiritual interpretations, yet progress in science in this area also influences the development of the individual. Precisely for that reason, there is growing discussion about the value that understanding the fifth dimension can have for every person on Earth – as well as for their spiritual growth and development. Spiritual interpretations of the fifth dimension can inspire individuals to explore their inner essence, to connect with universal energy, or to develop a greater sense of self-knowledge. Through such practices, people can strive to reach higher states of consciousness or harmony with their environment and the cosmos.

Entering the fifth dimension, in the spiritual sense, represents a process of transforming consciousness and the evolution of the soul toward a higher level of existence and understanding. This concept is tied to the idea that every human being has the potential to expand their consciousness and reach a state of enlightenment – which characterizes the fifth dimension as a level of being.

Key aspects of entering the fifth dimension in a spiritual sense

Awareness of unity: entering the fifth dimension involves developing an awareness of the oneness of all that exists. Understanding that we are all connected at the level of consciousness and energy, and that we are part of a universal whole, allows us to discover a deeper meaning of life and to open ourselves to love, understanding, and compassion toward everything around us. In the fifth dimension, consciousness becomes broader and more all-embracing, enabling us to view our existence from higher perspectives and to connect with the subtle energies that permeate all things. The boundaries between individuals fade, and the sense of unity with all that exists becomes more evident. It is a space where every thought, feeling, and deed creates faster and stronger manifestations, because we are in direct contact with universal energy.

Deep realization of purpose: we enter the fifth dimension as no one, and we leave as someone. This threshold encourages us to explore our spiritual potentials and to fulfill our highest purpose. In the fifth dimension, the ego is transformed and becomes a means of expressing the essential truth of our being. We are no longer limited by the duality of the mind, but recognize our essence as part of the infinite ocean of consciousness. Doors open to deeper self-realization and to connection with higher beings and dimensions of existence.

Challenges of transformation: entering the fifth dimension often requires releasing old patterns, emotions, and limiting beliefs. Through introspective self-work, self-reflection, and the practice of spiritual purity, it is possible to overcome challenges and open to new perceptions. This journey calls for love, courage, and a willingness to accept the essential truth of our unity with all that exists. It is a process of shedding illusions, drawing nearer to light, and realizing our full potential.

Higher levels of consciousness: the fifth dimension brings the possibility of developing higher spiritual abilities - intuition, telepathy, connection with universal energies. These capacities enable a deeper experience of life and open the door to unconditional love, compassion, and understanding. In this state, we become aware of our divine nature and fully accept our connectedness with everything that exists. Meditation, mindfulness, and spiritual practice help the individual attain inner peace, expand consciousness, and establish direct connection with higher dimensions.

Personal and planetary growth: entering the fifth dimension is not only an individual experience - it affects the collective evolution of the planet. Every being who rises in consciousness uplifts all humanity and contributes to global harmony, peace, and progress. Time in the fifth dimension becomes cyclical, and a human becomes a conscious being whose thoughts and deeds influence the entire universe. We become aware of our place in the cosmic order and accept responsibility for creating the world we live in.

In numerous spiritual traditions - Hinduism, Buddhism, Taoism, shamanism - the fifth dimension is linked to the soul`s development through many incarnations. Through these dimensions, the soul learns, grows, and strives for enlightenment, freeing itself from karmic patterns and attaining higher states of consciousness.

In a spiritual sense, the fifth dimension is an invitation to a deeper connection with oneself, with universal consciousness, with love and light. It is a path to discovering our divine essence and to living in alignment with the highest potentials we carry within.

Thus, the laws of nature play a key role in understanding and connecting with the fifth dimension, offering guidance for the development of consciousness, spiritual transformation, and the realization of higher levels of being.

Thought – forms

Thought-forms are energetic impulses radiating from the soul into the ether (etheric spheres) and into mass consciousness (the collective unconscious). They are the building blocks of 4D creation and the way things are brought into manifestation. Without emotion, will, desire, and energy, thought-forms have very little capacity to penetrate outer reality. Instead, they wander aimlessly through the mental spheres and, if not amplified, gradually dissolve into static energy fields (after being imprinted into the Akashic records).

Thoughts repeated over and over tend to crystallize into stronger thought-forms, just as a tiny snowflake (a single drop of water) crystallizes into a larger cluster containing many frozen droplets.

Gradually, a thought-form becomes substantial enough to penetrate outer reality, much like a snowflake becomes heavy enough to fall through the atmosphere.

Consciously or unconsciously, thought-forms can be projected from one person to another and appear in the mind`s eye (the third eye, Ajna) of the receiver as an image, symbol, or entity. Holographic mental projection is a technique developed by advanced human types, in which an image of a being is projected to another person, at another time or place. If the receiver is clairvoyant, that is, "awake," the thought-form may appear as the sender`s body "materialized" in the room - at least to the inner sight. In some cases, a mental projection can even be visible to the physical eyes.

Causal plane

The causal (karmic-causal) plane is the collective creation of individual souls. It contains the Akashic records and the building blocks of the etheric level. Artists perceive it as a crystalline world of perfect beauty. The causal spheres are like a control panel for the worlds of time and space. Minimal adjustments in the crystalline structure of the causal plane can create drastic shifts throughout the entire space-time continuum. This plane contains the very fabric, the very essence of evolution.

On the causal plane, highly developed souls come between incarnations to review their progress in evolution. From this vantage, the entire timeline of their evolution stretches before them. They can choose where along that line to incarnate next, depending on the lessons still to be learned through time and space. These are realms of great intelligence and wisdom, the home of the oversoul.

In understanding the fifth dimension from this angle, a significant contribution was made by **Dolores Cannon**, a renowned regressionist, hypnotherapist, and author whose work explores past-life regression, alternate realities, and higher dimensions of consciousness. Regarding the fifth dimension, Dolores Cannon offered unique insights through her work and experiences with clients who underwent regression sessions. In her view, the fifth dimension cannot be fully grasped through our three-dimensional perception, but rather as a field of energy and consciousness that transcends our usual concepts of space and time.

Dolores described the fifth dimension as a level of existence in which individual consciousness becomes all-encompassing and the boundaries between "I" and "we" dissolve. Here consciousness expands into universal love, understanding, and unity with all that exists. One becomes aware of one`s interconnectedness with the universe and all forms of life. She emphasized that the fifth dimension offers opportunities for the development of higher spiritual abilities - such as intuitive perception, telepathy, the "teleportation" of consciousness, and similar phenomena. Meditation and visualization can help expand consciousness and open toward higher dimensions. Likewise, the practice of empathy and compassion helps one attune to the higher vibration of the fifth dimension.

According to her findings, activities such as lucid dreaming or astral projection can offer insight into functioning beyond linear time and space - a prominent theme in her long-term work with clients. Many reported out-of-body experiences, encounters with angels and guides, or visions that afforded them a glimpse of the fifth dimension.

Dolores Cannon`s key message about the fifth dimension is the importance of **love, acceptance, and compassion** as the paths that lead to this higher level of consciousness. In that state, the essence of every being reveals itself clearly as a divine spark of universal consciousness, and the path to the fifth dimension becomes a journey toward the fulfillment of our highest purpose and potential.

In the fifth dimension, understanding the balance between **Yin** (feminine, receptive, intuitive) and **Yang** (masculine, active, rational) energies becomes essential for achieving inner harmony and wholeness. Alongside the yin - yang principle, awareness opens to the **masculine and feminine energies** which, as two complementary halves, unite into a whole. Masculine energies include strength, action, and rationality, while feminine energies encompass intuition, emotion, and creativity. In transitioning to the fifth dimension, it is important to integrate these energies in order to reach inner completeness.

Through a deeper understanding of the interplay among the fifth dimension, intuition, energetic principles, and spiritual polarities, one can expand consciousness, strengthen inner balance, and connect with higher dimensions of existence. Creating balance and harmony among these elements opens the door to healing, transformation, and the evolution of consciousness.

Life in the third dimension

The third dimension (3D) – is our earthly school of karma. It is the physical reality we chose so that, through lessons and experiences, we could fulfill our purpose. It is a space of challenges, opposites, polarity, and learning through experience.

Unlike 4D and 5D, the third dimension involves much suffering, but also opportunities for spiritual awakening through pain. The density of 3D reality enables deep karmic release and confrontation with one`s own shadows. Pain and suffering often become catalysts for awakening. You have surely heard stories of people who hit rock bottom – physically, mentally, and emotionally – and it was precisely then that they transformed. This is common in 3D: awakening through pain. In this school, we forget who we are so that we can remember. We heal old wounds, and we return for lessons until we learn them. The feeling of separation dominates – we divide ourselves from others, from the world, from our true being. At this level, we rely on reason, logic, and rational judgment. Love often becomes a transaction – an exchange of interests. The head rules the heart. When interests are not met, negative emotions arise: anger, sadness, shame, fear. These emotions shape us and our choices.

How many of us have stayed in jobs we do not love – out of fear of lack? Or in toxic relationships – out of fear of loneliness? How many times have we betrayed ourselves just to be accepted? 3D is a world of compromise, of sacrificing authenticity, and of false peace.

In 3D, the struggle between masculine (active) and feminine (intuitive) energy is pronounced. Masculine, linear consciousness dominates – thinking, planning, calculating. Feminine energy – gentleness, presence, pure being – is suppressed. We feel separate, alone, and lost. We may feel joy or love, but they depend on external circumstances. The real tragedy is precisely this – that we do not live from within, from the soul. What we need to do is – **change the channel.**

Transition through the fourth dimension – 4D

The fourth dimension is an intermediate phase, a spiritual awakening and expansion of space and time, a bridge between the third and fifth dimensions.

The fourth dimension is not a destination, nor a place we will "arrive" at – it is a state of consciousness we pass through to prepare for entry into 5D. The passage from 3D to 5D is possible only by first abiding in 4D. Here we are prepared for the fifth dimension on all levels of our being – physical, energetic, emotional, mental, and spiritual. We awaken and realize that we are more than the body. We set out on a journey toward our deepest self – our soul, a fragment of all-encompassing consciousness – and we learn how to remove the burdens and shackles of the 3D identity.

We move through emotional roller coasters, face our own shadows, and heal wounds partly inherited from our ancestors or carried from this life and others. We free ourselves from limiting and negative beliefs, from old patterns and roles that no longer serve us.

We realize that many things are not as they once seemed. We integrate the neglected capacities of the right hemisphere of the brain – holistic thinking, intuition, and creativity. We allow ourselves to express suppressed feminine qualities – ease, surrender, spontaneity, and compassion. We learn to unite reason and intuition in harmony. We become aware that, at every moment, we can choose where to direct our attention and energy. In the fourth dimension, we gain tools that help us choose love over fear, truth over falsehood, and creator-consciousness over the role of victim.

The 4D field – The Law of Karma (cause and effect) is the key law of the fourth dimension. Above it, the concept of karma loses meaning. Karma is not punishment, nor something to be "paid off," but the synthesis of the Law of Mind and the Law of Reflection.

The Law of Mind says: Thought is creative.
The Law of Reflection says: You will see in the outer world what you believe. In the case of karma, there is a time delay between intention and manifestation. The Law of Reflection is instant karma – what we think becomes what we see.
As the Bible says: *"As you sow, so shall you reap."* We sow thoughts (seeds), and we reap reality (manifestation). If you want a different outcome – change your thoughts. Imagine your mind is a projector, your beliefs are the film, and your life is the screen. To change what you are watching – change the film. The 4D field is a place of spiritual cleansing and reprogramming. Things are as we believe them to be. Our faith creates our reality.

Consciousness in 4D – In the fourth dimension it is possible for consciousness to occasionally slip back into 3D. That is natural. Our frequency varies – every thought, emotion, and word has its own vibration. Words like hope, beauty, gratitude vibrate high. Emotions like love, joy, peace – even higher. On the other hand, guilt, shame, hatred vibrate low. In 4D we learn how to attune to higher vibrations.

People on the healing path are, more or less, in the fourth dimension. Here we learn to feel, accept, and release. We balance masculine and feminine energy. We open to our soul and its connection with the universe. We begin to sense the energies and vibrations of people, spaces, and objects. We enter the world of imagination, creativity, and spiritual insight. We learn about the tasks of the soul, become aware of timelines, intuition, synchronicities. In 4D, time is no longer linear. We begin to understand the Law of Attraction – we do not chase, we attract. Our intentions and emotions shape reality. At times, it seems events occur before we speak them.

Body, energy, and awakening – On this journey, you may feel physical changes: mood shifts, fatigue, ringing in the ears, discomfort in the stomach. This is part of the process. The density of energy is changing, creating space for a new way of being. There will be moments when we slip into 3D: when we judge, when we cannot hear the heart. But empathy and compassion will grow. There is no need for worry – it is vital to remain gentle and patient with ourselves.

We will learn to love what we once could not. We will respond with more peace and presence. We will begin releasing the inner child`s belief that we are not enough. We will distance ourselves from societal stories that limited us. Our circle of people will naturally transform. We will start to value our time in silence and solitude more. These are signs of spiritual maturity – and preparation for entry into 5D.

Transition and the new frequency – We will often have emotional ups and downs. Old habits will try to return. That is normal. Being in a higher vibration is also a habit. Train new thoughts and feelings, learn to listen to the heart. At first, happiness may even feel stressful – because we are not used to that frequency. We may feel guilt for our joy. Yet this is a program that changes. Every moment of awareness in a higher vibration strengthens our path.

It is enough to feel that new frequency fully even once – the body, mind, and soul will remember. Then they will, by themselves, seek a return to that state. You will be tuned. Like a navigator – once it finds the route, it guides you on its own.

The Fifth Dimension - Coming Home

If you spend some time among spiritual people, you will surely hear about the shift to 5D consciousness. In those circles of spiritual explorers, people speak about a time of awakening and the creation of a New Earth. Different levels of consciousness, or dimensions, give you insight into your spiritual awareness.

But what exactly is 5D? What does the transition into the fifth dimension look like? And where are you currently on your level of consciousness? What do the different dimensions and levels of awareness mean: 3D, 4D, and 5D? Each dimension is a level of consciousness with its own unique vibration. These are not physical places, but states of consciousness we can attune to. Our reality is far more comprehensive and abstract than we can imagine.

Higher dimensions open broader perspectives on reality. Although they are numbered, there is no hierarchy among them - each has its meaning and purpose. Just as you must tune a radio to the right frequency for a given program, so must consciousness be tuned to the frequency of a given dimension.

In the third dimension, vibrations are lower and denser compared to the light-filled vibration of the fifth dimension. At present, many people remain predominantly in 3D awareness. This reality is characterized by duality: good and evil, right and wrong, strength and weakness. There are rigid rules, conditions, dependencies, and a constant race for success. Competition, profit, and self-interest dominate, while the well-being of people, animals, and the planet is often neglected.

Many live under stress, work for money to pay bills, go on vacation, and secure a pension. Material goods, status, and external recognition become important - all to fill an inner emptiness and a lack of love. Limiting beliefs shape our daily life: "I`m not good enough", "I always have to do everything perfectly", "Only those who work hard deserve recognition and love". Fear, guilt, shame, sadness, doubt - become our daily companions.

We see the world the way we experience ourselves. If we are conscious of lack - we attract it. If we carry anger - others trigger it. Everything is neutral, and our perception assigns it meaning. If we do not love ourselves, we seek love outside - and are often disappointed. The greater the expectations, the greater the pain when they are not met.

The fifth dimension represents a new energy, an elevated awareness, a new perception - a place of unity rather than duality. It is the space of understanding that we are all one, that we are part of the same universal energy. The illusion of separation dissolves. Awareness expands and you feel a deep connection with all that exists. At the foundation of everything lies unconditional love.

This transition from 3D to 5D is not reserved only for the few - it is happening collectively. Sooner or later, everyone will reach their own "walls" that must be cleared to move forward. This is the process of the evolution of consciousness.

The Fifth Dimension – Unity – We have learned, then, that the fourth dimension is a bridge between the worlds of matter and spirit. Crossing that bridge and entering the fifth dimension, we leave the world of duality and enter a qualitatively different world - a world of love and unity.

The fifth dimension begins at the etheric level - an invisible sphere above the astral and mental levels - and it leads us along the path of the heart. Of course, the process of moving from 3D to 5D does not end with a single stroke. At first you may only peek at this new state of awareness, while certain aspects of your being still dwell in 3D or 4D. And that is exactly how it should be. It would be too much pressure on the body and mind for this transition to happen suddenly. It must, and can, unfold gradually, step by step.

You may now be asking - what does life in 5D actually look like? How do you maintain balance between the higher dimensions and everyday earthly duties? Throughout the day we continually enter and leave different states of awareness. Sometimes we are more focused on the physical, sometimes on manifestation, and sometimes we find ourselves in a dreamlike state. The key is not to strive for every moment to be "5D", but to integrate this awareness into daily life. If you have managed to feel it even once, the soul will easily find its way back there. All it takes is time, attention, and energy.

Just a few moments of daily clarity, presence, and being **here and now** can completely change the way you experience reality. You will begin to see how your inner world shapes your outer world. Pay attention to how you respond - outwardly, but also within yourself.

By integrating awareness into as many moments of the day as possible, you allow it to become part of you. At any moment you can choose how you want to experience the present moment. This is the creation of a new way of being. You can dive deeper into the highest version of yourself and realize it - while you are still here, on physical Earth. You need only the faith that it is possible and the willingness to plant that seed - your intention. And like any plant, your new reality requires patience and dedication. Seed plus time - that is the key to success. Remember it. In the 5D state, everything feels immense, whole, connected, and suffused with unconditional love.

"**All is one**" is no longer an abstract idea, but a feeling in every cell of your being. You no longer need to diminish anyone to feel better. You do not need to conform to others' expectations or hide your authenticity. Being true to yourself becomes your truth and the only value that matters to you.

In 5D, your location is not important - only how whole you are. You sense the world through the heart. There is no need for "more" , because in this moment - everything is here. The eternal now. 5D is the awakened choice of what and how you wish to be - in every moment. It is the awakening of your highest self, living it, and remembering what you once knew.

Divine flow and the heart center – In the fifth dimension, thoughts manifest quickly because resistance no longer exists. The channel is open. And this happens when a person lives completely from the heart, not from the ego. Anything that is not in resonance with the heart becomes a wall you must overcome - climb over or dismantle. Every being must go through this - sooner or later.

The fifth dimension cannot be explained by the mind - it is understood by the heart, by energy, by feeling. As we have already said, we can meet others only at the level at which we have met ourselves. But emotionally and energetically you will be able to understand this. Surely you have at least once experienced a moment of bliss when everything flowed from the heart. You shared it and it returned to you - doubled. Your feminine and masculine energies are in balance. You feel deeply and give deeply. You create and you realize. You learn to fall and to rise again. You grant space to yourself and to others. Gratitude and acceptance become your natural state.

Your intuition, clair-seeing, inner insights - are no longer " something special " . They become everyday reality. You communicate more through energy than through words. You are aware of the vibration of everything - people, spaces, objects. Time becomes an endless NOW, and the process of aging is replaced by a process of transformation. Entering the field of the fifth dimension requires opening the heart. That is why rule number 1 of the fifth dimension is: **"5D is not thinking about something but being connected to it in thought - being one with it."** For entering 5D allows us to reprogram ideas of nation, religion, and race. It is absurd here to speak of such divisions of the human population, because frequency does not ask for skin color, but for a carrier who can hold it.

The cosmic flow of time – In the fifth dimension, time is no longer linear. Past and future become wave-forms within your DNA. This is how our karma has functioned until now. We simply did not know - we could not know - that our Destiny and lifetime are not a line; they are a sphere we can infinitely develop and expand at will. A sphere of time filled with our options and possibilities - numerous branches of time - and from each such branch we can grow a new sphere of time - the Momentum of Our Destiny, defined by purpose and quality.

The linear imprint of time has made us uneasy so far because time always seemed to be going somewhere. But dates and hours are an illusion, and even seasons and cycles are nothing but a cosmic hologram of time. We live on this planet for one and the same day. But we came to make this day perfect. For if we manage to live on Earth at least One Perfect and completely Free Day, then **all earthly time** will change - as will our whole life. We are here because we are the Masters of our time. We are present in the One Day and honing Mastery of Perfect Time and the ability to exist perfectly in this Day.

Every morning we begin anew. Day and night are a time cycle, a sphere that continually rotates within and around us. It seems to us that we have much time in the past and future, that we have many days. In truth, we have only one day of our life. And one night. Here and now. Now is all that exists. Feel it with your whole being. Live not as if you are living your last day, but as if you have only one day - and from the energy of that one day you can create whatever you wish, as much as you wish.

If we learn the nonlinearity of even one day of our destiny and grasp the uniqueness of each new cycle of our One day, then we will stop spending the energy of the One day on pettiness, emptiness, ignorance, selfishness, rush, and fuss. Absorb with every cell of your body each present moment, which for you is at once the only one. And by absorbing, perceiving, and understanding the time of each moment, each day and cycle, you begin to expand these spheres of time - the sphere of the present moment - here and now, the sphere of the day`s time.

Your task is to master **the perfection of this one day**. For if you master One Day, you set a cosmic change in motion. A new clock is born within you - **the Clock of Cosmic Synchronicity**. Time is all you have, and all you need. The perfect day does not come from outside. It is created from within. So remind yourself every day: you possess everything - your will, your body, your knowledge, your experiences, the Earth, the elements, your family, the precious lessons of destiny and karma.

All of this is your wealth. The air, the water, the Sun, the Sky. All of this belongs to you. And spring, and autumn, and summer, and winter - everything happens here and now, in the present moment of your remembrance, though in the linear version of events in the world of the third dimension. The plants, your home, the animals, the birds, all the chemical processes happening in your body. All the scents, colors, dreams - you have them all here and now. In the single moment of eternity of your existence on Earth. In your one day. All of it is now - within you. Feel it. Write it down. Give thanks.

The awakening of eternity – Your reality in 5D reflects your spiritual state - your level of peace, love, and serenity. If you want change, **live as though it has already happened**. Feel it. Enter it. Because 5D is already within you - in your mind and your heart. If this lesson is difficult to grasp, read it daily. Write your own truth. Clearly define the states you wish to release and the ones you wish to develop. The fifth dimension is a world of subtle, powerful, light-filled energies. Learn to accept them. To work with them. To follow them. They will guide you.

The unity of the heart is your unity with yourself. You are still an individual soul, but now infused with divine light. True unity comes when you have gone through the cleansing and only the essence remains. Love is that essence. **The path to 5D is not always easy**. But it is precious. And worthy of every step. Trust it. And trust yourself.

Exercise - Conscious Grounding in the Present (3D)

Third-Dimensional consciousness represents a mode of being focused on material reality and separation. In this dimension we experience ourselves as individuals separate from others (and from the Divine Source), relying first and foremost on the five physical senses. Life in 3D is often viewed as a struggle for survival ruled by fear and a sense of scarcity – we believe there isn`t enough for everyone, so life becomes a competition for resources, power and success. We build our identity on what we possess, how we look, and the role we hold in society, while deeper spiritual truths remain hidden behind that surface. In the third dimension the ego – mind is dominant, keeping us tied to the past or to worries about the future, rarely allowing true rooting in the present moment. And yet, 3D is the starting basis for the development of consciousness – the experience of duality (light and dark, good and evil) that offers our soul lessons through choices between love and fear. In fact, in every situation in 3D we can respond from love or from fear; only when we learn to choose love consistently do we begin to move beyond this plane of existence.

- Preparation: Find a quiet place where you feel safe. Sit upright (or stand, if that`s more comfortable) with your feet planted firmly on the ground. Close your eyes and take several deep breaths, relaxing your body more with each exhale. Feel your breathing slowly slow down and become rhythmic.
- Connecting with the Earth: Bring your attention to the weight of your body. Sense gravity drawing you downward, toward Earth`s center. Imagine roots extending from your feet or the base of your spine, penetrating deep into the ground. With each exhale, those energetic roots spread deeper and wider, giving you a sense of stability, rootedness and safety. Surrender to that feeling – as if the Earth were gently supporting and holding you.
- Sense awareness: Now bring attention to your physical surroundings. Listen to the silence or the sounds around you, feel the air temperature on your skin, notice the scents in the space. If you wish, open your eyes briefly and choose three objects nearby to look at. Observe each for a few seconds, noticing its shapes, colors and textures, then close your eyes again. You are aware that these objects exist outside of you and that you are the observer separate from them – you feel the clear boundary of your physical body and the outer world. You are fully present here and now, in your body.
- Detecting and releasing fear: Turn your attention inward. Notice whether you feel tension, restlessness or fear anywhere in the body. Perhaps it`s a weight in the stomach, a tightness in the chest, or any sensation of discomfort. Try giving that sensation a form in your imagination – for example, picture the fear or tension as a dark little cloud of

energy inside your body. Inhale deeply, and as you exhale imagine that dark cloud leaving you and traveling down your roots straight into the Earth. Mother Earth will receive and transform that energy, like compost that turns waste into fertile soil. Repeat this a few times: with each exhale, hand over to the Earth whatever you no longer need (fear, insecurity, tension). Feel your body and mind slowly shedding the burden.

- Embodiment: After several consecutive exhales release all remaining tension, then place your attention at the center of your chest. Feel your heartbeat or the rhythm of your breath – a sign that life is flowing through you in this very moment. Allow yourself to feel gratitude for that life energy in your body. You are now fully present, grounded and aware here and now. Notice the peace and strength this rooted state brings. Enjoy a few moments of quiet unity with the Earth and with your body, knowing this state of conscious presence is the foundation of all further spiritual growth.
- Closing: Gently deepen your inhales and exhales, becoming aware of the room you`re in. If your eyes are closed, slowly open them. Feel your feet on the floor and look around. How do you feel now compared to the start of the exercise? Remember this feeling of connection and calm, for it represents the vibration of the third dimension when it is made conscious – a safe base from which you can step toward higher dimensions.

You can practice this grounding exercise daily, especially in the morning after waking to begin the day centered, or in the evening before sleep to release accumulated stress. Also reach for it whenever you feel overwhelmed by fear, anxiety or racing thoughts – a few minutes of conscious grounding will help you return to balance. Regular practice will help you feel more stable, present and resilient to the challenges of everyday 3D life.

Exercise – Exploring the Astral Plane (4D)

The fourth dimension is considered a transitional, astral level of consciousness that connects the physical with the spiritual. It`s often described as the realm of dreams or the subconscious – a plane of lesser density and greater fluidity, where time and space are far more flexible than in the physical reality of the third dimension. In 4D we begin to perceive that everything is interconnected and that there is much more than the senses can register. At this level we realize that thoughts, emotions and intentions strongly shape our experience of reality – our inner world begins to mold the outer. The duality of good and evil still exists, but is infused with greater understanding: we more easily grasp the bigger picture and show more compassion, both to ourselves and to others. You can also imagine the fourth dimension as a gateway or passage: while dwelling in it, we can still slip back into old 3D awareness when lower vibrations overtake us, yet doors to the fifth dimension open at the same time. Many people touch this level through dreams, deep meditation or creative imagination – it is a space where transformation is easier, because the rules of reality can bend and shift in accordance with the energy of consciousness.

- Entering a meditative state: Sit or lie down comfortably in a quiet place where you won`t be interrupted (dim light is helpful). Close your eyes and begin breathing slowly and rhythmically. Relax each part of your body gradually – from your feet upward – until you feel calm and a pleasant heaviness in your limbs. Imagine your mind settling like the surface of a lake at dusk.
- Portal visualization: In your inner vision, imagine a door or passage that leads to a different dimension. It could be an old wooden door, a glowing portal of energy, or even a golden threshold at the top of stairs – choose a symbol that inspires trust. Approach that imagined threshold. Take a deep breath and, as you exhale, mentally affirm your readiness: "I open myself to exploring the fourth dimension." When you feel prepared, step through the door. Sense a gentle transition, as if a wave of warm energy were surrounding you as you enter a new space of awareness.
- New environment and feeling: Now find yourself in a fourth-dimensional landscape your soul creates. It might be a floating space filled with stars, a misty forest with

impossibly vivid colors, or any scene that comes spontaneously. Look around in that world of imagination: what is the sky (or vault) like above you? What is beneath your feet – do you even feel ground or do you sense lightness, as if you could float? Notice that the laws of physics are different here: you may feel a lightness in the body, as though you could lift off with only a small impulse of will. Breathe in this wondrous ambience with all the senses of your astral being.

- Testing reality`s fluidity: In the fourth dimension, thought has a direct effect. Try it: extend your hands in front of you and imagine you slowly lift off – like a bird pushing away from the ground. Notice how in this plane you really can rise, hovering without weight. Then imagine descending gently again. You can also call an object with your mind: for instance, picture a mirror or a lotus blossom appearing before you – watch how that creation of your mind materializes in the astral space. Observe with awe how things change faster here than in 3D, guided by your energy and intention.
- Interacting with symbols and guidance: As you explore this fluid plane, pay attention to any symbolic images or beings that may appear. You might spot an animal, a child, or a figure of light approaching – this could be your spiritual guide or an aspect of your subconscious bringing a message. Stay calm and curious as you observe whatever arises. You can ask your higher awareness a question, e.g., "What is most important for me to understand now?" – and wait for an answer to arrive as an image, a word or a feeling. The fourth dimension is a space of intuition and vision, so your soul may communicate insights here through metaphor. Remember any message or symbol you receive; give thanks for it, knowing it carries meaning for your path ahead.
- A glimpse of the fifth dimension: In the distance of your astral landscape, imagine a radiant golden-white light appearing. It pulses with unconditional love and draws your attention like a beacon. What you`re perceiving is an energetic portal to the fifth dimension – an even higher

level of awareness. Feel how that light fills you with joy and peace just by its distant presence. For now, simply know it exists and awaits your next step. Soak in the feeling of exalted love emanating from that far light, as a quiet preview of what you`ll experience when you`re ready to step into 5D.

- Returning to the body: After this journey, it`s time to come back to waking awareness. Lovingly say farewell to the scenes surrounding you in the fourth dimension, knowing you can return here whenever you wish. Consciously find the same door you entered through. Step back through it and feel yourself again within the space of your mind behind closed eyes. Gradually become aware of your physical body resting quietly. Begin to deepen your breath; with each inhale, feel your chest, arms and legs. Sense the weight of your body and the support beneath you. Gently wiggle your fingers, then your toes, and stretch. When you`re ready, open your eyes. Take a moment to write down or remember the key impressions from your astral journey. You`ve just experienced a passage beyond the limits of the 3D world – notice the difference in your awareness and energy.

The exercise of consciously exploring the fourth dimension is best practiced when you have ample time to relax fully and immerse yourself in imagination. For some, that will be several times a week, while others will feel called to such a journey only occasionally, when intuition shows it`s needed. Evenings or before sleep are ideal, as the mind is then naturally closer to the dream state (which eases access to the 4D world).

With regular practice of this meditation, the threshold between dreams and waking will become more permeable – your intuition will grow stronger, and fear of the unknown will diminish, because you`ll realize there are multiple levels of existence and that you are safe within them, guided by your inner light.

Exercise – Meditation of Unconditional Love and Unity (5D)

The fifth dimension of consciousness is a plane of existence suffused with pure light and unconditional love – a state of unity with Source and with all life. On this plane we finally transcend the illusion of duality: we no longer experience the world through clashing polarities, but recognize in every phenomenon an expression of divine harmony and higher meaning. When we act from 5D awareness, we know deeply that we are all one and that love and compassion are the universe`s fundamental vibration. The sense of separation and existential fear fall away – those lower patterns are replaced by unshakable trust in life`s flow and the divine intelligence moving through it.

At this level our higher awareness (higher self) is fully integrated into everyday being – our mind and heart work in harmony, guided by intuition and the heart`s highest wisdom. Living from fifth-dimensional awareness, our thoughts, words and deeds flow spontaneously from love, truth and authenticity. Human relationships gain a new ease, without judgment or the need to evaluate anyone – we understand each person is on their own unique path of growth. In short, 5D is a state of enlightened awareness in which we feel deeply connected with all beings, with the planet and the stars, and with Source itself. We are present in the Now, immersed in peace, joy and the creative current of life, aware of the miracles that surround us at every moment.

- Preparing a sacred space: Sit in a comfortable meditation posture (cross legged on the floor or on a chair with your spine upright). If you like, light a candle or incense to mark the beginning of a sacred practice. Place your palms together at your heart, or rest them on your lap facing upward in a gesture of surrender. Close your eyes and listen for a few moments to the rhythm of your breathing, allowing each inhale and exhale to grow deeper and slower. Consciously release tension in the body – relax the muscles of the face, shoulders and abdomen.
- Opening the heart: Bring attention to your heart center in the middle of your chest. Breathe there, as if you were inhaling through the heart itself. Imagine that with each inhale you draw warm, golden light into the heart, and with each exhale you release any residual pain or heaviness. If you wish, speak a sincere intention or prayer within: for example, "I open my heart to unconditional love. May the power of unity and

light work through me." Feel these words resonate inside you. Let your heart energetically "expand" with each beat, becoming softer and more receptive.

- Uniting Heaven and Earth in the heart: Now visualize above you a radiant source of white or golden light – it might be the Sun, a star, or the galactic center itself. Imagine a beam of that divine light descending through your crown and gently filling your head, neck and chest with warmth. That luminous energy carries the feeling of unconditional love, grace and joy. At the same time, imagine another beam of light rising from Earth`s center – its color may be emerald green or ruby red (the energy of life). Feel how that energy from below supports and nourishes you. Let both lights meet in your heart and unite into a single sphere of brilliant light. You are now the meeting point of Heaven and Earth in one being – your heart center becomes a luminous portal vibrating the highest love and life force. Sense that sphere pulsing with your heartbeat, spreading pleasant warmth through your whole being.
- Expanding love outward: Let the sphere of light in your heart begin to grow. With each inhale imagine it becoming larger, enveloping first your entire body (every cell shining with love), then the aura around your body. As the sphere expands further, it includes the room you´re in, then continues outward to encompass your home, your neighborhood, your whole city. See it becoming so vast that it wraps the entire Earth in a protective mantle of love. Now you are within that sphere, and the whole world is within your sphere – the boundaries between you and others have vanished completely. You, the planet and all living beings now breathe together in this field of unity. Feel immeasurable love filling this spacious sphere – love for every person, every tree, every animal, for Earth itself as a living being. Allow the sphere to spread onward into infinity: embracing the Moon, the Solar System, the stars of our galaxy… the entire cosmos. You feel merged with all that exists, as if your being were pulsing to the same rhythm as the heart of the universe.

- Unconditional love and gratitude: Now focus on the sense of unconditional love flowing through you. Silently speak an affirmation or blessing: "May all beings be happy. May all beings be healed. May all beings feel love and unity." Feel deep compassion radiating from your heart toward everything held within your sphere. If images of people (or beings) arise – including those with whom you`ve had difficult relationships – simply surround them with love. In the fifth dimension there is no judgment and no division – only understanding. Surrender for a few minutes to this wave of warmth, joy and sweetness… You may even feel tears of joy welling in your eyes, and that`s perfectly fine. Your heart is expanding and cleansing old wounds through love.
- Remaining in 5D state: Notice how you feel right now – calm, light, safe, connected? This is the vibration of the fifth dimension. Enjoy it as long as you wish. Know that in this state you are deeply connected with your essence and with the spiritual Source. In quiet, you can ask your higher self a question or request a blessing for yourself and loved ones. Be open to receiving a very clear insight or solution right now, as a whisper or a heart-born vision. Or perhaps only a deeper peace will arise – accept whatever the experience is, without expectations. You simply are – present and one with life.
- Return and integration: When you feel it`s time to close the meditation, gently draw your sphere back in: imagine it slowly narrowing from the vastness of the cosmos, back to Earth, to your city, to your body, until the entire sphere of light rests again in your heart. Though now centered in your chest, it still shines with the same intensity. Know that the flame of 5D awareness remains lit within you. Bring your attention back to the breath in your chest. Feel your physical body – the pressure of your feet on the floor or the weight of your body on the chair. Gently move your shoulders, neck and fingers. You may place your palms over your heart again as a sign of gratitude. When you open your eyes, keep a few moments of silence. Notice how you look around now –

softer, with more love and ease than before. Carry that quality into each next step.

You can practice the meditation of unconditional love and unity every day – even a few minutes of this state can transform your day. It`s especially recommended in the morning, to attune your vibration before you go out into the world, or in the evening before sleep, to end the day in peace and gratitude. Of course, you can also do it anytime you feel a need to reconnect with Source or to remind yourself of the wider perspective (for example, in the middle of a demanding day, take a 5 – 10 minute break to withdraw into quiet and return to this feeling of love).

By practicing these three exercises, you`ll gradually develop a felt sense of moving from the limited perspective of the third dimension, through the magical threshold of the fourth, into the spacious awareness of the fifth. Each of these phases brings its gifts: 3D offers rootedness and lessons of choice, 4D opens doors to intuition and wondrous insight, and 5D fills us with unity and love. This journey through the dimensions is deeply personal and sacred. May these guided exercises be faithful companions on your path to your own holy trinity – the unity of body, soul and spirit in the vibration of love, wisdom and light, worthy of the XXI century. Good luck!

NOTES

ASTRAL PROJECTION

"In the astral you don't leave the body —
you exist as pure consciousness, without name, form, or time."
Aleksandra Božović

WHAT IS ASTRAL PROJECTION AND WHAT IS IT FOR?

Astral travel (projection), AP, is an experience in which a person feels that their awareness or "astral body" separates from the physical body and can travel through different dimensions or astral planes. It appears in esoteric and spiritual teachings worldwide and is often linked with **out-of-body experiences (OBE)**. People commonly describe it as floating above the body, traveling through spaces that aren't physically accessible, and communicating with higher entities or spirit guides.

The term astral projection or astral travel describes an out-of-body experience that presupposes the existence of a subtle vehicle — known as the astral body or body of light — through which consciousness can operate apart from the physical body and travel through the astral plane. These experiences are often very intense and deeply personal.

The purpose of such journeys — where we are no longer only a physical body — is learning: **gaining knowledge** about oneself and about the extraordinary capacities of human beings in general.

The importance of these experiences and insights becomes clear when we see how much we've changed afterward. Many people feel that such experiences profoundly affect their lives.

This practice has a long history and appears in different cultures around the world. In some spiritual traditions, astral projection is a skill to be learned and trained, while others view it as a natural ability that can be developed. The general testimony of people who consciously experience OBEs — and of researchers who have documented their reports — gives us much information about the non-physical dimension. Unlike the physical dimension of our existence, the non-physical is multilayered, composed of several levels or dimensions.

The astral plane is understood as an informational field located right alongside the earthly world; it vibrates at a similar frequency and partly interpenetrates it.

In this chapter we'll address whether it is truly possible for the spirit to leave the body and visit other places where we witness real events, and what astral projection is actually for. There are various techniques for exiting into the astral, which means there is both knowledge and practice that use OBE for developmental, informational, and healing purposes. People also often have astral travel during sleep or in deep meditation. Experiencing astral projection in sleep is similar to flying; it differs from ordinary flying dreams because you can usually recall returning to your body — which is felt as constricting after the freedom of flight.

The human spirit can soar to unimaginable heights — figuratively and literally — but human fear also has enormous power and can seriously harm the spirit's currents. We may label something "supernatural" while lacking any knowledge of the nature of the Universe, calling supernatural anything beyond our imagination and understanding. Yet from ancient civilizations to today, people have engaged the "supernatural" in the most natural ways and practice astral projection daily without special preparation or ritual. Trained practitioners may simply close their eyes and relax for a moment to seek information that appears to their inner sight in images; some don't even need to close their eyes — insight arrives directly: as soon as they have a question, the answer comes.

The astral holds all human memories and knowledge, as well as various entities that can help you — or harm you. Practitioners warn that it isn't safe to communicate with entities and that while traveling you shouldn't touch anyone or anything, nor take or give anything to anyone you meet (who may appear pleasant or familiar). Many spiritual healers caution that astral projection without intention and awareness can lead to loss of control; for safe travel they recommend techniques that link the practice with the chakras to prevent frightening or harmful experiences. So don't do this as a joke (the

Universe has no sense of humor — that's a human quality and creation); approach the experience with an open mind and a clear intention. Typically, a dimension is populated by consciousnesses with the same tendencies — the same quality of energy, intention, thoughts, and feelings.

There are dimensions inhabited by beings not aware that they are no longer biologically alive.

Other dimensions, by contrast, are populated by advanced societies — communities of evolved consciousness fully aware of the cycles of successive lives we are in. These consciousnesses plan their next physical life according to goals that include helping humanity, furthering their own evolution, and assisting others in theirs. Although medicine acknowledges only unintentional astral experiences as a phenomenon of consciousness, practitioner accounts attest to the deeply transformative effects of this mystical and spiritually empowering practice.

History and origins

Astral projection has been discussed in many cultures throughout history. Regardless of culture, socioeconomic class, gender, language, nationality, religion, civilization, or era — from the earliest tribal societies to modern XXI century life — humans have mentioned the exit and later return of the subtle body to the physical body, describing numerous distinct features of the phenomenon with striking consistency. The idea of astral projection appears in many cultures:

Early evidence of OBEs appears in **ancient Egypt** 3,000–5,000 years ago. **Ba** was considered the part of the soul that could leave the body and travel. Egyptian priests knew of the astral body and called it **Ka**.

Descriptions later appear in **ancient Greece** in writings by philosophers such as **Plato and Herodotus**. In the **Indian Vedas** the experience is described as **svapna or svarūpa**; in the **Tibetan tradition** practitioners cultivate traveling outside the body through **dream yoga**; while Western esoteric schools explore astral dimensions in **Kabbalah, Hermeticism, and Theosophy**. Cases of conscious astral projection are also documented in the **Bible** — for example, Ezekiel 3:14; Revelation 1:10–11 and 4:2; and in Paul's letters, e.g., 2 Corinthians 12:2.

During the **Middle Ages**, under the repressive influence of the **Inquisition**, OBEs were studied and practiced in secrecy within esoteric and occult movements. The secrecy contributed to myths and untruths about the dangers of astral travel that persist today.

In the XXVIII and XIX centuries many pioneers influenced society by publishing works on the subject, including Swedish philosopher **Emanuel Swedenborg**, French novelist **Honoré de Balzac** (with his semi-autobiographical Louis Lambert), and the founder of Spiritism, the Frenchman **Allan Kardec**.

There are reports of various scientists and artists—such as **Nikola Tesla, Leonardo da Vinci, Van Gogh,** and others — who received ideas, experiments, and designs through astral travel experiences. Today there are many examples of people whose lives were changed by such experiences. Since the astral is understood as an informational field situated next to the earthly world, it is understandable that these experiences leave significant traces on a person and their life. When you travel astrally, your soul and consciousness leave the body to explore other realms; in that way you can visit other places and dimensions and bring back information of great significance to implement in your earthly reality.

Many practitioners use astral projection to **access the Akasha** and its records. In that world you receive information you might never reach from within the physical reality you're in. As with near-death experiences (NDEs), you can receive information on this plane that is otherwise very hard to access. Those who have had clinical death or near-death encounters can testify that insights obtained here can truly change your entire life and leave an indelible mark.

OBE (Out-of-Body Experience) – From the historical perspective, the most important conclusion from research and personal OBE accounts is that human beings are more than their bodies.

An out-of-body experience — also known as astral travel or astral projection — is as natural as sleeping or breathing. During an OBE, human consciousness operates independently of the physical body in a non-physical dimension. Sometimes this occurs with some awareness of what's happening, but often not — which means the person won't retain memories of it.

Someone who has an OBE gains undeniable personal evidence that the physical body is only a temporary "house" through which human consciousness manifests in the physical dimension. During an OBE (which usually happens while the body sleeps or is in an altered state of consciousness) the non-physical bodies separate from the physical one. If a person maintains awareness during this, they may see that their self-awareness is located in the non-physical body, not the physical. The strongest personal confirmation is when someone becomes lucid while out of the body and sees their physical body sleeping on the bed. This often happens in **near-death experiences**, where separation of the non-physical body results from a critical physical state. Thousands of documented reports from accident and cardiac-arrest victims, among others, confirm this phenomenon — sometimes referred to as bilocation.

Similarly, it is widely mentioned and accepted that the non-physical body is connected to the physical by an **elastic field of energy** known as the **silver cord**. The silver cord acts like a tether for the non-physical body, preventing it from getting lost in non-physical levels or failing to return to the physical body. It is the energetic intermediary between two vehicles of manifestation (physical and non-physical) and snaps only at the moment of biological death, when the non-physical body (the bearer of consciousness) departs and a new inter-life period (a rest period) begins. The silver cord is sometimes called one's **bioenergy or energy body**. In fact, this energy body is the conduit through which the energy fields generated by the chakras in the human body flow to the non-physical body and back.

That continuous — usually unconscious — exchange of energy maintains necessary bodily functions and keeps the body alive both in waking life and when the person is out of the body. Likewise, this energetic connection allows the non-physical body to travel far from its physical base.

Bioenergy is one of many terms used to describe the energy field that radiates from and surrounds every living being. It is also known as vital energy, chi, prana, aura, and life force. As a natural element, bioenergy is present in all human processes and relationships. What most people don't realize is that it's also a resource we can learn to control. Mastering your own bioenergy brings countless benefits. In the context of OBEs, energy control is a key component for inducing the experience, determines how **lucid** we can be outside the body, and is the resource that lets us perform tasks and maintain balance in the non-physical dimension.

Although astral travel resembles lucid dreaming, it is not the same. In lucid dreams anything is possible: you can become whatever you wish, wield various powers and magic, be wherever you want, and direct what will happen. Astral travel is quite different and more complex: it is a real experience of your spirit leaving the body in which you do not decide what happens and where you go. That's why thorough preparation is necessary before attempting it.

During an OBE, as awareness disengages from the physical brain and manifests in the brain of the non-physical body — where the memory of an individual's past lives resides — there is a heightened probability of recalling past lives and thus deepening our understanding of evolution, the processes of physical birth and death, and the cycles of successive lives. Likewise, recognizing that we do not die brings a host of new perspectives on past and present relationships and their interconnections, pathologies that have manifested not only in this life but across lifetimes, our multidimensional curriculum, and our purpose or task in this physical life. This makes the OBE an exceptionally rich, instructive, and fascinating experience. Still, most people, after leaving the physical body, remain in the layer closest to the physical dimension — the Earth's "crust."

A given dimension is typically populated by consciousnesses with similar tendencies in the quality of their energy, intentions, thoughts, and feelings. For example, some dimensions are inhabited by beings unaware that they are no longer biologically alive. Others are populated by advanced societies — communities of evolved consciousness fully aware of the cycles of successive lives. These consciousnesses plan their next physical life with goals that include helping humanity, further personal evolution, and serving others in theirs.

Sensations During an OBE – To better understand OBEs, consider common sensations associated with exiting the physical body. Data collected from participant reports in practical training courses on OBE held worldwide by the **International Academy of Consciousness (formerly the International Institute of Projectiology and Conscientiology)** indicate that common sensations during exit or re-entry include: falling, floating, and repercussion effects such as myoclonus (limb jerks), sudden awakening, projective catalepsy (a feeling similar to sleep paralysis), sinking, numbness, intracranial sounds (as if coming from inside the head), tingling, clairvoyance, rocking or swaying, buzzing, and serenity. Other reported experiences include perceiving non-physical beings; sensations like itching, cold, temperature shifts, bodily pressure, tears; as well as clairvoyance and a tunnel effect. Participants also mentioned unusual sensations such as waves passing through the body, pulsing, swelling, lifting, vertigo, stretching, dematerialization, and boiling.

Many scientists have conducted experimental studies. For example, in 1972 **Janet Lee Mitchell**, a researcher at the American Society for Psychical Research in New York, ran a series of experiments to deepen knowledge of "traveling vision" during out-of-body states. The subject was **Ingo Swann**, a noted clairvoyant and surrealist painter. Various objects were hidden on a platform 3.5 meters above the lab floor. After "projecting" his vision, Swann described the objects in words and drawings. An independent judge correctly matched eight of Swann's drawings to the eight target objects — highly unlikely by chance — supporting the "traveling" nature of his perception.

The following year, **Karlis Osis**, a parapsychologist, issued an open call across the US for people who could intentionally project and travel out of body to the ASPR offices in New York. From many volunteers, 100 were selected. Four target objects were placed at predetermined locations in the building. Although the experiment wasn't a complete success, 15% of participants provided clear evidence that they had visited the offices by non-physical means. In 1979, working with **Donna L. McCormick** at the ASPR, Osis tested **kinetic effects of projected consciousness**. The team set up sensors in a sealed chamber to detect a projected presence (in this case, **Alexander Tanous**), who attempted to perceive figures randomly produced by a custom optical device inside the chamber.

Of 197 trials by Tanous across 20 sessions, there were 114 hits and 83 misses. Whenever Tanous correctly described the displayed figure, the sensors registered the presence of "something" in the closed chamber.

While every human experiences some **separation of the non-physical from the physical body** each night during sleep, the great challenge is **to maintain lucidity** while outside the body so we know what's happening and can direct the experience — and then retain memory of it upon return. Fortunately, several mechanisms are known to facilitate lucid OBEs:

- Simple, practical setup: wear comfortable clothing; lie on your back; the room should be dark, quiet, with comfortable temperature; ensure privacy and peace.
- Concentrate on a target or an ethical purpose for the OBE.
- Be relaxed, well-rested, emotionally balanced, motivated; believe in success; release fears and doubts about the experience.
- Likewise, certain factors can hinder OBEs or reduce their quality. Avoid before attempting an exit:
- Highly exciting or violent films/books; conflicts with others; negative rumination; alcohol or any drugs; indulging negative emotions — especially fear.
- Attend to physiological needs beforehand; a full stomach or bladder makes it hard to forget the physical body, which is a prerequisite for an OBE.
- There are also factors and techniques that improve recall of the time spent outside the body. Persistent work strengthening will, memory, concentration, and sustained attention helps remembrance.

Because it's easier to induce OBEs in altered states than in ordinary waking alertness, those interested in lucid OBEs should take advantage of naturally arising positive states such as physical tiredness, lucid dreaming, the hypnagogic (alpha) state, or deep relaxation. Still, the most important qualities for achieving a lucid OBE are strong desire, mental focus, and determination. The effectiveness of these personal qualities cannot be overstated.

Beyond the above, countless other induction techniques exist. The effectiveness of any technique depends entirely on the individual;

everyone must experiment — through trials and errors — to find the method that suits them best.

BENEFITS OF ASTRAL PROJECTION

Astral projection is a practice in which a person steps out of the physical body and travels in the astral plane. People who work with this technique say it brings numerous benefits — spiritual, psychological, and emotional. It offers many potential advantages for spiritual growth, personal evolution, and exploration of subtle dimensions of existence. It does, however, require practice, patience, and mental stability. Those who engage in it should be open-minded yet cautious, to avoid illusions and unconscious fears that can color their experiences. While it's important to study, identify, and understand the sensations associated with out-of-body experiences (and the many related phenomena), it's equally important to view them within a broader context that properly recognizes the value of the experience.

So what, exactly, is the value of an OBE? The true purpose of an OBE is to accelerate personal evolution by giving people the chance to firsthand experience invisible, yet real, non-physical dimensions with which they are in constant interaction. As a tool of self-inquiry, OBEs allow people to discover what they truly are — that they are not merely physical bodies, but evolving consciousness. Here are some ways astral projection can be used and what it's used for:

Expansion of consciousness & spiritual growth – Experiencing reality beyond physical limits can open the mind to a deeper understanding of the universe and connection with higher dimensions of existence.

Overcoming fear of death – Many report a sense of freedom and the realization that consciousness can exist independently of the body. This can reduce or remove fear of death, revealing life as more than material existence.

Connection with guides and higher beings – Practitioners often describe contact with spirit guides, angels, higher aspects of self, or divine beings, bringing guidance, insight, and a sense of support.

Access to the Akashic Records – Sometimes called the "library of the universe," containing information on past, present, and potential futures. Some report reaching these records to receive answers about life and purpose.

Exploring parallel realities and past lives – Because time is experienced non-linearly, people describe exploring past incarnations, parallel universes, or alternate timelines, clarifying patterns, karmic lessons, and the purpose of the current life.

Heightened intuition & energetic sensitivity – Regular practice can sharpen intuition and sensitivity to subtle energies — awareness of the vibration of people, places, and situations — supporting wiser decisions and energetic self-protection.

Faster healing & energetic balance – Some believe AP provides access to planes where energetic healing is possible — revealing blocks and supporting their release — benefiting physical, emotional, and spiritual health.

Creative inspiration & new perspectives – Freed from material constraints, the mind may open to unexpected insights, artistic visions, and ideas that can be applied in daily life.

Travel through space and time – People claim to visit distant places on Earth, other planets, historical events, or communicate with extraterrestrial and higher-dimensional beings — without physical movement.

Deeper understanding of dreams & lucid dreaming – AP practice can develop lucid dreaming and improve dreamwork. Greater nocturnal awareness supports inner transformation.

CHARACTERISTICS OF ASTRAL TRAVEL

- **Separation from the body** – A sense of floating above oneself or moving through spaces impossible to explore physically.

- **Perception of other dimensions –** Encounters with beings and guides; movement through different energetic spheres.
- **Conscious control –** Many can direct their movement within the astral.
- **Return to the body –** Re-entry may be gradual or sudden, sometimes with a jolt or vibration.
-

Common ways to induce astral projection:

- **Deep meditation and relaxation –** Focusing the mind and entering profound relaxation.
- **Visualization techniques –** E.g., imagining climbing a rope or feeling yourself levitate.
- **From lucid dreams –** Using lucidity as a springboard into AP.
- **Spontaneous episodes –** Occurring in sleep, during trauma, or near-death experiences.

TYPES AND VARIETIES OF OUT-OF-BODY EXPERIENCE

There are countless OBE types, differing by how they **arise**, their **nature, and purpose**.

Spontaneous/accidental – Common during trauma, illness, or sleep; the experiencer didn't intend to leave the body and may know little about the phenomenon.

Intentional – Consciously induced through projection methods, meditation, visualization, etc.

Guided projection – Using hypnosis, audio frequencies, or energetic stimulation.

"Verified" OBE – Enough lucidity to perform practical tasks that can later be checked in the physical world.

"Relaxation/freedom" OBE – Marked by feelings of ease, joy, and often flight.

Near-death OBE (NDE) – Reports of traveling through light and other classic NDE features.

Meetings – Encounters with deceased loved ones, or with friends who are also consciously out-of-body, sometimes communicating during the experience.

Continuously conscious OBE – Awareness is maintained through every phase: ordinary waking, relaxation, separation, time spent out-of-body, re-entry, and waking post-return.

Paranormal phenomena are, to a large degree, part of everyday life. We may benefit from strings of synchronicity — feeling nudged to respond to a "signal," or acting as a messenger for someone we know, delivering something we don't fully grasp but is meaningful to them. Without a framework that includes non-physical dimensions and beings, we tend to attribute such events to chance, luck, or fate, and miss that we might be experiencing **clairvoyance or intuition**.

That's why personal and formal research is valuable: it helps us recognize and study non-physical dimensions and beings and, in turn, better understand the true nature of reality. The non-physical is so different from familiar material life that, during conscious OBEs, we encounter conditions foreign to our usual mindset. Out-of-body, we may fly, have a 360-degree field of vision, or, in some cases, leave Earth's atmosphere at astonishing speed. When the non-physical body isn't aligned with the physical (as in partial or full projection), a range of parapsychological phenomena and perceptions far beyond everyday experience can arise.

The ability to experience such phenomena is normal for consciousness projected outside the body with high lucidity, regardless of one's psychic skill level in ordinary waking life.

Examples of **projective phenomena:**

- **Bilocation** – Awareness of being in two places at once (e.g., seeing your resting physical body while in the non-physical body).
- **Permeability** – Passing through physical objects.
- **Internal autoscopy** – Viewing the interior of one's body — bones and organs — whether awareness is in the brain or outside the physical body.

- **Cosmic consciousness –** An exceptionally expanded state where one perceives order, balance, and logic in the universe, and joyfully recognizes unity with it (akin to nirvana, satori, samadhi).
- **Precognition –** Accessing information about events that have not yet occurred.
- **Retrocognition –** Accessing information about events that already happened, often relating to oneself in this or past lives.
- **Non-physical telepathy –** Mind-to-mind communication with people who are physical, projected, or non-physical.

An OBE offers insight into how physical and non-physical dimensions affect one another — making it a valuable tool for evolution and self-study. Understanding the mechanisms of this interaction helps explain aspects of our lives that otherwise defy explanation without appealing to belief alone.

Examples of phenomena not accounted for by conventional science include: a deep, instinctive conviction that an invisible force helped us at critical moments; life-altering intuitions and inspirations; bewildering synchronicities; and sudden, seemingly inexplicable waves of emotion. A model that includes interplay between physical and non-physical dimensions also accounts for documented phenomena such as poltergeists; "material" apparitions of the deceased who aid rescues or deliver vital information; and sensing the presence of a late relative in their former home.

Just as we relate to other physical beings—family, friends, colleagues, acquaintances, strangers—we also interact daily with non-physical beings. By developing awareness of their presence, our connections with them, and their actions and influences, we can understand them better and use that understanding to gain greater control over our lives.

Cosmoethical non-physical beings — consciousnesses at higher levels whose intentions are constructive for our evolution — are known by many names: helpers, spirit guides, guardian angels, disembodied teachers, mentors, protectors. Many of these terms carry mystical or religious overtones, yet such beings need not be tied to mysticism or belief. They are consciousnesses like us, displaying high maturity and lucidity during inter-life periods. They continue to evolve and will live physical lives again. They specialize in assisting those who need it. Their hallmarks are discretion, strong ethics, and respect for personal free will. Their presence doesn't impose a guru-disciple dynamic; instead it tends to increase our lucidity, discernment, and critical thinking.

Out-of-body experience is rich in opportunities for expanding and evolving consciousness. It's worth briefly noting some additional comments on the key benefits of OBEs. By undergoing a lucid OBE, people gain compelling, first-hand evidence of **life after death**. They may even recall a **life plan** (purpose) established before birth, which can help them set new priorities in this life. They can also remember **past lives** or **inter-life periods** while lucidly being outside the body.

Regular lucid OBEs enhance one's parapsychological abilities, extrasensory perception, and sensitivity to energy, and they foster energetic **self-regulation** and skills for **energetic self-defense**. Accumulating such experiences also helps people develop awareness of the nature of their energetic interactions with physical and non-physical beings; offer assistance to those in need by transmitting therapeutic energies; communicate directly with evolved non-physical beings that most people cannot perceive; deepen self-knowledge; and accelerate their own maturation.

ASTRAL PROJECTION PROCEDURE

Set your intention and call in protection – As with manifestation, it's important to set a clear intention: that you want to have an astral journey and explore the astral plane. During practice you can define specific areas to explore, questions you want answered, or issues you want to resolve. Invite your spirit guides, protectors, angels, or a higher power (depending on your belief system) to keep you safe on the journey. If calling on beings doesn't resonate with you, visualize a circle of white light around you — a protective "bubble" on all sides.

When we embark on this journey, we carry in our "suitcase" all of our **beliefs and convictions** neatly packed from physical reality. Here "world" is just a convenient word — this isn't traveling from continent to continent; it's a level of consciousness. When a human being reaches a certain level — expands awareness — that "world," that dimension, becomes accessible.

Because the astral world is far subtler than the physical one, **everything subtle within you — normally invisible — becomes visible and tangible there**. Your emotions, feelings, thoughts, beliefs, fears… can take on form in that state of consciousness. You bring with you everything you've been taught and all the knowledge gained through experience — your beliefs about the world, life, and yourself. In the physical world we say, "You can run from everything — except yourself." You can go to the other side of the globe and nothing will change — you'll still be unhappy, distrustful, insecure — unless you consciously decide to face and transform what you're running from, which is in you, not in the people or places you left.

So, in the subtle world you will still be you. Very quickly you'll come face-to-face with yourself, and above all with your fears. You may not see them, but you know they exist in you. Take a common example: fear of a particular animal — snake, wolf, lion — depending on where you live. If you think of that fear or wonder whether such an animal lives there, you'll instantly get a confirming answer. As soon as such a thought appears in this subtle world, it begins to take form — to manifest — and you'll see what you fear. If that manifestation increases your fear (very likely), you'll instinctively start thinking it will attack or harm you — and that's exactly what will happen. You enter into a struggle with a form — of a being and a fear — that you created. The rule here is: "As a mirror of your beliefs, you will find yourself in a world that can be heaven or hell."

Relax and drop into a meditative state – Assume a comfortable position, as for meditation — lie down or sit, as you prefer. If you like meditating with music, white noise, nature sounds, etc., play them and immerse yourself. To maintain continuous awareness while the body rests, lie down somewhere pleasant, slightly elevate your upper body (a pillow or two under the upper back and head, so saliva doesn't bother you), and close your eyes. Now place attention on your breathing. Breathe slowly, gently, into the belly. Keep the mouth closed; breathe through the nose. Simply watch the breath. If you're very mental, you can count:

- Inhale 5 seconds, hold 3,
- Exhale 5 seconds, pause 3.

That's one cycle. If counting isn't needed, just breathe as feels easiest — slowly and deeply — and follow the guidance above.

Do nothing else — don't try to visualize, fantasize, or focus on any sound except your breathing. Just watch the breath and initially guide it a bit — belly breathing, slow and gentle. After a while many people feel tingling on the skin or face — as if a tiny bug is crawling, or an itch arises. This is normal; the physical body is "checking" whether you've truly fallen asleep. If you scratch or move to satisfy the itch, the process restarts. The goal is to resist that urge and sink deeper. Don't move; center on your breathing. Within about two minutes the itch/sensation will pass. After a few more minutes you may notice the breath "disappears" — you stop perceiving it even though you're still aware. That's normal; you haven't stopped breathing—you're simply ceasing to perceive physical processes. This is an excellent sign. Stay aware; remain awake.

Astral projection with chakra balancing – Sweep attention through the body from feet to head, relaxing more and more. As you go, pause at each chakra, ensuring it's open and rotating properly. Balance each chakra by inhaling white light through it and exhaling through the crown, or simply by feeling yourself breathing through the chakra as its energy flow normalizes and "finds rhythm." With each exhale, say inwardly "my body relaxes" and feel the calm, pleasant vibration. By the end, feel aligned with body and spirit, energy streaming through you — relaxed and ethereal.

Soon you may feel waves, friction, or fluttering — as if you've become paper in the wind. In other words, you begin to sense the contours of your subtle body — your subtle energies. This is the next stage of separation from the physical body. When you notice your subtle body, it's crucial **not to do anything**.

In practice: Don't try to move or steer what you sense as your second body; don't manipulate it; don't do anything with it. Don't analyze what it is; don't summon ideas, thoughts, or fears. Just witness what you perceive — relax and enjoy. If you try to control it immediately or start analyzing and fearing, the experience will stop or end soon after. Most likely this is your first time feeling your subtle body, which is probably still delicate and undeveloped. Any interference or attempt at control can disrupt the process.

So instead of control, analysis, definitions, and fear — relax even more and simply enjoy whatever you feel. With luck you may also see, though many don't at first — they only sense. That's fine and normal. This is the beginning, the gate to out-of-body experiences, especially other dimensions like the astral. You're not there yet — you're in your subtle spiritual womb. You need to be "born," to strengthen and adapt. When you reach this point, you can imagine gentle swaying, spinning, or rising in an elevator to stimulate entry into the astral. Let it be decisive and strong, which can enable a quick, stable entry. You can also imagine grabbing the **silver cord** above your head with your hands and, by pulling, separating from the physical body.

Source energy manifests through the channels of our intuition, communicating with us via interconnection with all that surrounds us. Likewise, our astral/energetic being speaks through an open sixth and seventh chakra, through deep meditative states associated with gamma brainwaves, through 5D, universal wisdom, Zen, Nibbāna, Samādhi, or the Akasha Records—and knows what is, what was, and what will be. Our energetic being knows information even before events occur; it knows our spiritual tasks and tests before we do, even before our birth; it knows which other energies we will meet and recognize on that path, and what task our soul has in relation to them.

The astral/spiritual body is older than the physical body. The way our astral/spiritual (energetic) body communicates — with us and with others — is through intuition, telepathy, and energetic connectedness. That's why communication on the level of higher consciousness — the so-called 5D level — is free of the classic forms of communication we know (words, physical presence) and unfolds energetically instead.

It can be helpful to use a **quartz crystal** to raise and accelerate your vibration as preparation. Gently hold the crystal on the third eye just above the center of the eyebrows, eyes closed, and breathe deeply. Feel the vibrations. You may visualize gold, white, purple, or any color you wish. During meditation and astral travel, you can hold the crystal in your hand or place it on your chest or stomach. The crystal will strengthen and protect you because of its high vibration, since negative energies are of lower vibration.

Imagine the room you're in — Focus your awareness in the third eye (center of the forehead) and imagine, in as much detail as possible, the room you're in. Imagine yourself standing in the room or floating. This should be the moment in which astral projection happens — when you project your spirit outside your body. Some techniques recommend trying to float above your body by seeing and feeling your astral body separate from the physical (keeping the same shape and appearance), starting from the feet. If it's not easy to see yourself outside the body, try the rope method — imagine a rope hanging from the ceiling, grab it, and pull yourself out of your body; from there, look down at your physical body you just left. Practitioners suggest there is an energetic link like a cord connecting the astral and physical bodies, allowing you to go anywhere and eventually pulling you back (which can create feelings of tightness or discomfort on return).

So, when you become lucid in a dream and are aware of yourself and the dream, all you need to do is set an **Intention or Thought**, and hold to it — repeat it several times in the lucid state: "I want an out-of-body experience NOW." or ask, "What does an out-of-body experience feel like?"

Any of these intentions/questions in lucid dreaming will catapult you into an OBE. Simply stick with the intention — repeat it a few times in the dream. That's enough. In that state, intentions and questions are incredibly clear and strong, and they manifest immediately. That's literally all you need to do — the OBE begins right after, entering through the dream.

Use your mind to move your soul out of the body. In your mind, picture the room where you're lying. Move your "body" in your mind to stand up. Look around. Get up from the bed and walk across the room, then turn and look at your body on the bed. Your OBE is successful if you feel you're looking at your body from the other side of the room, with your conscious self now separate from it.

For some people this takes a lot of practice; for others it's as natural as breathing. If you have trouble lifting completely out, first try raising just a hand or a foot. Keep practicing until you can move around the room. Return to your body. Your soul always remains connected to your body by an invisible force called the **"silver cord."** Let this force guide your soul back. Re-enter your body. Move your fingers and toes — physically, not just in your mind — and allow full waking consciousness to return. Repeat several times to build the skill of entering and exiting the astral field.

Explore the astral plane — verify your projection. Once you can project within the same room, you'll want to confirm you were truly in two separate planes. Next time, don't turn to look at your body. Instead, leave the room and enter another room in your home. Examine an object there that you've never noticed closely in waking life. Note its color, shape, and size, gathering as many details as possible. When you've projected outside yourself, be curious — move and explore to see where you've arrived. Over time you can start planning where you'd like to go, what you want to explore, and which answers you seek — before entering the astral.

Through learning and practicing astral travel, we open the possibility of meeting and communicating with highly advanced beings. This can include highly evolved souls (ascended masters), angelic beings no longer needing 3D bodies, those we knew in past incarnations, and various spirit guides ready to share knowledge and help us rise. Angels or holy beings may guide you to different places, show you your past, present, and future situations, offer wisdom relevant to your path, and then return you to your physical body. Learning through astral travel can help you understand your divine essence more deeply, including your reincarnational history and potential parallel lives.

If you give yourself a mission or goal, make it something close at hand—for example, simply to feel your subtle spiritual body. Don't set distant goals; pick something near. This strongly supports success. Those who can meditate or sit in silence can feel many subtle bodies. Once you reach a **thought-free** state — inner peace — everything needed to feel your subtle body is to think one single thought and nothing more. **That thought is a wave**. Think of a wave — of water, or wind. Instantly, the thought transforms into a sensation you just continue to perceive. You'll feel as if you've become that wave, changing little by little. The thought is only a trigger; the key is the sensation.

As long as you feel such sensations, you can be sure you are sensing your subtle body (or one of them). By simply observing and not generating other thoughts — just witnessing — various changes will begin to occur in the sensations, and you may feel other subtle bodies as if "flipping through" an album of images. This may last a minute — or hours. It depends entirely on maintaining attention on the sensations, allowing them to present themselves without interruption by other thoughts.

In later sessions, go to locations less and less familiar. Each time, record details you never noticed before. After each session, physically check the details. After a few journeys, you'll be experienced enough to travel to completely unknown locations with confidence that you truly performed astral projection.

There are several ways to check whether you're in the astral. One excellent method is to pinch your mouth and nose shut and try to inhale — you'll still be able to breathe (remember, physical laws don't apply in the astral). To help yourself, it's recommended to create a work plan — keep it in mind while in the astral (though sometimes hard to recall). It helps you avoid the "What do I do now?" moment, because the instant you stop and ask that, you tend to snap back into the physical body.

As we see, in the astral we should keep moving, because stillness often ends the session. You can add items to your plan right away: Look at yourself in a mirror to **teleport** (at first somewhere close — e.g., outside the room or onto the street; never teleport into a closed space without doors or into a basement). Then, **fly** — yes, you can in the astral! Remember, your astral body isn't your physical one; it may not even look like you, and it doesn't have muscles in the ordinary sense. You'll need to fly by will, not by muscles.

Returning to the body — When you're ready to return, bring attention to your body — first see it, then feel it. Focus awareness on bodily sensations — your muscles, the weight pressing into the surface beneath you, your breathing. You may think or say, "I call my astral body back," to return to ordinary consciousness. Return to your body. In waking life, walk into the room you had projected into and find the item you examined during the journey. Can you confirm the details you noted when you explored it astrally?

Some say astral projection is dangerous — especially as you gain skill and explore unknown places — but it doesn't have to be. As long as you ask for protection in your way, it will be a good experience. Before projecting, it's helpful to imagine yourself bathed in bright white light — like a cloud around you or within you. This protects you from other thought-forms or negative energies. There is so much to explore, but know that nothing bad will come unless you believe it will. Remember: you carry yourself there — your beliefs, feelings, and fears.

The silver cord can never be severed; still, it's said your soul might be delayed in re-entering the body if you expend too much energy outside it. Even so, your soul and body are so intertwined that the soul naturally returns when the time is right. Your soul can also communicate with other astral projectors — try it with a friend who's practiced as much as you. (Some say **astral intimacy** is astonishing.) In any case, remember you always return to your body.

It's possible **to heal others** during astral travel — this is a very potent form of remote healing. Imagine the person who is unwell, perhaps lying in bed. It doesn't matter if they aren't physically in bed at that moment, because time and distance are empty in the astral. Always ask for protection, healing power, and guidance from whatever you pray to, and visualize light; you can ask during astral travel as you wish. See white, strong light in your hands; if you feel ready, place one hand on their forehead and the other on their abdomen and pour light into them. Your intentions must be pure, and you should feel nothing but love for them. Sometimes people will tell you something amazing happened — even if you never told them you might have been the source. Never try to enter the astral two days in a row — always rest in between.

Integrate the experience — When you're fully present and awake again, reflect on your experience — you may want to take notes and track what happens, to get to know yourself and your processes more deeply and learn to enter/exit astral projection more easily at will. Consider keeping an astral projection journal to record your progress — treat it as your ongoing research project to refine over time.

What if astral projection isn't working?

Astral projection doesn't have to succeed on the first try. You may have a conscious or unconscious resistance — or fear — that keeps you from relaxing, especially if you've had unsuccessful or unpleasant attempts before. Relaxing may lead you into sleep so the experience feels vague, or the whole thing may feel frustrating. Your motivation may also be the issue — astral projection isn't a trendy hobby, nor a matter of ambition, competition, or success. It's time set aside for relaxing and connecting with yourself, for deep exploration that shifts perception and widens perspective — something you enter for the experience and personal growth itself, because it matters to you, you're curious, and it might satisfy your desire for alternative sources of knowing and for spiritual and psychic experience.

There's no rush here — merely trying and relaxing is enough. Even if you don't have a vivid astral projection, balancing the chakras and cultivating energy awareness will still give you a deep experience and broaden your perspective.

LUCID DREAMS

When speaking about astral projection, we must also mention **lucid dreams**, which are quite different yet closely linked to astral projection. While both involve a sense of separating from the physical body and exploring other dimensions of awareness, they differ in nature, induction, and conscious control. Lucid dreaming is considered a state one enters accidentally or on purpose, and from there may have access to astral projection.

A lucid dream is a state in which a person becomes aware they are dreaming while still in the dream. In this state, the dreamer can take control of the dream, change the environment, interact with characters, and even wake up at will. This ability lets people explore their mind, overcome fears, boost creativity, and even improve skills used in waking life.

Some people regard lucid dreaming as an "entry point" to astral projection. There are reports of lucid dreamers who managed to transition from a lucid dream into an astral projection state. Lucid dreams are a state in which the dreamer becomes aware of the dream and can steer it, while astral travel involves the perception of leaving the body and exploring other dimensions. While lucid dreams remain within the sphere of mind and subconsciousness, astral projection is often viewed as an experience outside bodily reality.

The key difference is that astral travel is experienced as a "real event" occurring independently of the subconscious, whereas lucid dreams are recognized as mental projections. Lucid dreams differ from ordinary dreams in that they include **metacognition** — the ability to recognize within the dream that it isn't real — which opens the door to experiences not possible in waking life.

With the silver cord ensuring an unbroken link between the physical and non-physical bodies, it's possible to have a variety of lucid experiences outside the body. We can travel across physical levels or visit other dimensions, meet old friends or make new connections, exercise our will, and make choices. But how can we be sure that what we experience is real, and not a dream or another altered state triggered by fainting, exhaustion, fever, medication, hormones, or drugs?

Among the hallmarks of a conscious OBE, clearly distinguishing it from a **dream or hallucination**, are the following:

- Lucid dreamers/active OBE participants make decisions and use their mental faculties, whereas in a dream they remain passive and have no control over the experience.
- Environments and situations encountered during projection are real, while in dreams they may be distorted or nonsensical.
- Situations met during projection occur independently of an individual's creative abilities or imagination.
- Projections are harder to recall than dreams, since the experience occurs outside the physical brain and isn't recorded in it.
- During projection, people can see and even touch their physical body, while dreams unfold within the physical body.
- People report feelings of freedom, satisfaction, expanded awareness, and sometimes euphoria thanks to flying and passing through material objects, whereas dreams tend to provide more down-to-earth feelings and scenarios.
- People often perceive the exit and/or return of their non-physical body into the physical one, which doesn't happen in dreams.

BENEFITS OF LUCID DREAMING

Because lucid dreams are a state in which a person becomes aware they are dreaming and can partially or fully control the course of the dream, this ability brings numerous benefits — mental, emotional, and creative — as well as for personal development and spiritual exploration.

Lucid dreaming offers a range of advantages, from personal growth and overcoming fears to boosting creativity and learning. It lets people explore the depths of their psyche, rehearse real-life situations, have unforgettable experiences, and develop inner wisdom. With regular practice, lucid dreams can become a powerful tool for life transformation and for opening new dimensions of awareness. Here are some of the most significant benefits:

Self-knowledge and personal growth — Lucid dreams provide direct access to the subconscious. By analyzing dreams, we can uncover deeper layers of our thoughts, feelings, and unconscious behavior patterns. This introspective power helps us understand inner fears, desires, and motivations, leading to greater personal development.

Overcoming fears and trauma — Many use lucid dreams as a tool to face phobias and trauma. For example, someone afraid of heights can practice flying or walking along cliffs in a completely safe dream setting. Gradually, this can reduce fear and help overcome it in real life. Lucidity lets the dreamer take control of scary scenarios and transform them into positive experiences. Techniques for engaging "negative entities" in dreams aid psychological integration of fear.

Creativity and artistic inspiration — Lucid dreams can be an endless source of inspiration for artists, writers, musicians, and scientists. In dreams you can create new landscapes, explore innovative ideas, and receive insights hard to reach while awake. Many renowned artists and inventors — like Salvador Dalí and Nikola Tesla—used dreams to create their works.

Improved memory and learning — Lucid dreams can enhance memory and support learning new skills. In dreams, you can review lessons, study languages, practice an instrument, or develop motor abilities. Research shows the brain processes information in similar ways during dreams and wakefulness, so lucid dreaming can accelerate learning.

Rehearsing real-life situations — One of the biggest advantages is the ability to simulate real situations. You can rehearse conversations, practice public speaking, test a new sport, or try out different choices before applying them in the real world. This builds confidence and prepares you for challenges. Studies show that practicing movements in lucid dreams can improve motor skills in waking life. Athletes and musicians sometimes use lucid dreaming for mental training.

Exploring the unconscious and deeper levels of awareness — Lucid dreams allow exploration of one's own mind and contact with unconscious aspects of the psyche. People often use them to better understand instinct, inner wisdom, and the inner guide. It's possible to experience expanded states of awareness, supporting spiritual growth.

Better sleep quality and nighttime rest — Although some fear lucid dreaming might reduce sleep quality, experience shows that awareness in dreams can reduce nightmares and improve overall sleep. People who lucid dream regularly often feel more rested and alert upon waking.

Dream control and fun — An obvious benefit is the ability to fully direct dreams. You can fly, time-travel, visit imaginary worlds, meet historical figures, or create your own fantastic scenarios. This freedom offers unlimited possibilities for exploration and enjoyment.

Development of spiritual awareness and meditative abilities — Lucid dreams are often used in spiritual practice to explore higher states of consciousness, connect with inner guides, and inquire into the nature of reality. Some people have mystical experiences, a sense of oneness with the universe, and a deeper understanding of existence. Buddhists and shamans have practiced conscious dreaming for centuries within their spiritual traditions.

Reducing nightmares and gaining control over dreaming — People who suffer frequent nightmares can use lucid dreams to transform negative experiences. Once aware they are dreaming, they can take control and shift the dream into a positive outcome. This is especially helpful for those with PTSD.

CHARACTERISTICS & WAYS TO INDUCE LUCID DREAMS

Characteristics:

- **Awareness within the dream** – The key feature of lucid dreams is that the dreamer knows they are dreaming.
- **Control over the dream** – The level of control varies, but experienced dreamers can shape the environment, teleport, fly through space and time, and create objects and beings.
- **Inner reality** – Everything that happens in a lucid dream remains within the dreamer's mind and isn't connected to astral dimensions.
- **Heightened perception** – Colors, sounds, and sensations can be more intense than in ordinary dreams.

How to induce lucid dreams?

- **MILD (Mnemonic Induction of Lucid Dreams)** – Repeating the intention to become aware in a dream. Before sleep, affirm: "Next time I'm dreaming, I'll know I'm dreaming."
- **WILD (Wake-Initiated Lucid Dream)** – Entering the dream directly from wakefulness via relaxation and visualization; maintain awareness as the body falls asleep, often through meditation or focusing on mental imagery.
- **WBTB (Wake Back To Bed)** – Wake up after 4–6 hours of sleep, stay awake 20–30 minutes, then go back to sleep focusing on lucidity.
- **Keep a daily dream journal** – Write your dreams every morning to improve recall, spot patterns, and raise dream awareness (and thus the chance of lucidity).
- **Reality checks** – Techniques such as looking at your hands or in a mirror (they often look altered in dreams), pressing a finger into the opposite palm (it may pass through in dreams),

reading text, looking away and rereading (text often changes), and asking, "Am I dreaming?"

- **Breathing & relaxation techniques** – Deep meditation and breath control can increase the likelihood of lucidity by preparing and relaxing the body for the process.

NOTES

TELEPATHY

"Telepathy isn't the transfer of thoughts,
but the meeting of two consciousnesses that recognize each other
without a single word — for what is true
doesn't seek explanation, only a flash of truth."
Aleksandra Božović

THE BRIDGE BETWEEN MIND AND CONSCIOUSNESS

Telepathy is a fascinating and controversial topic that has intrigued philosophers, mystics, scientists, and skeptics for centuries. Telepathy is the ability to transmit thoughts, feelings, or information from one mind to another without using the known senses or physical means of communication. This connection often appears as an instantaneous transfer, which leads to theories about a **"quantum field of consciousness" or "morphogenetic fields."**

Although the idea is often linked to science fiction, there are numerous phenomena and experiences suggesting that telepathy may not be mere illusion but a real capacity lying deep within human consciousness. The very word telepathy comes from the Greek **"tele"** — distant, far — and **"pathos"**—feeling.

The French researcher **Frederic W. H. Myers** first used the term telepathy in 1882 at a meeting of the Society for Psychical Research, explaining that it best described a phenomenon previously called mind reading.

The science that studies such phenomena is **parapsychology**, considered a branch of psychology that investigates so-called parapsychological phenomena—perceptions and activities of people with paranormal psychological abilities. These are divided into two main groups: **extrasensory perception (ESP)** in the form of **telepathy** (transfer of thoughts) and **clairvoyance** (spatial and temporal, the latter including foretelling the future); and

psychokinetic phenomena (moving material objects by mental energy) in the form of **telekinesis, materialization, and levitation**. Among other things, **hypnosis** also falls under parapsychology and is increasingly used for medical (anesthesia) and psychotherapeutic purposes.

To understand telepathy, we must first delve into the nature of consciousness and the interconnectedness of all beings, and into objective versus subjective experience. Objective experience is how we perceive real, 3D, material events around us, while subjective experience is how each of us lives an event on a personal level. Research shows that some events don't fully belong to either category and are considered anomalies not yet scientifically explained or proven.

Psychokinesis is the ability to influence material objects — moving or reshaping them — by the power of the mind. People who can receive or send telepathic or telekinetic messages are considered **mediums** (Latin medium, means, intermediary), and this ability is also known as the **"sixth sense."**

Extrasensory experiences represent all those perceptions of reality without using the five basic senses (smell, taste, sight, hearing, touch). Such events are often linked to insights from the distant past or past lives, or even point to events in the near future. We know the phenomenon where certain places, smells, or sounds can trigger memories we didn't even know we had.

One of my clients had a particularly interesting phenomenon that remains unexplained to this day. She was born in Serbia and had never before been to Sarajevo, in Bosnia and Herzegovina. When she first went to Sarajevo, she began to tremble and felt a peculiar connection with the city. One day she found herself in the very center of the old town, where small artisan shops lined the streets. Standing in the square, tears began to stream down her face. She couldn't explain her reaction or why it was happening. At some point, images from a past she didn't consciously know began to appear — as if she had been part of it. She felt extraordinarily connected to the images, sounds, and smells that surged from her memory even though she had never witnessed such events.

Given that we all descend from those who walked this planet before us and that genetic transmission of information to future generations is scientifically supported, it's entirely possible she received information about her ancestors — or her own past life — that may have unfolded long ago in that region. Several times after this experience she visited the same place again, and the feeling was even stronger and more intense.

Beyond information transmitted from the past, we also know of events involving information from the future. You surely know the situation: you think about a friend or about texting them — and in that very moment you receive a message from that friend. In that moment you "out of nowhere" pick up information about the friend just as they thought to write to you. While the friend is thinking, you receive that information with your mind, but you don't recognize it as something sent by your friend; you experience it as your own thought. Meanwhile your friend types the message, and the instant their focus shifts from thinking of you to the text they're sending, the telepathic link between you snaps.

Because 5D is a quantum field of collective consciousness, it's quite possible in that space to "pick up" other people's thoughts and "hear" when they think or speak about us. Just as in today's world of advanced technology we have Wi-Fi devices that let us connect to the internet through time and space — even though we can't see the signal with the naked eye — we know it exists, passes through walls, and reliably works. Telepathic communication has existed for ages; its existence can't be dismissed simply because it isn't tangible or visible.

From a 3D standpoint these things seem inexplicable and we may label them "magic," while in the 5D world they're entirely normal. In 5D, communication via thought is the primary mode, since the quantum field is highly transparent and we can connect with the thoughts of all living and nonliving beings. If observing the surface of the ocean from shore gives only a superficial sense of its contents — that's like our 3D view. But when you dive into the depths, you can perceive the ocean's full content; in the same way 5D becomes clear.

Supporting this is a phenomenon **Albert Einstein** named — skeptically — **"spooky action at a distance,"** referring to aspects of quantum mechanics. The phrase points to **quantum entanglement** — one of the most enigmatic and fascinating concepts in modern physics.

At first glance, quantum entanglement sounds like science fiction: two or more particles can be so correlated that, no matter how far apart they are, a change in one's state instantly affects the other's state. This instantaneous correlation defies classical physics, which holds that information cannot travel faster than light.

This peculiar feature of the quantum world has opened the door to speculation about possible parallels with telepathy — the idea that thoughts or feelings might be transferred between minds in a similar way. To understand how this might work, we must first look more closely at the phenomenon of quantum entanglement.

Quantum Entanglement

Quantum entanglement is a phenomenon in which two (or more) particles remain mutually connected so that a change in the quantum state of one instantly changes the state of the other — even if they are at opposite ends of the universe.

Imagine a pair of electrons that were originally linked and became entangled. If we send one electron to Mars and keep the other on Earth, changing the state of the first electron automatically changes the state of the second — without any visible force between them and with no time delay.

This phenomenon has been confirmed many times in experiments, most famously through the work of physicist **John Bell** and later the 1980s experiments of **Alain Aspect**, which unequivocally showed that quantum entanglement is not an illusion but a reality.

Einstein believed in a universe that operates according to deterministic laws — in his view, every physical process must have a logical explanation within the bounds of space and time. When quantum theory suggested that particles could "communicate" instantaneously over infinite distances, Einstein found this unacceptable.

He held that quantum mechanics was incomplete and that some "hidden variable" must exist to explain this mysterious link. However, later research showed that quantum entanglement is not just a theoretical concept — it is a real and fundamental feature of nature. Although quantum physics does not provide direct evidence for telepathy, the idea of quantum entanglement offers an intriguing framework for thinking about how telepathy might function on a subtle level.

For all physical things to "exist," there must be some kind of **diffusion and interaction of information**. We must agree that thoughts are real and lead to powerful outcomes. Defining thought can be tricky and belongs to philosophical and metaphysical circles, but whatever it is, it's a kind of energy, registered by different sensors inside and outside our heads.

Here's how it goes: Information in the brain is transmitted by electrical current, gated by sodium-dependent channels in cell membranes. This process is rather stochastic and does not, by itself, explain rational thought. However, if these processes were also responsible for another interaction — the transfer of momentum between interacting particles in the cell membrane — this could lead to the creation of variably neutral Z bosons, one of the carriers of the weak force, which decay into a neutrino and an antineutrino. The Z boson is heavy and short-lived and dies soon after. Neutrinos and antineutrinos are almost massless and have a very small cross-section, which means they rarely — if ever — interact with other particles. Theoretically, they should never do anything significant in our bodies.

Let's assume our brain receptors are also capable of collecting neutrinos. Neutrino "flavor" could be used to encode information, in a kind of binary language transmitted, say, via neutrinos. Combined with instantaneous motion through a carefully mapped neural network, this could be analogous to the information traffic that takes place on the internet. Active neurons would be the routing network, while neutrinos would be the actual data packets. Reception and decoding would still remain a mystery.

This could explain why we sometimes have "random" thoughts or the fact that we cannot "feel" the flow of thought. If they are indeed triggered by a balanced reaction between neuronal voltages and neutrinos moving at the speed of light, then there is no way to catch them. This could also indicate why thoughts are so elusive. Neutrinos are hard to detect. And no human being sits inside a particle accelerator, which makes any attempt to simulate brain activity recorded via external sensors impossible.

How does this explanation relate to telepathy? Well, neutrinos (and antineutrinos) are not confined by the boundaries of our skull and could easily escape without being captured by our receptors. These neutrinos could then spread to another person's head and trigger a "hacking" reaction by producing unwanted chains of thought. Taken together, this brain-working method could explain many things — sudden, random thoughts, déjà vu — and also how we are able to "pick up" other people's thoughts.
There are several key parallels that explain telepathic connectedness among people:

Instant connection despite distance – Just as entangled particles are linked regardless of distance, some telepathy reports describe instantaneous communication between people far apart. Many have experienced a "sense" that a loved one is in danger or have received a mental image precisely when that person underwent a powerful emotional event.

Deeper connection at the level of consciousness – Some scientists, such as Rupert Sheldrake, suggest that consciousness is not limited to the brain but functions within a collective energy field connecting all humans. This idea, known as the theory of morphogenetic fields, resembles quantum entanglement — where a "field" linking individuals is what enables telepathic communication. In this view, living beings share a collective energy field through which information is transmitted intuitively or telepathically.

The impact of emotional bonding – Interestingly, quantum entanglement is not easily achieved — specific conditions are needed to "entangle" particles. Similarly, telepathic links often appear most strongly between people with a powerful emotional bond (mother and child, close friends, romantic partners).

Information beyond time and space – Telepathic messages, according to reports, often appear as sudden insights or feelings that come "out of nowhere." In quantum physics, the simultaneity of entanglement echoes this instantaneous exchange of information.

In addition, data transfer may be possible via **frequency resonance** — the idea that the human brain emits electromagnetic waves that can resonate with the waves of another mind, allowing the transfer of information.

Some scientists speculate that the brain, as a biological system, might use **quantum processes on a microscopic level**. Neuroscientists have discovered that processes involving subatomic particles and quantum wave functions take place inside neurons.

The quantum mind theory, proposed by researchers such as **Roger Penrose and Stuart Hameroff,** suggests that consciousness relies on quantum processes in microtubules — tiny structural components in brain cells. If quantum effects are indeed present in our brains, then it's not impossible that a similar principle could enable telepathic communication. Although telepathy has not yet been scientifically proven by traditional methods, quantum entanglement provides an intriguing theoretical framework for its explanation.

If the human mind can indeed connect with others in a way similar to quantum entanglement, it could have profound implications for communication, empathy, and our connectedness as a species.

While "spooky action at a distance" is now confirmed in physics, the question remains whether the human mind uses similar principles. **Telepathy** — whether as a quantum phenomenon or a spiritual ability—invites us to expand our understanding of consciousness and interconnection among people.

Perhaps the key lies in cultivating inner silence, attentive listening, and deeper connection with ourselves and others. As quantum physics shows, the universe does not always require explanations within classical logic — sometimes it's enough to open the mind and be present in the moment.

The concept of telepathy can be traced back to ancient civilizations. **The Egyptians, Greeks, and Chinese** mentioned mystical ways of communicating thoughts across great distances.

Hindu texts speak of **siddhis**, supernatural powers that include mental communication. In **Buddhist practice**, advanced meditators often describe the ability to read minds as a by-product of deep meditative states.

The Japanese have a term for this unspoken form of communication — **ishin-denshin** — which means "communication by the heart," or "what the mind thinks, the heart transmits," communicating "from one heart to another."

In spiritual practice, telepathy is often seen as an expression of deeper connectedness among people, grounded in a unified field of consciousness. Many meditative traditions teach that when one attains inner silence and harmony, the ability to "feel" the thoughts or emotions of others becomes more natural.

Spiritual teachers claim telepathy is not a "supernatural" ability but a natural gift that can be awakened through cultivating awareness, empathy, and openness to universal connectedness.

In the West, telepathy became popular in the XIX century, especially thanks to the work of parapsychology pioneers such as **Frederic Myers and William James**. During that period, experiments with hypnosis, suggestion, and mental thought transfer drew the attention of the scientific community.

Telepathy has fascinated not only mystics and occultists but also prominent psychologists and scientists. **Carl Gustav Jung, Sigmund Freud, and Joseph Banks Rhine** are among the key figures who seriously considered telepathy, each with a unique approach.

Joseph Banks Rhine at Duke University conducted 1930s experiments using symbol cards — **Zener cards** (a 25-card deck with circle, star, waves, cross, and square) — to test telepathic abilities. A sender would visualize a particular card while the receiver tried to "sense" which symbol it was. If a subject guessed five out of 25, that would be pure chance. Yet some subjects guessed as many as 18 correctly, which Rhine and colleagues took as evidence of parapsychological abilities. Rhine argued that some participants achieved statistically significant results beyond chance. He coined **ESP (Extrasensory Perception)**, encompassing telepathy, clairvoyance, and precognition.

His well-known work also included **Ganzfeld experiments**, in which one participant, placed in sensory isolation, tried to receive mental images from another participant. The sender visualized specific images while the receiver described whatever came to mind. Statistical results showed significant deviations from chance, which Rhine took as evidence of telepathic communication. Although Rhine conducted many rigorously designed experiments, his findings were controversial. Skeptics argued that positive results could be due to chance, suggestion, or inadequately controlled conditions.

Later, in remote viewing experiments, participants showed the ability to describe distant locations or events unknown to them. These experiments — especially those funded by the U.S. government under

the Stargate Project — produced intriguing results that captivated both scientists and mystics.

Carl Gustav Jung was one of the first prominent psychologists to regard telepathy as a serious psychic phenomenon. He believed telepathy could be part of a deeper unconscious process linked to the collective unconscious. Jung thought telepathy might be possible through archetypal connections within the collective unconscious — a kind of network of universal consciousness to which all people belong. He held that symbols and images in dreams often manifest unconscious telepathic communication. Jung used telepathy to explain spontaneous insights and "coincidences," later introducing **the concept of synchronicity**, in which telepathic events are not mere chance but part of a deeper connectedness among people and the world.

If we think of a friend and they immediately send a message, Jung would interpret it as the expression of an unconscious energetic link. He conducted numerous observations on how mental images and thoughts might be transferred between people.

In one example, Jung describes a situation in which his patient dreamed of a snake at the very moment he, unconsciously, was thinking of a snake during the session — an instance of telepathic resonance within the analytic relationship.

Sigmund Freud was initially skeptical about telepathy but later shifted his stance, especially after noticing telepathic elements in psychoanalytic practice. He saw telepathy as a possibility that unconscious thoughts and feelings could be transmitted between people. He believed individuals in hypnotic or emotionally intense states were more susceptible to telepathic influences and considered telepathy a possible extension of instinct and unconscious communication.

In later years Freud regarded hypnosis as a possible avenue to open telepathic communication. In one session he recorded a case where a patient in a hypnotic state spontaneously "read" the analyst's thoughts, which he interpreted as a form of telepathy activated through the unconscious. Freud struggled to reconcile scientific skepticism with personal encounters of telepathy. In a letter to Jung, he wrote: *"Though a skeptic by nature, I cannot deny that telepathic phenomena deserve serious study...."* While remaining cautious, he did not completely dismiss telepathy as a mental phenomenon.

Research has shown that telepathy most often occurs in stressful, tense situations among close friends and family members. It typically manifests when one person becomes "aware" that the other is in danger — through a dream or by "seeing" fragments of an event that has not yet happened. The person who "sees" then transmits their thoughts to the person in danger, and such "information" can influence the course of events. In folk traditions this form of telepathy is called a premonition, and in psychological research these cases are the most frequent.

Studies suggest telepathy is closely tied to a person's emotional state and that women are more telepathically connected than men — psychologists explain this by noting that women are often more attuned to their intuition. Beyond linking minds between two or more people, some studies indicate that such connection can also change physiological elements in the body. Recorded effects include increased production of red blood cells and changes in the brain waves of the person receiving the message.

TYPES OF TELEPATHY

Telepathy can be classified by the nature of the information transfer:

- **Instinctive telepathy** – Arises spontaneously, most often in crises or between people with a strong emotional bond (e.g., twins, parent – child).
- **Mental telepathy** – Conscious communication of thoughts, images, or words between individuals.
- **Spiritual telepathy** – A deeper, intuitive connectedness that involves the collective unconscious or universal consciousness.

Telepathy; whether ultimately explained by science or embraced as a spiritual ability reminds us of the invisible threads connecting all people. Perhaps its key lies in expanding awareness, empathy, and inner connection. Maybe telepathy isn't "mind reading" in the usual sense, but a deep listening at the level of the heart and soul. In a world filled with noise, cultivating a quiet inner voice may be the most important step toward discovering this latent potential.

Exercises to Develop Telepathy

Telepathy rests on deeper connection with yourself and others. The focus is on cultivating intuition, clarity of thought, and the ability to send mental messages.

Step 1: Mental Centering & Focus

First, it's important to cultivate inner silence so that your thoughts are clear and focused.

Exercise: "Conscious Breathing"

- Sit comfortably and close your eyes.
- Inhale through the nose to a count of 4, hold for 4, exhale slowly for 4.
- Feel each inhale bring calm, each exhale release tension.
- After 5–10 minutes, place your attention on the space between the eyebrows (Ajna chakra).

Goal: Achieve inner quiet and reduce mental "noise."

Step 2: Develop Intuitive Sensing

Telepathy often presents itself as intuition — the sense that you 'know' what someone is thinking or feeling.

Exercise: "Guess the Number"

- Agree with a partner that one person will think of a number (start 1–10).
- Relax, focus on your partner's energy, and try to feel the number rather than guess.
- As you improve, widen the range (1–50, 1–100).

Goal: Strengthen intuition through concentration and trust in inner insight.

Step 3: Sending Thoughts (Active Telepathy)
Exercise: "Telepathic Image"

- Close your eyes and visualize a simple symbol (square, circle, triangle).
- Imagine mentally sending it to your partner.
- Your partner closes their eyes and listens for inner images or feelings.
- Compare notes afterward.

Tips: Practice in deep relaxation. Start simple before moving to words, complex images, or emotions.

Step 4: Receiving Thoughts (Passive Telepathy)
Exercise: "Mind Scanning"

- Your partner silently chooses a concept (e.g., "tree," "dog," "bell").
- Close your eyes, relax, focus on their energy.
- Let images, words, or feelings arise.
- Trust the first impression — it's often the most accurate.

Key: Trust inner perceptions; don't force answers.

Exercise: "Word Projection"

Goal: Build the ability to receive telepathic thoughts via spontaneous insight; strengthen intuitive perception.

- Ask your partner to silently repeat a chosen word (e.g., "sun," "river," "home").
- Sit relaxed and imagine that word "floating" into your mind.
- Focus on the first images or feelings that appear.
- Your partner later confirms whether you received the word or its symbolism.

Exercise: "Zener Cards" — Rhine's Experimental Telepathy (Psycho-energetic Skills)

Goal: Strengthen mental "reading" of symbols and notice when your mind best "catches" telepathic signals.

- Use a Zener deck (or make cards) with: circle, cross, waves, square, star.
- The sender mentally transmits one symbol; you try to sense which one it is.
- Record results and review after a series of trials.

Exercise: "Telepathic Trance" — Telepathy in Hypnosis & Unconscious Communication (Freud)

Freud believed that telepathy operates most strongly through unconscious processes. This exercise uses deep relaxation to stimulate intuitive perception and is especially helpful for resolving repressed conflicts in interpersonal relationships.

- Sit comfortably and ease yourself into a light hypnotic state.
- While in this relaxed state, visualize the person with whom you have a conflict and imagine the message that person might send you.
- Questions such as "What feeling is this person sending me?" or "What words are coming to mind?" help with receiving messages.
- After coming out of the trance, analyze the symbolism of the messages and write down the insights this exercise brought you. The goal is to sense others' energetic messages through a hypnotic trance.

Exercise: "Energy Scanning"

The aim of this exercise is to develop sensitivity to energy fields and their messages — strengthening energetic sensitivity and telepathic perception.

- Have your partner close their eyes and imagine a specific symbol on the body (e.g., a heart on the chest or a circle on the forehead).
- Bring your hands close to your partner's body at a distance of 5–10 cm (about 2–4 in).
- Try to feel where the symbol is — this may show up as warmth, tingling, or a "magnetic" sensation.

NOTES

SEXUAL TRANSMUTATION

"When, from the sexual act,
you aim your energy at a vision —
your energy becomes the fuel
for creating new worlds."
Aleksandra Božović

In our prevailing consciousness, sex is mostly experienced through the lens of pleasure and reproduction. However, few people know that only a small portion of our sexual energy is released during the sexual act, and even fewer realize that sexual energy is the most powerful energy in our body — an energy we can use for various forms of healing and to learn how to manifest and attract the life we want. It sounds unbelievable, but let's continue…

Sexual union is a conscious and willing merging with your partner that leads to a spiritual and healing journey. It is a bond that exists beyond this physical world and is eternal, regardless of how the relationship in this lifetime unfolds. Sex with a partner brings a deep blending — when two people consciously engage in it as a way of uniting their physical, mental, and soul bodies. And when we speak of manifestation, we mean that moment when, through sex and union with a partner, we connect with the entire Universe and thus come to know that we ourselves have the ability to connect with the divine energy from which we can draw in everything we desire in life.

Intimate union is an instrument for raising your consciousness and joining both physical bodies with universal, cosmic energy. In that context, union implies sharing, exchange, co-holding, and spiritual oneness.

To understand what sexual transmutation is, we first need to understand the process of transmutation itself. **To transmute**, literally, **means to change form** — that is, to convert one type of energy into another. From that we can conclude that sexual transmutation involves turning sexual energy into creative and generative energy. In practice, this means shifting the focus from physical pleasure to thoughts of a creative nature.

Sexual transmutation refers to the idea of putting sexual energy in service of other areas of life — such as creativity, productivity, and personal development. This concept originates in **Napoleon Hill's** *Think and Grow Rich*, and was later developed by various figures within the self-help movement and spiritual schools. But what does sex have to do with wealth and other life goals? Can sexual energy be used for something other than sex?
Napoleon Hill writes:
"Sex desire is the most powerful of human desires. So strong is this desire that men freely run the risk of life and reputation to indulge it. When harnessed and transmuted into other channels, this motivating force maintains all of its attributes and may be used as a powerful creative force in all endeavors — including the accumulation of riches."

Sexual Transmutation Is Not Celibacy

What did James Joyce, Gustav Klimt, Pablo Picasso, Jim Morrison, David Bowie, or Alan Rickman have in common? They were all acutely aware of their sexuality. Some had one, others many partners. They were incredibly passionate about their art — and that is exactly how the world remembers them.

Techniques of sexual transmutation were practiced throughout history by many other great minds as well, among them Nikola Tesla, Dante Alighieri, Beethoven, Mother Teresa, Leonardo da Vinci, and many more. Many chose celibacy, believing it would bring greater focus and success in their work. This is how the famed **Nikola Tesla** lived. He believed that the energy he would devote to a woman would diminish his creative energy, so he chose to spend his time alone, working.

Have you ever heard of someone so devoted to work and success that it brings them a pleasure equal to what they feel in bed? Perhaps you yourself have felt an urge similar to an erotic drive when it came to something that deeply interests you — but wasn't sex. You probably have. Because the desire for progress, the desire to create, is in essence nothing other than the most basic human impulse — to bring forth new life and preserve one's existence on planet Earth.

However, celibacy is not necessary. The essence of transmutation is learning about and using sexual energy — not denying it.

Tesla believed sexual energy could be used to achieve greater mental and physical strength and that this technique helped him create numerous inventions. Da Vinci said sexual transmutation helped amplify his creative power. In fact, celibacy in many people can have the opposite effect — building up aggression, anger, or dissatisfaction. That's precisely why you can practice sexual transmutation in certain time windows, when such energy is useful in other areas of life. Say you're working on an important project with only a week left to finish it. You can use sexual transmutation during that period to improve focus and productivity.

The essence of sexual transmutation is not to live a monastic life — but to learn how to channel your energy. What you will learn here is what sexual transmutation actually is, how to generate more sexual energy that will help you achieve whatever you want in life — be it creative or artistic aims, goals in your business and career, a desired state of health, or even attracting a partner into your life. Since we're talking about the most potent energy known to the human race, knowledge of sexual energy — how to generate it and work with it — can bring multiple benefits to your life.

Renowned yogis, Taoists, and mystics hold that sexual energy is the psychological and spiritual propellant needed for creation and manifestation. The core idea is that sexual energy is a highly potent, creative source of power, but it shouldn't be limited only to the sexual act. Through sexual transmutation, this energy is redirected into other areas of life and used to elevate personal growth, creativity, productivity, and success.

Sexual transmutation does not involve suppressing sexual needs or abstaining from sexual activity. Instead, it's about consciously channeling sexual energy and using it for other purposes. This can happen, for example, through creative projects, physical activities, mental stimulation, or spiritual practices.

The advantages of sexual transmutation lie in unlocking the full potential of sexual energy. By directing this energy into constructive channels, one can gain deeper self-understanding, increased creativity, better concentration, greater productivity, and spiritual growth.

It's important to emphasize that sexual transmutation is a personal choice and that everyone can find their own method. There are no hard-and-fast rules for how it "should" be practiced. Each person has different needs and preferences, and it's essential to consider these individual factors when developing a personal practice. It's also important not to confuse sexual transmutation with sexual dysfunction or sexual abstinence. The aim of sexual transmutation is the conscious use of sexual energy — not its suppression or avoidance. All in all, sexual transmutation can be a powerful method for improving quality of life and personal growth. However, it is necessary to think deeply about the topic and clearly define one's goals and boundaries so the method is integrated into life in a healthy, positive way.

Sexual energy is a very strong and vital force present in every human being. It can be felt physically, mentally, emotionally, and spiritually. It entails understanding and consciously directing it into other spheres of life. Instead of being used exclusively for sexual activity, it can serve the pursuit of higher aims such as creativity, success, education, or spiritual growth.

Practicing sexual transmutation requires self-control and conscious choices about how to use sexual energy. It's important to be disciplined and decide deliberately how to channel this powerful force. Many techniques and practices can help with sexual transmutation. Common methods include physical activities such as yoga or Qi Gong; creative projects like painting or writing; mental stimulation through study and learning; spiritual practices such as meditation or prayer; emotional and interpersonal relationships oriented toward depth and connection; as well as setting clear goals and making a plan to achieve them.

A key aspect of sexual transmutation is not suppressing or denying sexual energy, but accepting it and using it consciously. In other words, it's not about stifling sexual energy but about **channeling it efficiently and constructively.**

The goal of sexual transmutation is to increase sexual energy and transform it into a positive life force that contributes to personal development, creativity, and productivity. The essence is that energy isn't wasted or scattered but used as a power for growth and transformation.

Each person has their own way of experiencing and channeling sexual energy. There is no "right" or "wrong" method of sexual transmutation. What matters is that everyone finds their own path and adapts it to their needs and beliefs. Mastery of sexual transmutation takes time and practice. It's a continuous process that requires regular dedication to achieve the desired results.

Although some practice sexual transmutation to restrain or control sexual desire, at its core it is about consciously and creatively directing sexual energy in order to live more fully and successfully. Ultimately, this is a deeply personal process, and everyone should find their own way to harness and direct this energy.

WHY IS SEXUAL TRANSMUTATION IMPORTANT?

Every living being on this planet, including humans, exists thanks to sexual energy. It is the energy of life and of procreation. It encompasses far more than the sexual act or the instinct to reproduce, because without it there is no life. Sexual energy is life, and life is sexual energy — there is no separation. It gives us life at birth, but it also accompanies us throughout our lives, regenerating our cells and giving us motivation.

However, the use of sexual energy is not limited to making love. Besides being a source of pleasure, this energy can be used for many other purposes — from writing a book, to learning martial arts, to spiritual practices, or building a company.

Sexual transmutation is considered important because it has the potential to improve one's individual life and personal growth. Here are a few more reasons why it matters:

- **Channeling energy:** Sexual energy is one of the most powerful energies in the human body. Consciously directing it into other areas of life allows it to serve as a strong driving force for creativity, productivity, and personal development.
- **Increased creativity:** Sexual energy and creativity are closely linked. By redirecting sexual energy to support

creative projects, it's possible to enter a state of flow and develop greater creative abilities.

- **Improved energy levels:** Consciously directing sexual energy can raise energy levels in the chakra system. Instead of energy being lost through sexual activity, it can be used to strengthen the body, mind, and emotions.
- **Greater focus and concentration:** By channeling sexual energy, focus and concentration grow, because energy is no longer tied up in sexual thoughts or actions but in clearly defined goals and tasks.
- **Overcoming addictive behaviors:** The conscious use of sexual energy can help overcome addictive patterns related to sexuality. By redirecting energy to other areas of life, the focus shifts from destructive to constructive behavior.
- **Spiritual growth:** In many spiritual traditions, sexual energy is viewed as a form of divine life force. Through conscious transmutation, one can use this energy to foster spiritual growth and expanded awareness.

It's important to note that sexual transmutation is not an absolute necessity. Everyone has their own relationship to sexual energy and chooses their own path. However, for those interested in consciously channeling and using sexual energy, the practice of sexual transmutation can be an exceptionally enriching and transformative experience.

The main reason someone succeeds — or fails — in life often lies less in their level of education, finances, or social status, and more in their ability to channel their sexual energy.

BENEFITS OF SEXUAL TRANSMUTATION

Those who've been persistent and mentally strong enough to channel their sexual energy into something else report many benefits. Here are the most significant:

- **Unlocking creative potential:** Channeling sexual energy can awaken the creative genius within. When it does, you may become far more successful and creative in whatever you do.

- **More energy:** When sexual energy is devoted only to sex, it's quickly spent — along with life force. By limiting dissipation, you keep more energy for other areas of life.
- **Self-mastery:** That burning need for sex… fades. Consciously channeling sexual energy gives you greater control over yourself and your actions. You'll also notice better focus and a stronger drive to build and create.
- **Emotional stability:** Sexual transmutation can help release negative emotions like frustration, anger, or sadness, supporting emotional balance.
- **Productivity:** Transforming sexual energy into creative power leads to a dramatic jump in productivity.

Exercises for Successful Sexual Transmutation

Here are several practical exercises to help develop this skill:

- **Become aware of your sexual energy:** Regularly set aside time to sense how this energy feels in your body and notice its peaks.
- **Meditation:** Sit comfortably and focus on your breathing. When sexual thoughts arise, observe them without judgment and let them pass. As a next step, visualize sexual energy and guide it through the body with your breath.
- **Creative projects:** Direct sexual energy into creative tasks—painting, writing, composing. When you feel a surge, use it consciously.
- **Physical practices:** Do yoga, Qi Gong, or similar body-centered work. Visualize energy flowing through you, refreshing every part of the body.
- **Journaling:** Track your sexual energy, observations, and progress. Write about feelings and goals.
- **Goal setting:** Define clear goals and decide how you'll direct sexual energy toward achieving them. Visualize your success.
- **Learning and growth:** Use this energy for study. Make a list of inspiring books, podcasts, or courses and commit to them with enthusiasm.

Most people may notice the first results after around ten days, but every experience is individual. The best approach is to try the technique and keep a personal journal, noting how you feel each day.

Remember: sexual transmutation is deeply personal. Experiment, be patient, and find the exercises that suit you best. Consistency and dedication bring lasting, powerful results.

NOTES

MEDITATION

"For me, meditation is the sanctum of silence —
a place where I ask for nothing and find myself."
Aleksandra Božović

There are processes within us that shape us every day into what we once — consciously or unconsciously — chose and decided to become. For something great to arise from within us, something in service to the world, a wakeful, devoted inner practice is needed. When we pass through the cleansing — releasing all that has piled up inside — we get the chance to write our new, desired reality on a clean page of the soul.

When we dive deep and become what the world recognizes us by, we find a beautiful jewel within — **our passion, our purpose, and the name** our soul carries. This inner journey serves not only us but the planet, humanity, life as a whole. Many don't know there are depths inside them to dive into. Busy with daily obligations, we plan our life while it is already unfolding in the background. We forget — or maybe never meet — that part of ourselves waiting to be noticed and heard. We often avoid being alone with ourselves, afraid of what we might find in our own silence. Yet sometimes the very thing we fear most is what sets us free.

That is when we shatter our biggest blocks, cast off the shackles of fear, and gain the courage to make decisions that **shape a life on our terms.** One of the best and most effective ways to plunge within is deep meditation. It opens access to our inner world and brings very clear insights and guidance for our further growth and life path.

Have you ever dived into the depths of your soul? The first step to awakening our mental intelligence is precisely awakening the body and spirit — and one of the most accessible ways to achieve that is meditation. It is one of the most important tools our time offers for reconnecting with ourselves.

Meditation is the practice of allowing spirit to separate from the body to the point of realizing that, in essence, we are spirit — one that existed before and will exist after this body completes its journey.

We simply express spirit through the body we've been given. When we realize we are energy, a spirit using body, gender, and skin color as instruments of expression, we begin fulfilling our spiritual task.

Meditation need not mean assuming a specific **"asana"** posture. It doesn't have to be sitting in silence with eyes closed as it's often portrayed. Meditation is an inner process — so the most important thing is finding a posture in which you feel comfortable and relaxed. What prayer is within many religions, the **meditative state** is within meditation. Its core meaning is directing attention: to the breath, to presence, to what's happening within us. It's a bridge between conscious and subconscious, between the material and the spiritual.

Meditation Through the Ages

Meditation is an ancient practice, deeply rooted in human history—a **transformative experience** that lets each person explore the depths of the soul, quiet the chaos of the outer world, and attain inner peace. Its roots reach back over 5,000 years. The earliest traces appear in India, within **the Vedas** — sacred Hindu texts — where meditation was a means of **spiritual awakening** and union with the universe. Over time it became central to **Buddhism** through the teachings of **Siddhartha Gautama — the Buddha** — as a path beyond suffering and toward deeper understanding of the mind.

In Chinese tradition, meditation developed through **Taoism and Confucianism**, emphasizing harmony between human and nature, the individual and the universe. In medieval Europe, **monks** practiced contemplative forms of meditation to calm the mind and draw near the divine.

What Is Meditation?

We can define meditation as a conscious process of directing attention to achieve spiritual clarity, emotional stability, and psychological balance. It may include techniques like breathing, visualization, mantras, observing thoughts, sensing bodily sensations, or silence — all with one aim: a deeper connection with oneself.

The primary goal is to quiet the inner dialogue and clear the mind of excess thoughts that drain us and create stress and anxiety.

TYPES OF MEDITATION

Meditation comes in many forms — each with its own specifics and benefits.

Mindfulness meditation: Focus on the present moment. Attention rests on the breath or bodily sensations; thoughts and feelings are observed without judgment. It brings clarity, calm, and acceptance.

Transcendental meditation: Uses repetition of a mantra to achieve deep relaxation and transcendence. Popularized in the XX century, it's especially effective for reducing stress and improving mental health.

Zen meditation (Zazen): From Buddhism; based on upright posture and attentive breathing. Thoughts are noticed as passing phenomen — without reacting to them.

Loving-kindness (Metta bhavana): Sending well-wishes — love, peace, joy — to oneself and others. It cultivates empathy, closeness, and connection with the world.

Meditation offers many benefits for mental and physical health. Research shows regular practice can reduce stress, improve concentration, increase emotional stability, and aid in managing anxiety and depression. It can also improve sleep quality by enhancing the body's ability to recover and regenerate.

Beyond physiological and psychological benefits, meditation strongly supports spiritual growth, strengthening connection with the inner "I" and expanding awareness of our place in the world. Through meditation we can gain insight into our thoughts, beliefs, and emotional patterns — revealing deeper truths of our existence.

In deep meditation, Alpha and Theta brainwaves are often present. Alpha marks relaxed alertness and focused attention; Theta relates to the subconscious and deeper introspective states. All our activities — sleep, rest, relaxation, problem-solving — are accompanied by brainwaves across different frequency ranges. Higher frequencies are linked with conscious states; lower ones enable access to the unconscious — our subconscious. Behind all thoughts, feelings, and behaviors lies neuronal communication via electrical impulses. When synchronized, they form brainwaves measurable by EEG.

Main ranges include Beta, Alpha, Theta, Delta, Gamma, and Epsilon (Y) waves. Meditation is more than a relaxation technique — it's a journey inward, a chance to discover the wealth within. As ancient civilizations recognized meditation's power, so can we use it today to strengthen mental health, emotional resilience, and spiritual clarity.

By practicing regularly, we can transform the inner landscape, create an oasis of peace amid daily chaos, and become more aware of the presence we carry. In a fast world, meditation is a lighthouse — a quiet reminder of the importance of inner peace, presence, and connection with ourselves and the world around us.

HOW TO MEDITATE?

For beginners, starting can feel confusing — but it's actually simple. Here are basic steps to help you begin:

- **Choose a quiet place:** Find a calm, comfortable spot where you won't be disturbed.
- **Comfortable posture:** Sit in any position that feels good. You don't need lotus pose — relaxation is key.
- **Focus on breathing:** Direct attention to the breath. Inhale slowly through the nose, exhale through the mouth. Feel the air moving in and out.
- **Gently return attention:** Thoughts will come — it's natural. Don't fight them. Let them pass and return to the breath.
- **Extend time gradually:** Start with 5 minutes daily. As you get used to it, lengthen your sessions.

Your body is the primary instrument for awareness and expressing energy. Through meditation we enter balance and return to ourselves.

While meditating:

- Focus on the breath.

- Stay in the present moment.
- Relax the entire body.
- Close your eyes.
- Watch the flow of thoughts without attachment — let them come and go.

At first you might feel sleepy, tired, or restless. That's okay. Return to the breath and continue. Over time, thoughts quiet down. The mind settles. You rest in the moment — aware, present, whole.

It's helpful to practice in the morning or evening, when the mind naturally leans toward relaxation, making meditation more effective. The aim is to increase time by just one minute each day, building continuity until you can follow and guide your thoughts for at least ten minutes.

With time you'll notice your attention holding longer on a single thought. Choose a thought, state, idea, or image that feels good and hold it firmly in mind. Gently withdraw attention from unrelated thoughts, returning to what you chose. This chosen thought or image can be your **mantra** — the word **"OM,"** the image of the Sun, a candle flame, or anything that helps you remain present. The mantra is an anchor for attention. At first, a few seconds of focus is enough. You're on the right path. With repetition you'll sustain awareness for up to ten minutes.

Then you're ready for the next step: complete release from thoughts. In this relaxed state, practice not accepting any thought — let it pass without holding on. Aim for the full silence of the mind. At first it's only a few seconds, but it becomes easier each time. The goal is to remain in thought-free awareness for at least ten minutes. This deep state opens the door to fields of limitless possibility.

That inner silence excites modern scientists and sparks our imagination. When imagination and emotion merge — the vision of what's possible with genuine feeling—reality is born. This is the beginning of manifestation: creating space in our beliefs for something that, as far as we know, doesn't exist yet. We create it through the power of consciousness and the subconscious. Remember: mental strength is an inexhaustible source of our potential. Thanks to the internet, you have access to many guided meditations and a wide range of binaural frequencies that support brainwave development.

Other specific contexts where meditation is used:

- Art
- Martial arts
- Scientific and technological invention

In art, meditation can spark creativity — the silent space new things arise from. In martial arts, it aligns practitioner and self, sharpens the mind, and nurtures a state beyond ego. In science and technology, we've all witnessed how many inventions the great Nikola Tesla discovered with the benefits of meditative practice.

Why Is Meditation Important in the XXI Century?

Beyond numerous benefits for body and spirit, meditation is an excellent relaxation practice and can help with anxiety. Anxiety is fear of the unknown — and today we live in a world flooded with information, interactions, ambitions, and constant pressure. Each piece of information we attend to stirs thoughts like a pebble forming ripples on water. Meditation is a powerful tool — a way to gather our thoughts, calm the mind, and regain inner control.

How do you know you're on the right track?

If it feels goodv — you're on the right track. Over time, the meditative state lasts longer. You'll feel it becoming natural to dwell in silence, anchored to your mantra and inner peace. That's the moment you accept yourself fully — without thoughts, without emotions, without identifying with body, roles, ambitions, fears. It's you — here and now — turned toward your own self, gazing into silence and the feeling of true presence. Good luck!

NOTES

THE POWER OF SILENCE: THE PRACTICE OF STILLNESS (DAYS OF SILENCE)

"In stillness you meet the you who
silently observes your silence and the flow of your thoughts.
Behind all your thoughts stands your Witness."
Aleksandra Božović

WHAT IS STILLNESS PRACTICE?

Stillness practice, or a day of silence, is a conscious **retreat into silence** for a set period of time (usually one day). The essence is the deliberate refraining from speech and outer noise in order to turn attention toward your inner world. It is not mere absence of sound, but a disciplined exercise that creates the conditions for the mind to quiet down so we can become aware of our own thoughts and feelings.

In the yoga tradition this is called **mauna — a vow of silence** that leads to quietude of the mind and a deeper connection with oneself. Put simply, when you intentionally keep silent, you free the energy you would spend on speaking and direct it toward listening within. Like the calm surface of a lake that reflects reality clearly, the silence of the mind lets you see things more clearly and make deeper contact with yourself.

The basic principles of stillness include **outer and inner silence**. Outer silence means not speaking and avoiding unnecessary external sounds (e.g., music, television), while inner silence means observing your own mental "chatter" without reacting. The goal is not to force the mind into emptiness, but to create conditions for thoughts to settle on their own. Through this practice you cultivate inner peace, presence in the here and now, and better self-awareness. Many spiritual traditions emphasize that silence has a "voice" of its own — the voice of deep peace and insight. That's why stillness is often used as a technique of meditation, self-reflection, and spiritual growth.

To enter a spiritual process, you must pass through spiritual solitude. Spiritual solitude is a major component of self-evolution. It is the process of releasing any kind of need or fear and focusing on, and facing, the deepest level of your being. It is where you meet your true self without any outer interference. It is learning to know your deepest core — your light and your shadow. To learn who you are, why you are here, and what you want. To discover your possibilities and build your world from the ground up, leaving your trace behind. Learn not to be tied to or caught by your ego or defined by your identity. Learn not to reject or postpone your personal growth, or to enter another attachment hoping the shadows will vanish or grow fainter. As Tesla once said: **"To be alone is the secret of invention. To be alone, that is when ideas are born."** Ideas about the world and your place in it. Ideas about the deep feeling of your being. Without a deeper sense of being, it's easy to distract yourself with any low-frequency gratification. What truly moves us is that no kind of low-level pleasure can feed our need for a higher level of conscience. Work on yourself — for yourself.

Silence Across Traditions

The practice of ritual silence appears in almost all major spiritual traditions, speaking to its universal value. Throughout history, silence has been regarded as a path to wisdom and higher states of consciousness. Here's how some traditions cultivate silence:

Buddhism — Noble Silence – Buddhism nurtures the concept of noble silence. Nearly all Buddhist schools include some form of silence as part of practice. For example, on **vipassanā** meditation retreats participants spend **10 days in complete silence**, without conversation or distractions, to face themselves. According to the oldest texts, the Buddha himself often praised the value of silence. Noble silence means the quieting of body, speech, and mind — suspending needless talk and activity so the mind can settle. In the

Plum Village tradition (Thich Nhat Hanh's school), communal meals begin with 20–30 minutes of silence so people can eat mindfully and in peace. The purpose of this silence is to create the conditions to observe one's own mind and heart — to ask, "What is happening in me?" When we are not constantly engaged in conversation, we notice our inner life more easily. Silence cultivates mindfulness: it lets us "lower the shutters" of the senses for a while and look within, bringing spiritual growth and release from suffering. Hence Buddhists say we need time both for speech and for silence.

Yoga and the Hindu Tradition — Mauna (Vow of Silence) – In yoga and Hindu philosophy, **mauna (silence)** holds a special place: a conscious vow of silence to deepen spiritual practice. Tradition says outer silence leads to inner silence of the mind. When we restrain speech, the "inner dialogue" gradually quiets. Practicing mauna is the discipline of muting external noise to hear the inner voice. A famed example is the sage or yogi who refrains from speaking for years — not as "monastic oddity," but to direct all energy toward spiritual aims.

A known example is **Swami Nirmalananda**, who observed daily silence for **11 years**, using time for writing letters and meditation rather than speech. In this tradition, silence is believed to bring peace of mind **(Śānti)** and union with the Absolute. Mauna is not always absolute — a beginner might start by not speaking for a few hours a day and deepen over time (in some yoga retreats, along with silence, reading, writing, and even eye contact are avoided so mental waves can truly subside). Through dedication to silence, thoughts grow clearer and the inner senses sharpen, enabling deeper meditative experience and insight.

Christianity — Monastic Silence – In Christian tradition, especially monastic, silence has long been considered a virtue and a means of drawing nearer to God. From the early Desert Fathers in the III century, monks practiced long periods of silence to focus on prayer. **Monastic silence** is encouraged for cleansing the heart, humility, and **listening for the voice of God**. Many monasteries observe **"great silence"** during parts of the day or night — times when nothing is spoken except prayer. This practice is not only for vowed monastics; lay people on spiritual retreats can also participate in periods of silence for contemplation. In both **Eastern Orthodoxy and Catholicism**, silence is seen as a way to know oneself and open the soul to divine grace. Even the early **Patriarch Theophilus of Alexandria**, around the year 400, wrote that monks should love silence as much as faith, because "nothing is more important than these two things. **The Bible** includes messages like, "Be still, and know that I am God," indicating that higher encounters can be felt in the quiet of the heart. Many modern Christian monasteries offer **silent retreats** where participants spend days in prayerful quiet, finding deeper peace and clarity of faith.

Whether it's a Buddhist monk in meditation, a Hindu yogi under a vow of silence, or a Christian monk in contemplation — silence reappears as a path to truth, peace, and spiritual strength. Traditions use it to bring a person closer to their essence and to the divine within themselves and the world.

BENEFITS OF PRACTICE OF STILLNESS (DAY OF SILENCE)

Stillness benefits the whole person — body, mind, emotions, and spirit. Many who have practiced days of silence describe the experience as refreshing and transformative. Below are the key benefits of silence, supported by both subjective reports and scientific findings:

Physical benefits: Silence literally heals and rests the body. When you immerse yourself in calm, stress and tension decrease, which has a measurable impact on bodily functions. Research shows that even a few minutes of complete silence can lower blood pressure and heart rate. In one study, just 2 minutes of silence after listening to music led to a significant drop in heart rate and blood pressure — silence was even more relaxing than soothing music.

Over the long term, quieter environments protect the heart: people exposed to constant noise tend to have higher blood pressure, so it's no surprise that silence supports cardiovascular health. In addition, spending time in silence (especially in nature) can reduce the production of stress hormones like cortisol and encourage the release of "feel-good" hormones, contributing to stronger immunity and better sleep. Silence helps us physically unwind, release accumulated fatigue, and even improve the quality of rest and sleep.

Mental benefits: On the mental plane, silence is like balm for the brain. In an age of nonstop information and constant stimulation, quiet gives the brain a break and improves cognitive function. Without external noise, the brain can concentrate better — it spends fewer resources filtering irrelevant sounds and can focus on the task or thought at hand. A 2021 study found that people working in a quiet environment had lower "mental load" and less stress while solving demanding tasks compared to those working with speech or background noise.

Thus, silence improves focus and cognition — which can boost productivity, learning, and creativity. Interestingly, scientists have also found that silence can stimulate **neurogenesis**, the creation of new brain cells. In an animal experiment, mice exposed to two hours of complete silence daily showed growth of new neurons in the hippocampus — the brain area tied to memory and emotion. This suggests that a calm environment may support regenerative processes in the brain. While human research is ongoing, silence already stands out as a key factor in mental health: it recharges our "mental batteries," clarifies thinking, and even sparks creative insight (because in quiet, new solutions often "flash" across synapses).

Emotional benefits: Silence is soothing for our emotions as well. Many people initially fear being overwhelmed by a whirlwind of thoughts or feelings in the quiet, but facing that inner noise actually brings relief. As we gradually settle into calm, the "running thoughts" associated with anxiety slow down. As one psychologist and mindfulness educator notes, when we learn to be quiet, we stop spending energy on incessantly running the "hamster wheel" of our own thoughts. Silence gives us space to simply observe those thoughts instead of being consumed by them. Gradually, the mind settles — which opens the door to mindfulness, a present-moment awareness proven to help with anxiety and mood.

In silence, away from external stressors, people often feel tension subside and emotional balance return. During a day of silence you may experience a range of feelings — from restlessness to peace — but having time to notice them without interruption makes it easier to let them go. Many report more calm, patience, and optimism afterward. Silence can also help us process suppressed feelings: in the quiet, things we've swept under the rug can surface, giving us a chance to see them clearly and emotionally cleanse. Overall, regular the practice of stillness builds emotional resilience — it reduces stress reactivity (for example, lower levels of cortisol — the stress hormone — have been recorded in people who spend more time in quiet settings) and strengthens the sense of inner contentment.

Spiritual benefits: Silence has long been considered a gateway to spiritual growth. In deep quiet, many feel a stronger connection with themselves and with something greater — whether they call it **God, the universe, or simply a sense of purpose**. Through practice of stillness, you cultivate introspection — you become your own observer. As the outer world grows still, the inner voice of conscience and intuition becomes clearer. Many spiritual teachers say that in silence we hear the "voice of the heart" or the voice of God. Monastics, for instance, believe silence is a path to a closer relationship with God and to truly understanding oneself. In silence something almost paradoxical happens: we feel more deeply connected to others and to the world. When our personal story quiets, a sense of universality and oneness with life appears.

The spiritual peace that silence brings helps "refuel the soul," evoking gratitude, purpose, and love. It's no accident Gandhi wrote that half the world's troubles would vanish if people recognized the value of silence.

In silence we discover our inner strength and truth—we become, as he said, **"seekers of truth who must be quiet,"** because only in silence does truth resound clearly. Spiritually, many also feel after a day of silence a renewed faith (religious or simply faith in life), a clearer vision of their values, and a compass for the road ahead.
Silence, then, is not emptiness but fullness — a space where life-changing insight can arise.

Examples: If you wonder what the practice of stillness looks like in practice and whether it truly works, here are a few inspiring examples from well-known figures and seasoned practitioners who have woven regular days of silence into their lives. Their experiences show that quiet brings remarkable insight, strength, and peace — even in the midst of intense circumstances.

Mahatma Gandhi — silence as a source of strength: The famous Indian leader Mahatma Gandhi advocated a weekly practice of silence. Every Monday throughout his decades of public life, he dedicated a "day of silence": he would not utter a single word all day. He didn't necessarily spend the day meditating; he simply refrained from speaking — freeing himself from the obligation to voice opinions or make decisions that day. In this way, he said, he "quieted" external pressure and regained inner clarity. Interestingly, aides noticed that on Tuesdays, after the day of silence, Gandhi gave particularly powerful, eloquent speeches without notes — as if silence had refreshed his mind and sharpened his expression. Silence helped him remain calm amid upheaval — he himself said it was a simple practice that preserved his peace of mind.

Near the end of his life, after a fifteen-day period of the practice of stillness, he wrote the famous line: **"One cannot help but feel that almost half the world's suffering would disappear if we restless mortals understood the virtue of silence."** For Gandhi, silence was not an escape from reality but a tool for facing it — he believed it gave him the composure and wisdom to lead a nation to freedom. His example teaches that even the busiest person can (and should) find time for silence, because we return from it stronger and clearer.

Yuval Noah Harari — 60 days of silence a year:
A contemporary example of the power of silence is Yuval Noah Harari, the Israeli historian and **bestselling author of Sapiens**. Harari openly says that much of his creativity and clarity come from long stretches of meditative silence. Each year he goes on a lengthy **silent retreat of 30 to 60 days**, completely disconnected from the outside world. During that period he meditates daily in silence, without conversation, technology, or distractions. Harari says this committed practice has cleared his mind and improved his ability to focus, allowing him to see the "big picture" of the history he writes.

Before he began meditating, he admits he would likely still be a specialist in medieval history, confined to a narrow focus; meditation (and especially silence) opened his mind to much larger themes. He meditates about two hours a day and firmly believes that deep annual silence deepens his insight and creativity. For Harari, silence is the secret of productivity: **"A clear mind creates clear goals."** His example shows that in a modern world overflowing with information, retreating into silence is not a luxury but a source of competitive advantage — it enables you to think more deeply and originally than others.

Jack Dorsey — a tech leader in search of calm: The business world isn't immune to the appeal of silence either. Jack Dorsey, co-founder and former CEO of Twitter, is known for attending ten-day **Vipassana meditation retreats** where he spends time in noble silence. He has completed this ten-day silent course several times and says it is invaluable to him. He shared publicly that those 10 wordless days are **"the most challenging, yet the best thing"** he does for himself.

Imagine: a man who led one of the noisiest social media platforms in the world finds his calm in complete silence. Dorsey says that after tihovanje he feels renewed gratitude and focus, and that the practice helps him better manage the stress of an intense business life. He also keeps up shorter daily meditations in silence to maintain that centeredness. His example sends a strong message to modern professionals: the greater the pressure, the more you need quiet time to recharge. Dorsey and similar Silicon Valley leaders have shown that silence is not counterproductive; it actually improves mental clarity and strategic vision.

HOW TO BEGIN YOUR DAY OF SILENCE?

You might be wondering: "How can I, with all my obligations and in a noisy world, bring a day of silence into my life?" The good news is that it's doable with a bit of planning and preparation. Here's a practical step-by-step guide to organize your first (or next) day of silence and what to expect:

Set a date and inform your close ones: Choose a day you can devote to yourself — ideally a weekend or a day off without work or family duties. Let family or housemates know in advance what you're doing and ask for their support. Explain that you won't be speaking that day and will need a quiet atmosphere. If you have children or household responsibilities, arrange for a partner or relatives to cover for you so you can withdraw into silence. Planning ahead prevents interruptions and misunderstandings.

Prepare a space for silence: Decide where you'll spend the day. It might be a dedicated room at home arranged as a calm nook, or somewhere in nature (a cabin, the mountains, a nearby monastery or park) where you can be alone and undisturbed. Make the space comfortable and inspiring: soft light, a candle, cushions, a blanket — anything that helps you feel serene. Remove distractions: switch off the TV, radio, computer, even a loudly ticking clock. Put your phone and tablet away or power them down completely. A digital detox is a key part of the day — notifications and social media are just another form of noise. If possible, spend some time outdoors: birdsong and wind deepen calm and a sense of connection.

Set an intention: On the eve of your day of silence, take a few minutes to write down or clearly envision your intention. Why do you want to spend a day in silence? Rest from stress, reflect on a big decision, deepen your spiritual practice, or simply get to know yourself better? Your intention will steady you when the day feels challenging. It can be as simple as: "I devote this day of silence to hearing my inner voice," or "Silence brings me peace and clarity I will nurture." You can note it in a journal and read it in the morning as your guiding star.

Beginning the day — enter gently: When the day arrives, start calmly. Wake without rushing, ideally naturally (no alarm unless necessary). Remind yourself of your intention and that from this moment you're entering noble silence. You might begin with light stretching or meditation to set a peaceful rhythm. If you live with others, offer a smile or hug instead of "good morning" — they'll know your vow has begun. The first hours may feel unusual because we're used to beginning the day with talk or noise; enjoy the freshness of this novelty. Notice simple things: the taste of a warm drink, morning light, subtle sounds you usually miss. This mindful start will steady you for the rest of the day.

Throughout the day — welcome the experience without expectations:
Continue not speaking at all — no whispering, humming, or muttering under your breath. Early on your mind will likely be "loud." Thoughts may surge: "Am I doing this right? What do I do now? Oh,

I forgot to say…" — totally normal. Don't be discouraged; stirred water settles with time. If you feel you must say something, pause and ask whether it's truly necessary. Remember you chose silence and the world will keep turning without your words today. If you must communicate something essential at home ("Please pass…," "I'm going for a walk"), keep paper and pen handy and write it. Keep communication minimal and necessary. Also avoid news, books, and media content — the aim is to reduce input so the mind can run in "quiet mode." If anything, read a short, uplifting passage on spirituality or a guided meditation text — sparingly, as support rather than filler.

Plan light, mindful activities: A full day of silence doesn't mean 24 hours in lotus. Move and do ordinary things — just slower and more consciously. Prepare a few simple activities you can do quietly: a walk in nature or a park, gardening, gently cooking a simple meal, drawing or painting, yoga or stretching, gazing out the window, or simply sitting in meditation. Whatever you do, do it attentively and unhurriedly.

If you cook, make it a small ceremony: notice colors and scents, the sound of the knife, the texture of food as you eat. Treat the whole day as one big mindfulness practice. If you walk, keep noble silence in motion — don't answer the phone, don't play music; listen to your surroundings and notice details as if for the first time. These activities help you stay present without feeling idle or impatient.

Introspective practices during the day

A period of silence is ideal for inner work and self-reflection. Try brief mental exercises now and then.

Breath awareness: Sit comfortably, close your eyes, and follow 10 inhalations and exhalations, noticing where you feel the breath in your body. This simple practice returns you to the present whenever the mind wanders.

Body scan: In silence, sweep attention from feet to head, noticing tension and sensation without judgment, letting the body soften section by section.

Also, listen to your inner dialogue: what are your thoughts constantly "saying"? Imagine yourself as an observer on a riverbank while thoughts drift by like leaves. You don't have to stop them — just watch in quiet. Insights emerge this way — recurring worries may reveal themselves, or creative ideas surface once given space. If strong emotions arise, try staying with them rather than suppressing them. If sadness or anger comes without a clear reason, allow it — perhaps even tears. Silence supports you, it doesn't judge. Through such introspection, silence becomes your therapist and teacher.

Silence journal: While the core rule is not speaking, you may write. In fact, journaling can be very helpful. Keep a "silence journal" to note thoughts, feelings, or insights. Do it without breaking the spirit of the day — write for yourself, slowly and deliberately. Some like to jot down morning expectations or fears ("Today I notice I'm afraid of X…") and evening reflections ("After my day of silence, I realized Y…"). Writing can be a refuge if inner chaos swells — rather than breaking your vow, pick up a pen and empty your heart onto the page. The act of writing in silence is calming. Later, the journal becomes a treasured record. You may be surprised how much wisdom and clarity your thoughts hold when they arise from quiet. It also helps integrate the experience.

Closing the day and integrating silence: As your day winds down, exit gently. No need to snap the spell. Many keep a closing ritual: sit for meditation or a gratitude prayer, acknowledge what you experienced, and what you're thankful for. Look back — how was the day? What was hardest, what most beautiful? Notice how you feel now versus the morning. Then gently bring back your voice: perhaps first whisper an affirmation or prayer, simply to feel the vibration after a long quiet. When you speak to loved ones, do it softly, choosing words with care. You may find yourself speaking more slowly or quietly — that's fine; it means you value each word. Share a little if you wish — or simply keep listening, carrying your calm into the exchange.

Integration means taking a piece of silence into daily life: maybe add short quiet periods to your routine (e.g., 15 minutes of morning meditation, or one tech-free silent evening per week). Use journal insights to make changes (if you found phone-free time nourishing, perhaps limit social media). The point is to let the day of silence ripple into everyday life.

Be gentle with yourself: Perhaps the most important tip — approach your day with kindness. There's no "perfect" way; every attempt is valuable. You may break silence once ("thank you" might slip out) — don't scold yourself. Smile, return to quiet, and continue. If frustration or impatience arose, that's normal. They're part of the lesson. Each time gets easier. Celebrate the fact you gave yourself this experience — it's an act of love toward yourself and your mind.

Even if it felt like "nothing special" happened, trust that your mind rested at some level and that the fruits of silence will ripen gradually. Be proud: in a world drowning in noise, you created an oasis of peace.

Exercises for Deeper Introspection and Spiritual Integration

A day of silence can be very profound and may at times stir important life questions or insights. To make the most of the experience, it's helpful to do a few additional introspective practices before and after your silent day:

Before you begin — a letter to yourself: The evening before you enter silence, write a short letter to yourself. Note how you currently feel, what has been troubling or preoccupying you lately, and what you hope to receive from tomorrow's experience. This letter will serve as a reference point — after the day of silence you'll be able to compare your "before and after" states. You'll often be surprised by how much your perspective shifts in such a short time. Something that felt huge yesterday may seem solvable — or less important — after a day of quiet, and vice versa a new realization may surface. Don't read the letter the next morning; save it for the end of your silent day or the following day.

During silence — a question for contemplation: If you'd like to steer your introspection, set one key question in the morning and let the answer reveal itself gradually. For example: "What matters most in my life right now, and am I giving it enough attention?", or "What is my body telling me when I finally give it quiet?", or a spiritual prompt such as "Who am I without my stories and roles?" There's no need to obsess over it all day — plant the question like a seed and let it be. During moments of stillness, revisit it and see what arises. By day's end you may receive impressions or insights as an answer. This is a technique many sages used — entering silence with a question and patiently waiting for inner wisdom to speak.

Afterward — reflection and integration: The next morning (or that evening, if you have the energy), take time to reflect. Read the letter you wrote before your retreat. Then, with a fresh mind, journal: How do I feel now? What did I learn about myself? You can make two lists: **"Insights from Silence"** — note significant thoughts or feelings you observed; and **"Actions/Integration"**— concrete steps you want to take based on those insights. For example: "I realized how nourishing my quiet mornings are — I'll stay offline for the first hour each day." Or: "I noticed an old fear still quietly lingers — perhaps it's time to work on it therapeutically or through conversation." These integration notes help turn silence into lasting change rather than a fleeting zen moment. Also, celebrate your success — treat yourself (a warm bath, favorite tea, or simple rest) and thank yourself for the effort.

Longer-term practice: You might establish a rhythm — say, onc silent day per month, or at least a few quiet hours each week. Some choose more — an annual multi-day retreat, or combining silence with a meditation course. Find a cadence that fits your life. Each time will be different, deepening and bringing new insights, like peeling layers of an onion and revealing a more authentic you.

The practice of silence — of a whole day without speaking — is a gift you can give yourself at any age and in any setting. At first it can feel challenging to step out of the comfort zone of chatter and constant stimulation — but the benefits are priceless. Silence is like a kind teacher who patiently waits for us to settle, then shows us what we carry within. In quiet you'll find rest for the mind, clarity for life decisions, relief from stress, and a deeper bond with your soul.

Trust yourself in the process. You may be surprised how rich an inner world you've neglected while chasing outer noise. In silence you tell yourself you are worth listening to — that your inner voice deserves full attention. From that grows a great transformation: more peace, more meaning, and more everyday joy.

Let silence become your ally. Walk slowly — one minute of silence today, ten tomorrow, then a full day when you feel ready. And remember the words of Gandhi, who found refuge in silence during the greatest struggles of his life: **"A seeker after truth must be silent."** In that sentence lies the secret — the truth of your being is revealed in silence, along with the strength to live it. I wish you a beautiful journey into the world of quiet and back — richer for an insight that changes your life.

NOTES

GRATITUDE JOURNAL

"One 'Thank you'
doesn't change the circumstances
— it changes your awareness.
And awareness is the beginning of every miracle."
Aleksandra Božović

I'll guide you in this journal through a morning and evening gratitude practice. At the start of each day, with a few simple steps, you'll turn your thoughts toward what you're grateful for and set a tone of optimism. In the evening, a short reflection before sleep will help you recognize the beautiful moments the day brought. The journal includes prompts to guide your thoughts, space to write your personal experiences and feelings, plus affirmations and inspiring quotes to keep you motivated.

The goal is for your gratitude journal to be simple enough for everyday use, yet empowering and fulfilling. There are no right or wrong answers — this is your personal journey. Feel free to adapt the suggested exercises, and write as much or as little as you like. What matters most is that you enjoy the process and take a small daily step toward a more positive, grateful outlook.

Let's begin this journey together!

Morning Gratitude Practice

Morning is a special time — a new beginning full of possibilities. Set aside a few minutes each morning to consciously lean into gratitude. This practice will help you start your day with a smile and optimism, filled with energy and a positive mindset. Before you dive into tasks, get comfortable, take a deep breath, and focus on the present moment. Now take your journal and consider:

What are you grateful for this morning? – Write down three things — small or big — that you feel grateful for as you begin the day. They can be very simple: a warm cup of coffee, the morning sun through the window, the new day ahead, or simply a calm morning and your life as it is. The point is to remind yourself of all the good you already have right now.

What would make today even better? – Think about what you'd love to experience or do today so you'll feel fulfilled this evening. Maybe it's quality time with family, finishing a task, or taking a moment just for yourself. Write one or two things that would make today great for you. This brief positive intention will help you notice good opportunities as the day unfolds.

Today's affirmation: Create or choose one short positive thought to repeat during the day — something that encourages you and anchors you in gratitude. For example: "Today I choose to see something good in everything," or "I'm open to all the lovely things this day brings." Write your affirmation in the journal and read it aloud or silently. Let it be your personal motto for the day ahead.

Space for thoughts: Below these prompts, leave a blank area where you can add anything you wish — how you feel this morning, what you're looking forward to, or any thought that arises. This is your safe place to express yourself. Write freely.

As you finish your morning practice, you'll notice your energy and mood already lifting. Even if a challenging day awaits, you've reminded yourself of the good you have and the good that can come. With that mindset, you're ready to step into the day with a grateful heart.

Evening Reflection Practice

When evening comes, it's time to slow down and look back on the day behind you. Writing a few lines of gratitude before bed is a wonderful way to end with positive thoughts — research shows that expressing gratitude at night can improve sleep and calm the mind. So, before you turn in, take your gratitude journal and spend a few minutes reflecting.

Relax, close your eyes for a moment, and recall the moments today that brought a smile or a sense of peace. Now open your eyes and answer these prompts:

What are you most grateful for today? – Think back over your day and write at least three things you're grateful for. These might be goals achieved, lovely moments, something new you learned, or even a tough situation you handled well. Nothing is too small or too ordinary to deserve gratitude.

Who brightened your day? – Recall a person or people who contributed to your happiness and good mood today. Did someone support you, say a kind word, or do something thoughtful? Describe who it was and how they made your day better. Nurturing gratitude toward others strengthens relationships and reminds us we're not alone.

What brought you peace or a smile today? – Remember a moment when you felt true joy, calm, or contentment — a tea break, a sunset, a loved one's hug, an inspiring passage you read. Write down that moment and how you felt. This helps us notice the precious small moments that often go unnoticed.

How do you feel at the end of this day? – Finally, note your current mood as you write. Do you feel calm, lighter, joyful, or tired? Briefly describe your thoughts and feelings now that the day is ending. This introspection helps you consciously acknowledge all emotions — positive or negative — and frame them within gratitude and learning.

Space for thoughts: Here too, keep extra space for any other impressions from the day — anything you want to remember. You can also write a message to yourself for tomorrow, set a worry down on paper, or simply write: "Thank you for another day."

As you finish your evening practice, put your pen down and feel gratitude flowing through your thoughts. Congratulate yourself — whatever kind of day it was, you made time to recognize the good in it. With such grateful thoughts, you can drift into sleep more peacefully and wake ready to continue this positive cycle.

Inspirational Quotes on Gratitude

Sometimes we all need a reminder in the form of wise words about the power of gratitude. Here are a few to read whenever you need motivation or a fresh perspective. You might copy them onto a special page, place them somewhere visible, or simply revisit them for inspiration:

- "Enjoy the little things, for one day you may look back and realize they were the big things." — Robert Brault
- "Be thankful for what you have; you'll end up having more. If you concentrate on what you don't have, you will never, ever have enough." — Oprah Winfrey
- "Feeling gratitude and not expressing it is like wrapping a present and not giving it." — William Arthur Ward

Daily Affirmations

Affirmations are positive, present-tense statements that aim to reshape your thinking and empower you. By saying (or writing) affirmations each day, you gradually build confidence, optimism, and gratitude. Here are a few you can use each morning — or whenever you need a boost. Adjust them or create your own; what matters is that they ring true in your heart and feel good:

- Today I choose to see the good in everything around me, and I'm grateful for it.
- My heart is calm, filled with gratitude and joy as I begin a new day.
- Each day I notice more blessings in my life, and I give thanks for every one of them.
- I deserve happiness and love; I'm grateful for all the good life brings me.

Repeat your affirmations several times (out loud or silently) and feel their meaning. They're there to remind you of your strength and worth. It may feel unusual at first, but over time you'll notice your mindset shifting — your mind becomes more inclined to see the positive and be grateful for what is, rather than dwelling on what isn't.

A single positive thought in the morning can set the tone for the whole day, right? Use quotes and affirmations as daily fuel for your motivation. Charge yourself with positive energy and let gratitude lead the way.

Through this journal, day by day, you're building a gratitude habit that can enrich your life in countless ways. Remember: each entry is a step toward a more conscious, fulfilled life. Be proud of yourself for sticking with the practice. Keep discovering the beautiful moments around and within you — every day filled with gratitude is a step closer to a happy, fulfilled life.

Thank you for walking the path of gratitude with me. I wish you an abundance of reasons to give thanks today and every day to come.

NOTES

THETA HEALING

"In the theta state you don't just change a belief —
you enter the space where word becomes energy,
and energy answers with truth."
Aleksandra Božović

Touch the Divine Within

There is a light within each of us. A place where holy silence runs deepest, where feelings merge with intuition, where there is no fear or doubt — only the pure truth of the soul. Theta healing leads us right there — to the space between breaths, the space in which transformation happens. Not by force, not by analysis, but through love, energy, and luminous awareness.

You have surely wondered what it would be like to change a limiting belief — not by laboriously repeating affirmations for months, but deeply, quietly, in a few minutes — directly from your inner source? Theta healing is exactly that: a method that uses the natural theta brainwave state to connect you with yourself, the Source, and the power of change.

In this chapter we'll open the door to a technique that relies not on effort, but on awareness, intuition, and deep connection with yourself. Theta healing is not a "magic wand," but it is a gentle, intuitive, and highly effective method of inner work.

WHAT IS THETA HEALING?

Theta Healing is an **ancient energetic self-development technique** that was rediscovered and developed in 1995 by American healer **Vianna Stibal**. It's commonly defined as a healing technique that works on the **mental, emotional, and physical levels**. At its core, it's a method that combines work with the unconscious mind, meditation, and contact with the divine source (however you experience it), with the aim of healing, transformation, and releasing deeply rooted beliefs.

The technique takes its name from **theta brainwaves**, within whose range this healing work takes place. Theta waves are low-frequency waves **between 4 and 7 Hz**, typically present during deep meditation or sleep. In this state, the mind is relaxed and the subconscious is open — which allows access to old patterns, traumas, and beliefs, as well as their replacement and healing. It's the state in which children up to the age of six are almost constantly. In it, patterns are learned — identity, beliefs about self, the world, love, safety… And this is precisely why working in the theta state is so powerful — because we return to the very space in which those beliefs arose and change them from within. Numerous scientific studies of theta brainwaves and their influence on our lives have been conducted; **Colgin** notes that theta waves are the most intriguing brain oscillations being studied today, while **Lynch and Baudry** (1984) call them the "magic rhythm."

Theta waves are associated with deep relaxation and calm. They are present during meditative states, but also during sleep — REM sleep is a theta wave state. This sleep phase is characterized by rapid eye movements, which also occur for theta practitioners when entering the theta state. Theta brainwaves are emitted by the subconscious mind. The subconscious holds our long-term memory and is also a storehouse of creative inspiration, suppressed creativity, and repressed psychological content. Theta waves allow us to experience deep meditation in the brainwave pattern of meditation. **The key to the depth and bliss people seek in meditation is found in theta waves.** In the theta state we establish the strongest spiritual connection. In that state, everything we are not in touch with — and which is in some way buried deep in our psyche, whether positive or negative — may be closed off and inaccessible (if we don't possess the appropriate combination of other frequencies to access it).

Thus, this technique removes the causes of problems that lie in the subconscious. The process uses low-frequency theta brainwaves. These waves are usually reached in deep meditation, but Vianna found a method that does not require entering deep meditation and still accesses subconscious content so that negative material (blocks, traumas, fears…) can be changed in a simple way, significantly improving quality of life. Think of your childhood, your dreams, wishes, plans, and imaginings. How much of it came true, and how much was blocked by "invisible forces and influences" you met along your path? Those influences did not come from someone or something outside, but from you — from your subconscious.

Because Theta Healing is a technique that creates physical, mental, and spiritual healing, it is primarily based on working with the beliefs we carry in our **subconscious** mind — beliefs that limit or restrain us. Our brain functions like a biological super-computer in which all information is recorded. The way we interpret that information becomes our belief system. When the body, mind, and soul accept a system as real, it becomes a program. Programs can work for our benefit — or to our detriment. When you are in the theta state, your conscious mind temporarily lowers its "guard," and the subconscious becomes more accessible. In that space it is possible to:

- identify limiting beliefs (e.g., "I'm not good enough"),
- connect with emotions and the body without blockage,
- "rewrite" those beliefs with new, supportive patterns,
- invite in feelings you may never have felt (e.g., unconditional love, safety, acceptance).

The process unfolds through guided meditation, in which the practitioner (or you yourself, once you learn the method) enters the theta state and, through dialogue with the unconscious, recognizes what needs to be released, forgiven, learned, or invited.

Put briefly: Theta healing helps you reclaim your own power — to become what you have always wanted to be and what you truly are at your core. When you experience that you can have influence over what happens in your life, you understand how to guide the process of creating your own reality. It is a method in which you are in a meditative state, trying to reach yourself and find answers — because all answers are in fact hidden within you. Alongside you is your coach or therapist, who supports you in every way and guides you with the questions they ask. It is a conversation in which you fully surrender, turn inward, and begin, in a sense, to "dig" through your subconscious to find answers.

Digging is the core Theta Healing technique for uncovering the **root belief**. The process unfolds through conversation with the client to discover and change deep, fundamental blocks, negative beliefs, and feelings that create a problem or illness. It's important to emphasize that a theta practitioner changes a belief, feeling, trauma, or fear only if the client verbally accepts and approves it. There is no arbitrary or unilateral reprogramming by the practitioner. Often what we think is the problem is not what actually holds it in place. A person may say, "No one sees me." Behind this, there may be a childhood trauma of not being emotionally seen by parents, from which a belief was born: "I don't deserve attention," or even "Existence hurts me." By asking intuitive questions such as:

- What's the worst that could happen if you let this go?
- When did you first feel the exact same thing?
- What is this emotion trying to teach you?

...we find **the source** — and then, with the person's permission, we perform an **energetic exchange**. We release the old belief and, in its place, bring in feelings that may have been unfamiliar until then: safety, being loved, trust in life, dignity, belonging, and the like.

To better understand this technique, it's first necessary to clarify what the negative contents of the subconscious are — subconscious blocks and negative beliefs — and how they influence everyday life.

Subconscious blocks – People create their own lives — and everything that happens to them — through the power of their subconscious. The subconscious contains beliefs and feelings that are often the opposite of conscious desires and beliefs. This subtle mismatch between the conscious and subconscious parts of the human mind often confuses people and prevents them from understanding the true cause of various problems, illnesses, and life blocks.

Subconscious blocks: These are most commonly fears, phobias, and various traumas acquired in childhood and throughout life. In addition, there are traumas and feelings from the **fetal period** that we took on from our parents, inherited from the family, and even from the people to whom we belong.

There are also other "invisible" subconscious influences (blocks): vows, oaths, obligations, and attachments that, intertwined with beliefs, create a powerful constricting pattern by which we think and function.

Traumas and fears – We usually think of traumas as unpleasant experiences we personally went through. However, many arose indirectly: something unpleasant seen in life — or even in a film — can create, in the subconscious, a feeling as if it was personally experienced.

The subconscious lacks the logic to discern what is beneficial and what is harmful for an individual. It only records, like when you type text and save it to a computer disk. The difference is that you read the text on the computer when you reopen the document, while the content recorded in the subconscious is active even when you sleep. You simply have no control over when and how it will activate, what unusual associations and combinations it will make in the subconscious, and how it will influence everyday life.

Negative beliefs – A belief is a subjective truth. A person thinks that what they believe and experience is the truth and reality for everyone else as well. All kinds of beliefs — helpful and limiting — are formed through upbringing by parents and environment, and later through education. Practically everything can influence the formation of beliefs: TV, art, belonging to various groups, and all the content we encounter over the course of life.

Duality of beliefs – Beliefs often involve a split — ambivalence (holding two opposing opinions about one phenomenon at the same time) that puts a person in a "vicious circle," with no clear idea how to get out or free themselves from such beliefs.

Example: Many times I've met people who say: "I want and love to be successful and wealthy," "I love money because I can do good and humane things," etc. At the same time, in their subconscious there are opposite beliefs: "I hate money," "Money is cursed," "Money is dirty," "If I'm rich, I'll be robbed," and so on. In people who have achieved success and made money, such beliefs lead to highly unfavorable situations: e.g., loss of money, loss of a job, dissatisfaction. They can also cause family and interpersonal problems. The individual remains torn and doesn't understand why they are not satisfied with the success they worked so hard for.

The same holds for family, romantic, professional, and partner relationships: positive attitudes clash with a subconscious that may be opposed to conscious thinking. We want to be loved, satisfied, successful, fulfilled, and happy — yet subconsciously we may carry self-hatred, guilt, deep dissatisfaction, emptiness, resentment, anger — toward ourselves and others.

In short, whatever their origin, we experience beliefs as our own, and we behave accordingly. Based on our beliefs, prejudices, illusions, and delusions about ourselves, life, success, failure, money, partnership, God, etc., we make decisions, choose paths, fight or give up, create friends and enemies — yet rarely, if ever, do we pause to examine whether what we believe is right or not.

Manifestation of subconscious blocks and negative beliefs – The manifestation of subconscious content appears in life through various problems and symptoms that disrupt quality of life: lack of self-confidence, stage fright, obesity, depression, stress, anger, emotional instability, inability to express one's potential, guilt, jealousy, worry, lack of motivation, shyness, feeling rejected, obsessions, financial problems, poor relationships, various addictions… The list is almost endless.

HOW DOES THETA HEALING WORK?

Theta waves open our awareness and bring us into the field of infinite possibilities, known in the theta technique as **the Seventh Plane of Existence**. Other authors, such as **Joe Dispenza**, call it **the quantum field.** Whatever we call it, one thing is certain — this is a field of pure energy and creation, wisdom, unconditional love, instantaneous healings, manifestation, and the highest truth. Coaches or therapists who use the Theta Healing technique are trained to detect and change non-supportive programs and beliefs in the subconscious mind. These belief systems stretch across the **past, present, and future**. They are the foundation of Theta Healing work.

After the programs are detected, "digging" follows, through which **the trauma** in which the program, i.e., the belief, arose is located. Trauma is any event that shaped us. Sometimes it is neglect, abuse, abandonment, and often it is something that was denied to us — something everyone else had but we didn't — some "small thing" from childhood that felt like a mountain at the time. There are no levels of trauma. Anything that marked us and left a scar needs and deserves healing.

When we reach the point of origin of the program, a healing process follows in which we recognize what truly happened, what it was teaching us, we release all negative feelings tied to that event, release guilt, grant forgiveness, and release the belief — coming to know that it is possible and permitted for us to live without it. The event does not disappear, but our energetic attachment to it does, by which we gain the wisdom of the experience and freedom.

Beyond changing beliefs, an important part of healing is **working with feelings**. The whole story of manifestation rests on the fact that we will succeed in manifesting something only when we already feel as if we have it. A person who wants to attract love into their life will hardly succeed by only removing non-supportive feelings. They also need positive programs and the feeling itself for reality to align in the best and desired way for them. By working on feelings and emotions, a person learns how to feel loved — because someone who believes they are unworthy of love probably doesn't know what it feels like to be loved. When our subconscious mind holds supportive programs and the corresponding feelings, life sends us situations in which we can experience them.

The witness to this process is the visualization we go through, so we can say Theta Healing is a quantum technique — because there is no change unless there is a witness that it truly occurred. Everything happens in an instant, and the changes in life are concrete and very rapid. Theta Healing rests on the philosophy of **the Seven Planes of Existence**:

- First Plane: minerals, Earth.
- Second Plane: plants.
- Third Plane: humans and animals.
- Fourth Plane: souls and ancestors.
- Fifth Plane: spirit guides, angels, divine beings.
- Sixth Plane: the laws of the universe (Law of Attraction, free will, time…).
- Seventh Plane: the Creation of All That Is — the source of pure unconditional love.

Using this method, we work from the Seventh Plane — from pure creative awareness, where anything is possible. There we do not judge, diagnose, or analyze — we witness the change. That is the key: to believe, to ask, and to witness. In Theta Healing, we also often work with **"downloads"** of feelings. These are **energetic transmissions** — installations of feelings you may never have truly experienced. For example:

- "Do you know what it's like to feel safe in your own body?"
- "Do you know what it's like to be loved unconditionally, from within?"
- "Do you know what it's like to live in alignment with yourself, without needing to prove anything?"

If a person says they don't, we transmit the feeling, knowledge, and vibration of that feeling through the Seventh Plane. This often changes a life. Many of us live in programs we did not choose, lacking the experiences we needed. Theta Healing restores those feelings as the foundation for a new identity. In advanced modules, work is also done with DNA activation — that is, refreshing the soul's latent abilities: intuition, clarity, vitality, creativity.

The mode of work in Theta Healing unfolds in several ways: **belief work** — identifying and replacing unconscious patterns that limit you; **emotional work** — releasing deep fears, sadness, anger, feelings of rejection; **ancestral work** — healing inherited patterns and family programs; **body work** — energetic work on the **physical level**, activating self-healing; finally, **manifestation** — aligning with desired realities through clarity, faith, and presence; and **establishing even balance** — balancing the four belief levels: genetic, historical, soul, and core.

One client carried a deep belief: "If I earn more, I'll become selfish and people won't love me." Although he worked hard, he never crossed a certain income threshold. Through a theta session, he discovered that as a child he had watched a parental argument about money and, in that moment, decided that money brings discord. In the theta state, that belief was brought to awareness, pulled out, and gently replaced with a new one: "I can be successful and loved. Money is a means for good." Within three months, the client accepted a better-paid job he had previously avoided — and felt good about it.

How can Theta Healing help remove blocks and improve quality of life?

Theta Healing makes it possible to remove subconscious blocks, negative beliefs and feelings, traumas and fears, and with this technique one can "heal" and change any segment of life or any state we are in. Still, it should be emphasized that problems and symptoms may be similar among different people, but the cause is unique to each individual. Finding and removing that cause is precisely the goal of Theta Healing. As a result of working with this technique, deep changes arise in the person, in their relationships with others, and in their everyday life.

We are often unaware of how badly certain experiences have affected us. Through the Theta Healing process and through the coach's questions, you will understand what exactly troubles you — what you never got over and what hinders you at work or in family, romantic, or friendly relationships. When you realize this and see what limits you, you will also know how to act going forward.

We truly are the creators of our lives, whether we do it consciously or unconsciously. Our life is a reflection of our programs, beliefs, and patterns. **Louise L. Hay** said, **"The thoughts we choose to think are the tools we use to paint the canvas of our lives."** So let us be those painters, those creators who will make what is most beautiful for themselves, who will allow it to happen, and who will live their life in the best way — in light, energy, love, peace, and harmony.

One client had felt for years that she was invisible and that no one valued her existence. Through a systematic theta digging, she reached a childhood moment when she tried to comfort her mother and was ignored. From that she formed the belief: "My presence has no significance." After the transformation, for the first time she felt what it is like to stand in her own energy and be noticed without effort. Within seven days, three people contacted her for collaboration — without her writing to anyone.

Theta Healing is not reserved only for sessions with therapists and coaches. Once you learn to enter the theta state, you can use it for:

- setting intentions,
- manifestation,
- intuitive guidance,
- contact with the soul and your Higher Self,

- forgiveness and releasing the past,
- consciously creating the future.

This method is not a religion, not a dogma, not an "instant fix." It is a tool and a path. A path toward trust in life, toward reclaiming personal power, toward spiritual authority within. It doesn't change you — it reminds you who you truly are beneath layers of fear, past, and expectations.

If something in this text touched you — that is no accident. Perhaps right now is the perfect moment to dive into your own depths and find what you've long been seeking — yourself. Theta Healing is not the miracle. You are the miracle. And I'm lovingly reminding you of that.

Exercise - Meeting Yourself

Close your eyes. Inhale slowly and deeply. Imagine a stream of light energy flowing from your heart, traveling through your body, exiting through the crown of your head and rising into the sky. You pass through clouds, stars, layers of light… until you reach a pearl-white light. Ask:

- "Creator of All That Is, show me my next step toward healing."
- Stay there. Listen, observe, feel. Nothing may come right away, but your being has already received the message.
- Take one more breath and return.
- Write down what came to you. This is your soul's message.

Exercise: Working with Feelings of Inadequacy

Close your eyes. Take three deeper breaths.
Imagine you are in a bubble of light. You feel peace and safety.

- Ask yourself: "Which voice in me says I'm not good enough?"
- Allow an image, memory, or emotion to surface. Don't analyze — just observe.
- Say to yourself (or to that image): "Thank you for protecting me. I now choose differently."

- Imagine that emotion leaving your body like a shadow or vapor.
- Breathe in light. And say: "I am enough. I am. I love and accept myself."

This exercise is a gentle version of theta work and can be practiced daily as part of a self-healing process.

The reason theta healing works is that it doesn't try to "fix" you — it reminds you of what you already are. It doesn't push; it allows. It doesn't seek you outside; it guides you within. In the theta state, you access the part of you that knows, that is already whole. You don't look for solutions there — you become the space through which the solution arrives.

This method invites you to reconnect with yourself — without strain, without struggle. You don't have to know how. You don't have to have all the answers. It's enough to open. Because when you enter that quiet, soft place within — where the mind isn't harsh and the soul holds your hand — healing happens. It doesn't have to be dramatic. It can be gentle, like a smile.

If something inside you whispers, "Maybe it's time to let go…," then theta healing is your ally. Not as the answer to every problem, but as a quiet light on the path back to yourself.

NOTES

THE SILVA METHOD — THE SECRET POWER BEHIND YOUR SUCCESS

"There are inner rooms of the mind
you don't reach by thinking —
but by sinking to a deeper level.
Where reality doesn't exist yet,
and waits for your intention to bring it to life."
Aleksandra Božović

This chapter is devoted to the Silva Method — a unique program for developing personal potential through mind training. The method emerged in the mid-XX century thanks to the vision of a hands-on pioneer, **José Silva**. A radio technician from Laredo, Texas, Silva began experimenting in 1944 with hypnosis and meditation to help his children improve concentration and school performance. After years of trying techniques with family and friends, his approach proved so effective that in 1966 he delivered his first public training under the name **Silva Mind Control**. Since then, the method has spread worldwide — an estimated 10+ million people have attended Silva trainings and learned to apply the techniques in their daily lives.

The core idea was revolutionary for its time: **blending ancient principles of meditation with modern mental training**. Silva believed that most of us use only a small portion of our mental capacity at a conscious level, and that guided relaxation can grant us access to deeper states of awareness and activate the brain's latent potential. His program soon became part of the broader human-potential and self-help movement. By the early 1970s, Silva seminars were running across the U.S. and then Europe (eventually reaching our region, where they introduced many people to guided meditation for the first time). Although the name later evolved from "Mind Control" to the Silva Method, the essence remained: a practical training that teaches ordinary people to relax the mind on cue and direct it toward achieving goals.

It's worth noting that the Silva Method has long drawn attention from both scientists and the general public. On one hand, many were thrilled with the results — participants reported less stress, sharper concentration, and even intuitive insights that helped decision-making. On the other, skeptics criticized Silva's emphasis on intuition and ESP-like abilities as pseudoscience. Silva himself stayed modest and mission-focused, presenting the method as a non-dogmatic, non-religious practice: you don't need to be religious or "esoteric" — anyone, regardless of beliefs, can use these mental exercises. That practicality and openness helped the Silva Method adapt and endure into the XXI century, where it remains a powerful tool for personal growth.

KEY TECHNIQUES OF THE SILVA METHOD

The Silva Method consists of a set of simple yet highly effective mental training techniques. As your coach through this chapter, I'll walk you through the most important ones — how they work and why they help. What makes this method special is the combination of deep relaxation and active visualization. In other words, it's not just about relaxing; it's about using that relaxed state to work dynamically with images, affirmations, and goals in your mind. Here's an overview of the key principles and techniques:

Entering the alpha state of consciousness: In ordinary waking life our brain operates mostly in beta waves, which are fast brain rhythms associated with outward attention — and often stress.

Stress can be defined as the body's natural ability to cope with challenging situations. Nature built in a **"fight-or-flight"** response that helps us survive real danger: pupils dilate to assess the threat, nostrils flare to take in more air, the heart and brain get prioritized blood flow, and the adrenal glands release adrenaline to speed circulation of blood and oxygen. Many physiological processes do their part so that, once the challenge passes, the body can naturally return to balance.

The Silva Method teaches you how to deliberately slow your brain waves to the alpha level (7–14 Hz) — a light trance similar to daydreaming or the moments before sleep. Why does this matter? In alpha, the brain turns inward: calm increases, creativity expands, memory improves, and even the body's self-healing accelerates. Put simply, alpha is the threshold of the subconscious where we can "reprogram" negative patterns and free our intuition. The first step in every Silva technique is to learn, through guided meditation, to enter this relaxed, receptive state on command. So we begin with relaxation — how to, anytime and anywhere, follow a precise procedure to drop into the relaxation level, slow the brain to alpha, and harvest its benefits.

The alpha range of 7 to 14 Hz (some authors define it as 8 to 13 Hz) carries many benefits. Put simply, on alpha the immune system functions better, and in about 15 minutes of such relaxation the body clears the stress hormones we generate in a day.

Next, both **brain hemispheres** synchronize — the **left** (logic, language) and **the right** (imagination, intuition). When they work integratively, we "see both the tree and the forest," which leads to better decisions and more creative solutions.

Simply spending time in this relaxed state improves memory, concentration, recall, and access to previously learned material. We gain access to the "libraries" of the subconscious, which lets us effectively change limiting attitudes, habits, and behaviors. At the same time, aging processes slow while healing processes speed up.

Yet the modern person, instead of saying "I'm safe now, it's over," keeps replaying the event — what might have happened, what could happen — retelling the story and keeping themselves in a constant state of stress.

Such unprocessed stress is responsible for over 90% of illnesses. If you live with chronic fatigue, a racing heart, digestive issues, nervousness, overeating, poor concentration, mood swings, restlessness, skin problems, or insomnia — it's time to do something to release stress before it compounds into more serious conditions. You might say, "That's normal." It isn't. It's common, but not natural. You might say, "There are pills." Yes — and while they solve one problem, they often create another, bigger one. The real way out is learning how the mind and brain work so you can return yourself to a natural mode and regulate your reactions — healthily.

With the rise of visual media — film, TV, advertising — stressors multiplied, and modern people feed their bio-computer many images that trigger stress responses without even realizing it. In programming jargon: "garbage in, garbage out." Feed a computer poor components and software and you'll get poor outcomes. Likewise, if we feed our bio-computer ugly, disturbing content, we create an ugly, disturbing (sometimes even harmful) reality. The main stress drivers are fear, worry, and guilt. If you know the brain operates through mental images, you also know it's enough to think fearful, worrying, guilt-ridden thoughts — even without any real-world basis — to trigger the same responses.

More and more, the sheer volume of information we're exposed to is cited as a cause of stress. That's why experts believe today's human, to be healthy and successful, must develop two skills:

- the ability to eliminate stress, and
- the ability to use intuition.

Mastering relaxation gives you both — and the techniques deepen and prove them. The sequence of techniques first restores balance, then solves problems and supports decision-making.

The mental screen and creative visualization: Once you've reached deep relaxation, the Silva Method teaches you to use imagination in a precise way. The central concept is the mental screen — an inner "canvas" where you project images. On that screen you first visualize the current problem or desired state, then **consciously transform** the image toward your preferred outcome. This technique is the heart of the Silva Method — indeed, **Shakti Gawain**, author of the bestseller Creative Visualization, said: "The most important technique I learned through the Silva Method was creative visualization… it proved incredibly effective." Through guided images on the mental screen, we learn how to manifest goals (e.g., a desired result at work or improved health) and how to solve problems by resolving them mentally first. One of the more advanced applications is the Mirror of the Mind technique — imagining the problem in one mirror, then creating a new image of the solution in a second, "positive" mirror.

Affirmations and positive thinking: While we visualize, the Silva Method encourages the use of affirmations — short, **positive statements** that anchor the desired reality. In the relaxed alpha state, positive messages penetrate the subconscious more easily. For example, if you want to boost self-confidence, you might use: "Every day, in every way, I'm getting better and better." Coupled with a vivid mental image of success, these words become a mental program your mind adopts. The Silva Method integrates principles of autogenic training and autosuggestion from psychology, then adds the creative layer of imagery and intuition. All course segments — whether better sleep, dream recall, or pain control — include positive mental programming that gradually shifts your inner dialogue toward optimism.

Anchoring state — The Three Fingers Technique: A favorite Silva tool, thanks to its practicality, is the Three Fingers Technique. It's an example of a **mental anchor — a gesture** linked to a specific mental state so you can call it up later. In Silva, students learn that when they touch the thumb, index, and middle finger together, that gesture becomes a signal to instantly enter a calm, concentrated state. Of course, you first "train" the brain in meditation to respond to the signal.

Once practiced, in a stressful moment or before a key task you simply bring the three fingers together, take a breath, and your mind automatically slows its waves and regains meditation-like focus. In seconds you can restore composure, beat stage fright, or cue a mental skill. Many students study in alpha while holding the three fingers together, then repeat the gesture during an exam to recall the material. One study even found this simple exercise can reduce test anxiety and improve recall.

Intuition and mental projection: As you progress, the Silva Method goes beyond personal goals into cultivating intuition and empathy. In the second part of the training you learn exercises for so-called **remote perception** (projecting consciousness beyond the body): for instance, imagining your awareness "projecting" to another place, into a plant, a loved one, or even inside your own body. While that may sound unusual, the aim is wholesome — to connect more deeply with the world around you and with your own subconscious. Advanced techniques include creating a mental laboratory (your inner sanctuary where you "consult" with intuitive advisors) and casework — exercises in which you try to sense an intuitive solution to someone's health or other challenge.

It was physician **Dr. O. Carl Simonton**, a pioneer in mind–body cancer care, who said that Silva Mind Control gave him a powerful tool to teach patients how to engage mentally in their own healing.

So, in the Silva Method intuition isn't treated as a supernatural gift reserved for a chosen few — it's trained as a natural capacity of every mind that, when calm and open, can arrive at the right insights.

Many doubt that intuition can be developed and taught. While some doubt, others use it successfully. Intuition — our subjective inner sense — is innate to all of us. Research has found that people who use both brain hemispheres to solve problems and make decisions get four out of five decisions right. When decisions are made solely on rational, logical grounds, the average drops dramatically — only one in five is right.

How do we recognize true intuitive information? If I say "practice," you might roll your eyes — but that's the most precise answer. Still, here's a guideline many people find helpful when they confuse intuition with some other inner signal. Intuition is quiet and, in most cases, favors movement, progress, change, and creativity; that loud inner shout of "Stop! Don't!" is fear — not intuition.

A distinction I often share with clients is this: **"Intuition leaves you feeling stirred; fantasy doesn't. Intuition gives you a ripple of excitement because you know, from within, that what you sense will unfold — so you feel energized by it, positively or negatively, depending on the nature of the event you sense. Fantasy feels light and fluttery, without that accompanying sense that change is actually coming."**

Freeing yourself from bad habits & self-healing: The Silva Method also includes concrete protocols for habit control. Through guided visualizations, you can reshape subconscious associations. For example, if you want to quit smoking, at the alpha level you repeatedly "run the film" in which a cigarette is linked to an unpleasant taste or the sense of losing your health, and then you visualize yourself breathing freely, jogging strong, and living free of the habit. With repetition, the subconscious accepts the new message and the habit weakens.

Similarly with pain-management techniques — students learn to mentally anesthetize a body part (the "glove" technique) or to imagine white blood cells attacking illness. Many report these practices help ease chronic headaches or speed recovery from a cold — of course, alongside medical care. We don't claim this replaces a doctor; it's an added way to activate the body's healing abilities when the mind supplies positive suggestions.

As you can see, the Silva Method is rich with techniques — from very down-to-earth and practical to slightly more esoteric. At the core lies **the triad of mind, body, and spirit**: relax the body, center the mind, and you elevate the spirit. Below are several concrete exercises you can try yourself to taste what Silva seminar participants experience.

Practical Exercises for Self-Practice

In this section you'll find step-by-step guidance for several time-tested Silva techniques. Try them at home, in quiet. Carve out 15–20 minutes a day just for you, and let's begin.

Deep Relaxation & Entering the Alpha Level: This exercise is the foundation of the entire Silva Method. Choose a comfortable place where you won't be disturbed. Sit or lie down, close your eyes, and take several slow, deep breaths. Now gently direct your closed-eye gaze slightly upward toward a point above the brow — this cues the brain to relax (interestingly, closing the eyes and turning them upward naturally activates alpha waves).

Begin slowly counting backward from 50 to 1. As you count, imagine walking down steps or feel your body growing heavier. By the end, you'll feel pleasantly drowsy — stay aware. You're now in a lighter alpha state. Count down again from 10 to 1, very slowly, whispering the numbers in your mind — sinking deeper with each number. At "1," say mentally: "I am now at my level of mind, fully relaxed and focused."

Remain here a few minutes, enjoying the calm and quiet. If thoughts arise, let them pass. When you're ready to finish, come out in reverse: count 1 to 5, and at "5" open your eyes with the autosuggestion that you're energized and well rested. With practice (ideally each morning or before sleep), you'll need less time to enter alpha. This is the base on which all other techniques are built.

The Mental Screen Technique ("Mind Movie")

Once you're comfortable entering alpha, you can actively work on goals through guided imagery. Enter relaxation again (a few minutes of breathing and counting).

Now imagine in the darkness behind your closed eyes a mental canvas or screen in front of you. Some see a chalkboard, others a movie screen. First, project the current situation or problem you wish to change.

For instance, if your goal is to feel more confident at work, display a scene where you currently feel unsure: see yourself on the screen staying silent in a meeting and not sharing ideas. Then say, "Erase!" and let the image fade or the screen go white. Shift your attention slightly to the left — imagine a new screen appearing there (Silva calls this moving from the "blue" to the "white" mirror, but a simple new frame works). On this second screen project the desired outcome: see yourself speaking calmly and confidently, colleagues listening and nodding. Make it vivid — add color, the sound of praise or gentle applause — and, most importantly, feel the pride and confidence.

Live in that scene for a few moments — your brain treats it as real. Now affirm, for example: "I am calm, confident, and I express myself clearly." Repeat several times. Take a deep breath, open your eyes, and trust that you've planted the seed of success.

This is the Silva Mirror of the Mind when done formally with blue and white frames. The essence is: in a meditative state, show the problem, erase it, and replace it with the solution. Repeat daily. Many "law of attraction" books are inspired by this — here you're training both the subconscious and the will, a powerful combination.

The "Three Fingers" Technique for Focus & Calm

Here's how to program your mental anchor. First, pick a situation or goal where you want maximum poise and success — an exam, a presentation, a sports event, even pain control. Enter your relaxed alpha level as before. On your mental screen, show yourself in this future situation going exactly as you want it to: if it's an exam, see yourself relaxed, reading questions with a smile, realizing you know the answers; if sports, envision the perfect jump, swing, or shot, along with the feeling of triumph.

While holding that vivid success scene, physically touch the tips of your thumb, index, and middle fingers together (one hand or both, as you prefer). Press lightly and say to yourself: "Whenever I join these three fingers, I instantly reach my level of mind and function with full concentration and confidence."

Repeat three times, with full belief, while you still feel the emotion of success from the visualization. Then relax your hand, end the imagery, and come out of meditation counting 1–5. To lock it in, repeat the process several more times (Silva recommended about ten repetitions over a few days). After that, your Three Fingers Technique is "installed."

In real life, when stress rises or focus is needed, discreetly join the three fingers, breathe, and you'll feel the same wave of calm clarity you rehearsed. It's wonderfully portable — on a call, in a meeting (a single hand in your lap is enough) — and the only thing others will notice is your sudden shift into confidence.

The "Glass of Water" Technique for Subconscious Insights

Here's a very simple, charming exercise the Silva Method offers for solving problems and dilemmas. You need only an ordinary glass of water. Do it in the evening before sleep. Fill a glass with water (if you like, you can spend a couple of minutes entering a light meditative state, but it isn't necessary if you're already tired). Close your eyes, gently angle your closed gaze slightly upward, and form in your mind the question or problem you want answered.
For example:
"What is the next best step for my career?" or "How can I improve my relationship with __?" Try to keep it to one clear thought. Now take the glass and sip half of the water while adding this suggestion (silently or aloud): "This is all I need to know the answer. I will now fall asleep, and in the morning I will wake up with a clear insight." Set the remaining half by your bed and go to sleep.

The next morning, as soon as you wake, take the remaining water, drink it, and say: "Thank you. I know I have the answer." — even if it isn't on your mind immediately, trust that the solution has been set in motion. Pay attention during the morning to your first thoughts, or to any "coincidences" that day — you might overhear a sentence that gives you an idea, or suddenly have an "Aha!" moment.

The essence is that this little ritual engages your subconscious while you sleep: water here is a symbol and a medium that "holds" your intention as you drift into alpha at bedtime. Many people love this technique because it's easy to do, and they often report that within a few days their thoughts clear or answers arrive through dreams. Even if it doesn't work the first time, repeat it the next night — it costs nothing, and your mind is working for you while you sleep.

Of course, practices like this yield the best results when you do them regularly. The key is discipline and ease — don't approach it with a tight "this must work" grip, but with playful curiosity, as though you're running a mental experiment. Remember: you're training your awareness. Just as the body grows stronger with regular workouts, the mind becomes more receptive and creative through repeated mental training.

Well-known examples: Real stories can be the most inspiring — people who applied the Silva Method and achieved remarkable results. Over the decades, the program has drawn many successful individuals: best-selling authors, athletes, and physicians. Here are a few names you'll recognize, each of whom, at some point, dipped into Silva techniques and drew strength from them:

Louise L. Hay — you've likely heard of her classic You Can Heal Your Life. The author and motivational speaker was an early Silva participant. In her memoirs she acknowledged that she owes her first insights — and the initial momentum she gained as a writer — to the Silva Method. She learned to visualize healing and to use affirmations while in deep meditation, which later became the backbone of her own self-help approach. In fact, her global movement of positive affirmations was sparked in part by what she experienced as a young Silva seminar attendee. She later shared that marriage of meditation and affirmation with millions of readers, passing the light forward.

Dr. Wayne Dyer — often called "the father of motivation," Dr. Dyer attended Silva training in the 1970s and was impressed enough to recommend it frequently in his talks. He said, "I encourage you to enroll in the Silva Method and take yourself to a higher level of health, wealth, and happiness. You owe it to yourself." Dyer believed everything begins with an idea — very much a Silva lesson: an idea planted properly in the mind can grow into reality. Many of the concepts he wrote about — manifesting desires, inner alignment, outcome visualization — align with Silva techniques. Those close to him recall his morning meditations and mental projections.

Shakti Gawain — the author I mentioned earlier was a young artist when she discovered the Silva Method. She learned to pair her creative visions with relaxation techniques, a shift so powerful that she wrote Creative Visualization. In one interview she said: "The rational mind is like a computer, while the intuitive mind gives you infinite possibilities. Thank you, Silva Method." Her bestseller inspired millions to change reality with guided imagery — a direct echo of Silva's philosophy.

Jack Canfield — coauthor of the Chicken Soup for the Soul series and a leading corporate trainer, is also a Silva graduate. He once said: "The Silva Method is one of the most profound approaches to human potential I have ever discovered… I highly recommend you enroll and take your life to the next level." Canfield used visualization and mental goal-programming to create the success of his book (initially rejected by many publishers). He pictured — in detail — selling millions of copies and mapped the steps while in meditation. We know how that story ended: a global phenomenon. He often teaches leaders and entrepreneurs the law of attraction and mental techniques rooted in the Silva training he mastered.

These are just a few well-known users. There's also **Dr. O. Carl Simonton**, the physician who integrated Silva-style visualizations into care for cancer patients, and **Richard Bach**, author of the cult novel Jonathan Livingston Seagull, who said: "Mental discipline and creative visualization lie behind the power of the Silva Method." Even elite athletes emphasize mental preparation: for example, Olympic diving champion **Greg Louganis** publicly shared that visualization and mental training — akin to Silva techniques — helped him overcome fear and execute perfect dives. Whether or not all of them formally took a Silva course, it's clear that champions across fields discover the same principle: relaxed mind + clear image of success = results. The Silva Method was a pioneer in teaching these principles systematically — now a near-standard in sports psychology and executive coaching.

Reading these stories, you might wonder: "Will these simple steps bring me such dramatic change?" Every person and experience is different, of course. But the fact that so many diverse figures — writers, doctors, speakers, entrepreneurs — found value in the Silva Method suggests something universal at work. It's the timeless truth about the power of the mind: when we calm it and aim it, our limits move. As one successful founder, **Robert Stiller**, put it: "Silva shows there is no limit to what the mind can do."

The Silva Method is that bridge between mind and spirit which inevitably touches the body as well. Through mental discipline we arrive at spiritual peace — and through that peace we influence physical reality (health, relationships, success). In today's fast, digital age, this method reminds us of the value of slowing down and looking within. Technology offers many tools, but the most powerful tool we already carry — our mind. Silva teaches us how to sharpen it, and how to gently persuade it to work for our goals instead of against us (you know those sabotaging thoughts of doubt — time to transform them!).

No "supernatural" ability is required to benefit. You don't need to see visions or believe anything mystical. Give yourself a few minutes a day for these mental exercises, with an open mind and heart. Results may be subtle at first — sleeping a bit better, a touch more patience in traffic, a serendipity that resolves something that bothered you. They can also be dramatic — landing a dream job after mentally rehearsing your interview, or recovering faster from an injury because you visualized tissue healing each day in relaxation.

As your coach and the author of this book, I encourage you to experiment. Bring a childlike spirit to the Silva exercises — playful and curious. Keep a journal of your experiences. Celebrate small wins: every time you steady yourself with the Three Fingers Technique instead of snapping from nerves, that's a big step. Each time intuition whispers the right fix after a Glass of Water night or a Mirror of the Mind session, thank yourself and the Universe. That's how you grow trust in your own abilities.

The Silva Method is more than a set of techniques; it's an invitation to partner with your own mind. Rather than being run by the mind's worries and limits, we learn to guide it — with love, not force. I hope you've felt that warmth and possibility in this chapter.

Now it's your turn: close your eyes, take a deep breath… and step into your inner world. You may be pleasantly surprised by what you find there. Wishing you a beautiful journey into silence — and back — enriched by the insights that change a life.

NOTES

HO'OPONOPONO: THE POWER OF FORGIVENESS AND INNER HEALING

"Healing doesn't begin when you change the world — it begins when you cleanse the room within you through which you experience it."
Aleksandra Božović

Imagine a simple method that helps you release the weight of negative emotions, heal old wounds, and bring more peace into everyday life. As a coach for emotional work and personal transformation, I often meet people who carry guilt, anger, or pain from past events. Perhaps you recognize an unhealed place in yourself, too — a family conflict, a strained relationship with a loved one, or an inner restlessness that follows you.

The good news is that there is an **ancient Hawaiian technique** designed precisely for such situations, called Ho'oponopono. In this chapter we'll get to know this warm, transformative practice — what Ho'oponopono is, how it arose, why it works, and how to apply it in daily life. You'll be guided through the history of the traditional Hawaiian reconciliation practice, then its modern form popularized by **Dr. Ihaleakala Hew Len** (with the well-known four phrases: **"I'm sorry, please forgive me, thank you, I love you")**, and you'll learn practical steps, exercises, and tips to experience the power of this method yourself.

WHAT IS HO'OPONOPONO?

Ho'oponopono (pronounced ho-oh-po-no-po-no) is an ancient Hawaiian practice of reconciliation and forgiveness, rooted in the belief that true healing is possible through releasing negativity and taking responsibility for one's own life. The name comes from Hawaiian: **ho'o** means **"to make, to cause,"** and **pono** means **"right, just."** Ho'oponopono is therefore often translated as **"to make right" or "to set things in order."** In other words, it is a process of "correcting" the imbalance caused by quarrels, hurts, or negative thoughts so that harmony and peace can be restored.

Traditionally, Ho'oponopono was practiced within Hawaiian families as a rite of reconciliation and spiritual cleansing. It helped repair damaged relationships and inappropriate behaviors among family members — people believed that through shared prayer and conversation, divine help would arrive to "correct" the conflict at its root. In older Hawaiian communities, the family would gather in a circle, led by the eldest or by **a local healer (kahuna)**, to speak openly about the problem. Everyone present would sincerely admit their mistakes, express remorse, and extend forgiveness to one another. Illness and misfortune were thought to arise from stress, guilt, mutual blame, and especially a lack of forgiveness. The goal of the Ho'oponopono ritual was therefore to clear negative emotions and tensions within the family so that balance and health could return. If the family could not resolve the dispute on its own, they would turn to a neutral facilitator — a respected spiritual leader — who would guide the process without judging either side. Only when everyone had forgiven everyone else was the dispute considered truly resolved; the rite would end with a solemn prayer and sometimes a symbolic meal, celebrating renewed unity.

Ho'oponopono has been practiced in Hawaii for **over a thousand years** as a way to heal oneself and one's relationships. Generations passed on this skill of familial forgiveness and reconciliation, knowing it worked not only as a way to communicate ("I'm sorry," "I forgive you"), but also as a way to restore self-respect and inner balance for each person involved. When each participant releases anger and guilt, respect returns — toward others and toward oneself. Here lies the essence of the Ho'oponopono philosophy: **inner peace begins with forgiveness.**

From Traditional Ritual to a Modern Method

Over time, Ho'oponopono evolved from a family ritual led by elders into a contemporary, individual approach to personal growth and healing. A key figure in this shift was Hawaiian healer **Morrnah Nalamaku Simeona**, who in 1976 adapted the traditional practice for the modern world. She moved the focus out of the family circle and shaped it into **a method of self-help** — a process an individual can apply alone to resolve problems both personal and broader in scope.

Removing the need for the entire family to gather physically, Morrnah developed a 14-step Ho'oponopono process that includes prayer, meditation, confession, repentance, and forgiveness. The emphasis was no longer only on mutual forgiveness in a group, but also on inner, spiritual cleansing of the individual. Her version — **Self-Identity Through Ho'oponopono (SITH)** — highlighted taking responsibility for everything we experience as individuals and relying on Divine energy to transmute negative memories into light. Simeona traveled the world teaching this method; thanks to her, the first Ho'oponopono seminars appeared outside Hawaii (for example, in Germany and elsewhere in Europe).

Ho'oponopono reached global popularity through the work of **Dr. Ihaleakala Hew Len**, a student of Morrnah Simeona. Dr. Hew Len, a Hawaiian psychologist, simplified the techniques he learned and shared them with a broad audience in the late XX and early XXI centuries. He became known for an almost unbelievable story of applying Ho'oponopono in a clinical setting. According to his account, in the mid-1980s he worked as a psychologist at a state psychiatric hospital in Hawaii, on a ward for forensic patients — people who had committed serious crimes but were found not responsible due to mental illness. The ward had a reputation as an extremely difficult place: patients were violent, staff turnover was high due to stress, and the atmosphere was grim. Dr. Hew Len accepted the job without meeting the patients directly. Instead of classical therapy sessions, he sat in his office, read their files, and applied Ho'oponopono to himself for each patient. What does that mean?

Simply put, while reviewing a file he would address the Divine in thought, apologizing and asking forgiveness for anything that had

contributed to that person's state. He would continually repeat the four key Ho'oponopono phrases:
"I'm sorry. Please forgive me. Thank you. I love you."

The results of this unusual "therapy" astonished everyone. Over time, even though they never met him, patients began to calm; aggressive behaviors subsided; some who had been restrained or on heavy sedatives for years became stable enough to be freed from those measures. Even severe cases improved to the point that some patients were discharged as healed. Within a few years the ward that had once been synonymous with chaos became peaceful — eventually it was closed because there were no more patients. The story sounds legendary and is sometimes retold with a measure of skepticism, but Dr. Hew Len consistently maintained that all he did was apply Ho'oponopono principles to himself, trusting that change within would be reflected without. He never presented himself as a traditional kahuna or a guru; he often said he was "a regular guy working on himself," and that anyone can do the same.

According to this philosophy, everything that appears in your experience is, in part, your responsibility, because it is happening to you — within your field of awareness. There is no strict division between "outside" and "inside"; what you perceive "out there" (in relationships, situations, others' actions) reflects stored memories, beliefs, and emotions you carry within. When you accept that responsibility, a natural urge arises to say "I'm sorry" — to express remorse for all the negativity (conscious and unconscious) that contributed to the problem. Then you ask for forgiveness — "please forgive me" — which frees you (and others) from the chains of guilt. Next comes "thank you," a sincere expression of gratitude as though the solution has already arrived, and finally "I love you" — sending love to yourself, to others, and to the situation itself.

These four phrases form the heart of the modern Ho'oponopono process. You can experience them as a prayer or mantra, repeated many times (silently or aloud) until you feel an inner shift. Dr. Hew Len teaches that by repeating these words we address our Divine essence (the Inner Child and the Divine, in the method's terms) with the intention to clean the "programs" — negative memories and subconscious beliefs. When those programs are erased or lightened, what remains is the zero state — a state of clear consciousness and limitless possibility in which we experience peace, inspiration, and connection with others.

In essence, modern Ho'oponopono blends ancient wisdom with simple affirmations to let each of us become our own healer. You no longer need a physically present mediator or to wait for everyone involved to gather; it is enough to work on yourself, and the change will be reflected outward. This idea — that by changing ourselves we change the world around us — appears in many other spiritual traditions, but Ho'oponopono offers a concrete, practical tool to put it into practice through daily acts of repentance, forgiveness, gratitude, and love.

HOW AND WHY DOES HO'OPONOPONO WORK?

After everything described so far, you may be asking: how can speaking these four sentences lead to real change? To understand why Ho'oponopono works, we can look at it from two angles — spiritual and psychological — which beautifully intertwine in this practice.

The spiritual aspect (100% responsibility and oneness): As mentioned, Ho'oponopono rests on the view that "there is no 'out there'" — everything we experience is part of our subjective reality. This doesn't mean blaming ourselves for everything that goes wrong; it means taking responsibility as the first step toward change. When we say "I'm sorry" and "Please forgive me," we are addressing a higher power (God, the Universe, or our Higher Self, depending on our beliefs), acknowledging that something within us — even if unconscious — may have contributed to the situation at hand. In doing so, we release the burden of judgment — we stop blaming external circumstances or other people and turn toward our own role. In the moment of sincere remorse, we open the door for divine energy to work through us and cleanse harmful energetic patterns.

After that, we express gratitude ("Thank you"), trusting that a solution will arrive, which directs us toward a positive outcome instead of spinning inside the problem. Finally, love ("I love you") brings the highest healing vibration — unconditional love for ourselves and others, powerful enough to soften even the hardest heart. Many spiritual teachers say that repentance, forgiveness, gratitude, and love are the most potent forces in the universe — Ho'oponopono unites them in one brief practice. When done with faith and devotion, this prayer/meditation "erases" negative vibrations and returns us to our natural state of harmony — what is often called the divine zero state.

From the spiritual side, you could say Ho'oponopono works by grace: we do our part (repent, ask forgiveness, give thanks, and offer love), and we leave the rest to God/the Universe to arrange. In Hawaii it is believed that such sincere prayers are heard, and that divine energy transmutes negative memories into light, bringing healing to everyone involved. It's a mysterious process — some call it the miracle of forgiveness — but its beauty lies in its simplicity and sincerity.

The psychological aspect: Even if we view Ho'oponopono from a purely psychological angle, its effectiveness still has a clear logic. Imagine you've been deeply hurt by someone's actions. Your mind loops through blame or self-pity; your heart feels heavy. If you remain in that state, the hurt takes root — stress rises and relationships suffer. Now imagine pausing to say (even silently) "I'm sorry" — first to yourself for the pain you're carrying, and then to "the part of the universe" that participated in the situation. Already you're stepping out of the victim role and taking a step. Next you add "Please forgive me," which can also mean "forgive me for contributing to this conflict with my negative thoughts." Notice how your stance softens? You're no longer gripping anger or resentment; you're beginning to let them go. Then you say "Thank you" — perhaps it feels odd at first to be grateful in such a moment, but you're acknowledging that every experience can teach you something. Gratitude shifts perspective: instead of asking "Why is this happening to me?" you're saying "Thank you for the lesson; I understand the message." And finally, you say "I love you" — most likely exhaling deeply and feeling relief as you speak the words. Love is the opposite of fear and anger; when you fill yourself with love, negative emotions lose their power.

What happens within you at that moment is a genuine psychological shift: you move from anger or hurt into calm, understanding, and compassion. Your approach to the problem changes — you're no longer reactive, but open to solutions. That inner change often invites change in the other person or in the circumstances. For example, when you practice Ho'oponopono around a conflict with someone, it's very possible that the other person soon softens or behaves differently toward you because you have changed your energy. Even if the other side doesn't change immediately, you will experience the situation differently — with less stress, clearer insight, and more empathy.

From a scientific standpoint, forgiveness and gratitude are well-researched concepts with proven positive effects on mental and physical health. Psychologists teach that grudge-holding and anger can contribute to anxiety, depression, and psychosomatic illness, while forgiveness reduces stress and improves well-being. Similarly, practicing gratitude has been shown to increase optimism and life satisfaction. Ho'oponopono brings several such therapeutic elements together in one practice — and that is one reason many who try it feel significant relief.

Speaking the four sentences can function as a form of affirmation or meditation focused on positive values. It halts negative inner dialogue (blame-shifting, mentally reliving trauma) and replaces it with simple, soothing repetition carrying a positive charge. This helps break the cycle of destructive thoughts and emotions — the mind redirects itself toward forgiveness and love, which directly leads to emotional ease and better focus. Many clients describe Ho'oponopono as lifting a weight off their shoulders or clearing darkness from the heart. Because of this subjective feeling of cleansing (some call it "erasing bad energy"), we often say Ho'oponopono works like a mental-emotional detox.

In short, Ho'oponopono works because it changes us from the inside — and thereby indirectly changes our outer world. Whether you embrace its spiritual dimension (appealing to divine grace) or regard it as a psychological tool for reframing, the result is similar: you release emotional burdens, forgive yourself and others, fill with gratitude and love, and create space for positive change.

WHAT IS HO'OPONOPONO USED FOR?

Ho'oponopono can be applied to virtually **any area of life** where you sense disharmony, pain, or blockage. Traditionally it addressed family conflicts and healing strained relationships. Today, modern practitioners use it across a wide range of situations — from emotional healing and personal growth to improving relationships, even supporting success at work or fostering better health. Here are key areas where Ho'oponopono can help:

Emotional cleansing and mental health: If you struggle with anger, hatred, sadness, fear, or guilt, Ho'oponopono is a tool for gradually releasing them. With regular practice, you slowly clear "emotional programs" that may have accumulated in your subconscious for years. This can be especially helpful for those facing anxiety or depression rooted in unresolved emotions. Repeating the four phrases has a calming effect — it soothes the inner critic and heals the wounded "inner child." Over time, you'll find it easier to forgive past mistakes and notice greater self-acceptance and self-love. In essence, this method can be seen as a form of self-compassion meditation that nourishes inner well-being.

Personal development and spiritual growth: Many people use Ho'oponopono as a daily spiritual practice to maintain inner balance and continual growth. Repeating "I'm sorry, please forgive me, thank you, I love you" can become part of your morning routine or evening meditation, resetting your mind to a neutral or positive state. Day by day, you release limiting beliefs ("I'm not good enough," "bad things always happen to me," etc.) and replace them with gratitude and love. As inner blocks clear, creativity, clarity, and motivation often rise. People report that while practicing Ho'oponopono they experience "synchronicities" — unexpected coincidences and opportunities that support their goals. Spiritually, Ho'oponopono cultivates humility ("I acknowledge my responsibility"), forgiveness, and continual letting go of expectations — qualities that ease progress on any path of self-improvement.

Healing relationships and family patterns: One of the most obvious applications is improving relationships. Whether it's marital conflict, a cooled friendship, tension with a colleague, or deep family trauma, you can use this technique to bring the energy of forgiveness and reconciliation. Instead of waiting for the other person to change or to say "sorry," you take the initiative at the energetic level. By repeating the four phrases while visualizing a person or situation, you change the way you approach the conflict. Ho'oponopono invites forgiveness, love, and harmony into strained relationships, bringing relief and healing. Even if that person is no longer in your life (or has passed away), you can resolve attachment and find peace.

This method can help even when open communication isn't possible — for example, if the other party refuses to talk or is physically distant — because Ho'oponopono, according to practitioners' experience, bridges distances. When you sincerely send "forgive me" and "I love you" to someone's soul, it often happens that they intuitively feel the shift. Of course, Ho'oponopono doesn't replace direct conversation and practical action in relationships, but it creates the best inner foundation for those talks and actions to unfold in a healthy way. Many couples therapists, relationship coaches, and family counselors now recommend this technique alongside classical methods precisely because it softens hearts and prepares the ground for honest dialogue.

Physical health and well-being: There is also a belief (in traditional Hawaiian wisdom and in modern holistic medicine) that accumulated negative emotions and unforgiven hurts can, over time, contribute to physical ailments. As the saying goes: "What troubles you within can hurt you without." Ho'oponopono is therefore used as support in the body's healing process — not as a substitute for medical treatment, of course, but as a complement that addresses emotional roots. By practicing Ho'oponopono you reduce stress, which positively influences many health parameters (blood pressure, immunity, stress hormones, etc.). Some people report relief from chronic pain, migraines, or other discomforts after regular practice, because they finally "let go" of old emotional wounds that may have fed physical tension. Even if you're unsure about that connection, Ho'oponopono will certainly help you cope mentally with health challenges — and a positive spirit and calm mind always aid the body's recovery.

Work, Finances, and Other Goals: Interestingly, some people have begun applying Ho'oponopono to areas like career and financial goals, with the idea that inner blocks can also stall our outer success.

For example, if you have self-sabotaging patterns (you keep procrastinating, feel you "don't deserve" success, or fear failure), you can use this technique to work through those inner obstacles. You say "I'm sorry" — to yourself, for clinging to those self-defeating beliefs; you say "Please forgive me" — asking forgiveness from yourself and the universe for having limited your own potential; then "Thank you" — expressing gratitude in advance for the success that will arrive once you release the blocks; and "I love you" — sending love to your vision, to your future success, and to yourself regardless of the outcome.

This process helps you release fear and doubt, replacing them with trust and self-respect. Of course, you still need to work diligently toward your goals, but Ho'oponopono can dissolve the inner resistance that so often holds us back. Some entrepreneurs report that, since practicing Ho'oponopono daily, they've made better business decisions because their thinking is clearer and they're no longer driven by hidden fears. In a team setting, the method can also be used to improve the collective atmosphere — for instance, a manager can "energetically" cleanse conflict in the team by mentally applying Ho'oponopono, which then helps them address the issue with concrete actions and less pressure.

In general, Ho'oponopono is a universal tool: it can be applied to any situation in which you sense negativity or "stuckness." From deep emotional traumas to everyday minor frustrations — whenever you feel knocked off balance, you can reach for this method to return to center. Think of it as an emotional first-aid kit: a four-ingredient remedy ("I'm sorry, please forgive me, thank you, I love you") that's always with you, has no side effects, and can bring relief to the soul in many situations.

HOW TO APPLY HO'OPONOPONO IN DAILY LIFE?

Theory and understanding are useful, but the true power of Ho'oponopono reveals itself in practice. The good news is that this technique is extremely simple and flexible — it doesn't require special conditions, lots of time, or any props. You can do it anytime, anywhere, which makes it ideal for everyday use. Here's how to weave Ho'oponopono into your day and apply it to concrete life situations:

A short Ho'oponopono meditation in the morning or evening – Consider starting (or ending) your day with a few minutes of Ho'oponopono. Sit comfortably in a quiet spot, close your eyes, and take a few slow, deep breaths. Then bring your attention to your heart and begin silently repeating the four phrases: "I'm sorry. Please forgive me. Thank you. I love you." Repeat them gently, at a pace that feels natural. You can use whatever order resonates with you — the sequence isn't crucial; the sincerity behind each word is. As you repeat, try to really feel the meaning of each phrase.

For example, you might mentally add a brief intention to each one: "I'm sorry (for whatever negativity lives in me, known or unknown). Please forgive me (for my mistakes and those of my ancestors that influence this reality). Thank you (Divine energy, for cleansing all of this). I love you (life, myself, all people — I fill this situation with love)." You don't need long — five to fifteen minutes is enough. You'll notice a sense of calm and lightness. In the morning, you'll enter the day with more inner peace; at night, you'll release the day's worries more easily. The key is not to rattle off the mantra mechanically, but to practice with conscious intention for cleansing and reconciliation. Some people pair Ho'oponopono with breathing — e.g., on each inhale think "I love you," on each exhale "Thank you," alternating with the other two phrases. Find the rhythm that soothes you.

Repeat the phrases "on the go" throughout the day: One great advantage of Ho'oponopono is that you don't need to carve out special time — you can integrate it into daily activities. For instance, during your morning routine, instead of mentally diving into your to-do list, devote those few minutes to Ho'oponopono. While brushing your teeth or showering, repeat in your mind: "I'm sorry, please forgive me, thank you, I love you." While commuting or walking from the parking lot, keep the phrases going silently. Household chores — washing dishes, vacuuming, cooking — are wonderful opportunities to anchor the mind in something positive instead of worry.

Many people practice Ho'oponopono during routine tasks and find it lifts their vibration, turning even the most ordinary job into a kind of meditation. You can repeat the phrases in order or at random

— even focusing on just one can help. For example, while dusting you might repeat only "Thank you," feeling gratitude for having a home to clean. Or when stuck in traffic, instead of getting irritated, you can repeat "I love you" (addressing life, your Higher Self, even the drivers around you!). You'll notice how this approach greatly reduces everyday stress.

Emergency use in moments of stress or conflict: Life inevitably brings challenging moments — an unexpected argument, a colleague's harsh comment, frustration over bad news, or your own mistake. That's exactly when Ho'oponopono is your "first-aid tool." Next time you feel your blood pressure rising, try this: before you react (or at least before you continue reacting), take a brief pause. Breathe deeply and say inwardly, "I'm sorry… please forgive me… thank you… I love you." Cycle through the phrases several times until the initial surge of anger or panic subsides. This is especially helpful mid-discussion: while someone says something hurtful, instead of exploding, repeat inwardly "I'm sorry, forgive me, thank you, I love you." This doesn't mean passively accepting injustice; it means protecting your inner peace so you can respond wisely. Once the emotional storm settles, you can speak or decide far more constructively.

For example, if you receive criticism at work that stings, before snapping back or withdrawing, apply Ho'oponopono for a couple of minutes — perhaps in the restroom or on your way back to your desk. Chances are you'll see the situation differently afterward: anger gives way to understanding or at least neutrality, a much better starting point for next steps. Use this "quick application" for internal stress too — if deadlines overwhelm you and anxiety spikes, take a five-minute break, find a quiet spot, close your eyes, and practice Ho'oponopono. You'll be surprised how quickly you "reset" — the mind clears, and what seemed impossible a moment ago now feels manageable.

A Ho'oponopono journal (a written exercise): If writing helps you process thoughts, keep a Ho'oponopono journal. Use a simple notebook to occasionally work through forgiveness on paper. When you have an issue or a person you want to "clean," write down everything you feel about it. For example: "It hurts that my sister insulted me in front of our parents. I'm angry and disappointed. I want to forgive her, but right now I feel rage." By acknowledging your emotions on paper, you've already said "I'm sorry…" to yourself. On the next page, create four headings: I'm Sorry, Please Forgive Me, Thank You, I Love You. Under each, write a few lines in the spirit of that phrase, addressing the person/situation and yourself. Under "I'm Sorry," you might write: "I'm sorry this anger lives in me; I'm sorry we're not at peace." Under "Please Forgive Me": "Please forgive me for judging you and for the times my words hurt you." (ask forgiveness for your part, too). Under "Thank You": "Thank you for the lesson this brings; thank you for being in my life." Under "I Love You": "I love you and wish you peace; I love myself and release this anger with love."

Write whatever feels authentic — there's no wrong way. Often after a few pages, perspective shifts: you understand the other person more, and you view yourself with more empathy. This exercise is powerful because it combines therapeutic writing with Ho'oponopono principles. Keep the entries, or tear/burn them as a symbolic release — do what feels right. What matters is giving yourself space to see, express, and let go through forgiveness and love.

Creative visualization with Ho'oponopono: You can amplify the practice by adding imagery. The mind responds strongly to pictures, so use them during Ho'oponopono. While repeating the phrases, imagine light or a color surrounding you and filling the space. Some imagine golden or white light descending like a shower as they say, "I'm sorry, please forgive me, thank you, I love you." Others visualize holding a loved one's hand in a peaceful place and speaking the words telepathically. Be creative — imagine placing all your worries in a balloon and releasing it into the sky while saying "thank you, I love you." Or picture yourself on the ocean shore (fitting, since Ho'oponopono comes from the Pacific) and each wave washes away a layer of sadness or anger while bringing calm.

With clients, I often guide a meditation in which they visualize standing in a circle with those they want to forgive. They ask each person for forgiveness and send each one love (mentally). At the end, they imagine the whole circle repeating "I love you" together and dissolving into light. Many describe feeling a lighter heart afterward and being able to speak calmly with those they were in conflict with. Don't underestimate the power of imagination — paired with the

Ho'oponopono mantra, it becomes a strong tool for reprogramming the subconscious.

Patience and repetition: As with any healing process, consistency brings results. Sometimes you'll feel relief after a single Ho'oponopono session, but for deeper or older issues you may wish to return to it multiple times. Be gentle with yourself. If an old emotion resurfaces, it's not a sign "it isn't working," but a reminder there's more to cleanse. Think of peeling an onion — each round of "I'm sorry, please forgive me, thank you, I love you" removes another layer of dissatisfaction or pain. Continue until you feel you've reached the heart — where peace resides. Sometimes it's quick; other times it takes time — but it's worth it. Meanwhile, every practice counts — you'll feel at least a little better each time than before.

You can also treat Ho'oponopono as a way of life: a mindset where problems aren't seen as punishment or something fixed, but as an opportunity to take responsibility and grow.
Whenever you face a challenge, big or small, remember you can say to yourself: "Okay, I may not have consciously wanted this, but it's here in my experience — I accept responsibility to resolve it. I'm sorry this has come to be, I ask forgiveness from all involved, I'm grateful for the chance to make it right, and I love all that is as it returns to balance." Even this single thought shifts your mindset from helplessness to proactivity.

Over years of practicing and studying Ho'oponopono, I've witnessed many moving examples of how this method helps people turn situations around — or transform their inner state. Below I'll share some inspiring stories — from public figures who've spoken about Ho'oponopono's impact to experiences from my own clients — that show what it looks like when the "miracle of forgiveness" truly happens.

World-renowned motivational coach **Tony Robbins** has mentioned Ho'oponopono in interviews as a beautiful, simple technique for entering a "beautiful state of mind." He's even retold Dr. Hew Len's story to his audiences, emphasizing forgiveness and personal responsibility as keys to ending suffering. The Robbins foundation has released bracelets engraved with the Ho'oponopono phrases as a reminder of the practice — showing how highly he values that philosophy.

Another interesting example from the celebrity world is TV host **Scott Evans**, known for Access Hollywood. In one interview Evans revealed that before every important on-air appearance he takes a few moments to say the Ho'oponopono prayer: "I love you. I'm sorry. Please forgive me. Thank you."
He says this ritual helps him stop negative thoughts and self-sabotaging doubts right before the cameras roll — instead of being flooded by fears like "I'm not good enough" or "the audience won't accept me," those words bring him back to confidence and calm, ready to shine in front of millions. He kept the habit because he noticed it keeps him positive and focused. Evans's example is a great reminder that Ho'oponopono can be used practically, "here and now," to shift your state from nerves to ease — even in high-stress moments like live TV.

As a coach, I've had the privilege of witnessing small "miracles" when clients apply Ho'oponopono in their lives. One of the most touching is the story of my client, whom I'll call Ana.
Ana came to coaching in deep pain over her relationship with her father. For years it had been difficult and distant. Their last serious argument had been more than three years before, and they had barely spoken since. Ana felt tremendous bitterness — she told me some of his words had hurt her so much she couldn't even imagine forgiving him. At the same time, a part of her longed for closeness with him, especially as he was getting older. But pride and hurt stood like a wall between them. She asked me, "How do I forgive him when I don't feel he deserves it? And yet, this situation eats me up more than it does him…" — she knew the weight of not forgiving rested on her shoulders more than on his.

I suggested she try Ho'oponopono as homework between sessions, explaining that forgiveness isn't a gift we give someone else — it's a gift we give ourselves to regain peace. I taught her a short meditation using the four phrases while envisioning her father. At first she met resistance — "It's hard even to say 'I love you' to him in my mind… it doesn't feel true." I encouraged her not to force anything, but to start where she could: if "I love you" didn't come, begin with "I'm sorry" and "Please forgive me." She first did meditations addressing her inner child — the little Ana who had ached for fatherly love. She wept as she told herself, "I'm sorry you went through that;

please forgive me for neglecting you so long; thank you for holding on; I love you, little one." This phase was very emotional and helped her feel compassion for herself instead of only anger toward her father.

In the weeks that followed, Ana set aside time each day to speak the phrases to her father in her mind. She often visualized him as a young man (as she'd seen in old photos, from before she was born) — he looked more carefree and open-hearted. She imagined standing before him, gently saying, "Dad, I'm sorry… please forgive me… thank you… I love you." At first a wave of sadness would rise — sometimes she'd stop, sobbing as layers of accumulated disappointment surfaced. I encouraged her to continue, slowly and tenderly with herself. After about a month of daily practice, she noticed a big shift: she no longer felt that sharp anger when she thought of him. She scheduled an extra session with me, eager to share the news — one evening, while doing Ho'oponopono, she felt a strong urge to call him. She didn't that night, but the next morning she gathered her courage and phoned him for the first time in years.

She told me, "As soon as he heard my voice, he cried. I cried too. He apologized first, in his own awkward but sincere way… and I told him, 'forgive me for everything,' as well. We talked for an hour. It felt like ice melting — I can tell our relationship won't be the same as before." Her eyes filled with happy tears as she spoke. It didn't become perfect overnight, but the wall fell. They began talking weekly, and she visited him the following month. She kept practicing Ho'oponopono because, as she said, "I want to keep my heart open." Soon the old misunderstandings were resolved through conversation, with far more mutual understanding than had ever been possible.

This story always reminds me how powerful sincere forgiveness is — even when it begins as a one-sided inner act. Ana started forgiving her father in the workshop of her own soul — and the outer situation changed as a result. Sometimes you don't even need to say "I forgive you" aloud to the other person; it's enough to perform the act in your heart, and the energy between you shifts. In Ana's case, her father later admitted he had carried his own guilt and sadness all along but didn't know how to approach her. Her subconscious change (through Ho'oponopono) seemed to give him permission to let his guard down. Today they're slowly but surely building a new relationship — based on understanding and acceptance. Ana says she feels "released from the curse of family drama," far lighter in other areas of life, which has sparked positive changes in her roles as mother and spouse (because a huge burden lifted from her soul).

There are many similar stories: a client who used Ho'oponopono to make peace with himself after a divorce and open his heart to a new relationship; a woman who carried guilt for years after ending a pregnancy, but through the practice finally forgave herself and found peace; a young man with low confidence at work who "cleaned" his fear of authority with the phrases and was surprised to notice his boss treating him much better. Each case shows that whenever we apply love and forgiveness, something transforms — at the very least, our experience of the world, which practically means our whole world.

To close this chapter, I'd like to offer a few practical tips and encouragements, especially if you're just getting ready to bring Ho'oponopono into your life. Any new self-work habit can feel a bit daunting or strange at first, but with the right guidance it becomes a natural, pleasant routine. Here are a few pointers from my experience — both personal and professional — on how to get the most from this beautiful technique:

Start slowly and simply – Don't pressure yourself to dive straight into long meditations or your hardest traumas. Begin with something easy — say "Thank you" and "I love you" to yourself each morning as soon as you wake up. Or choose one situation a day (traffic, a checkout line) where you'd usually get irritated, and dedicate it to the Ho'oponopono mantra instead. You'll feel the effect in small doses, which will motivate you to go deeper.

Make the practice your own – There's no rigid rule for how to do Ho'oponopono. Some prefer a formal approach (light a candle, sit in silence, and repeat the phrases a set number of times), others repeat them while jogging in the park. Anything that feels good to you and reflects the essence is right — and the essence is a sincere intention to transform negativity into love. Follow your intuition. If you feel like humming a tune with the phrases — hum. If you want to include them in prayer — please do; that's still Ho'oponopono. Some people blend it with, say, Orthodox prayers ("Lord, have mercy… I'm sorry, forgive me…"). Others create little rituals, like mentally "washing" worries down the drain while washing hands, whispering "thank you, I love you." Be creative and authentic. The more the practice fits you, the more likely you'll keep it up.

Don't force emotions you don't yet feel – If you're working through a tough forgiveness — like my client Ana — and feel resistance to saying "I love you," start with what you can honestly say now. Maybe it's just "I'm sorry I feel this way," or "Please forgive me for my part in this." As you clear layer by layer, the other phrases will gather strength. One day you'll be surprised to hear "I love you" flow out effortlessly — from a heart full of understanding. Be gentle with yourself — forgiveness is a process, not a single event.

Let relief guide you – Ho'oponopono isn't a chore — it's a gift. If you notice you're turning it into a rigid rule ("I must repeat this mantra 108 times because I read it somewhere"), pause and remember the point — release and relief. Do as much as feels right in the moment. Sometimes that's two minutes; sometimes you'll want twenty. Check in with yourself: "Do I feel lighter? A bit calmer?" If yes — wonderful. Continue a little longer if you wish, or finish with gratitude. If you don't yet feel a shift, maybe continue a minute or two more. The key is sensing the burden lift, even a little. If that happens, you're on the right track.

Trust the process, even when outer results aren't immediate – People sometimes say, "I repeated Ho'oponopono for a week and that person still hasn't apologized," or "I haven't gotten a raise yet, even though I've been cleaning limiting beliefs." It's natural to hope for external outcomes, but try to hold a wider view. Change happens first within us (that's the essence), and the outer follows at the right time — perhaps in ways you didn't expect. Maybe that person never says "I'm sorry," but you notice their attitude improve. Maybe you don't get that raise, but a new opportunity opens where you're valued more. Release attachment to a specific outcome, but trust that every sincere Ho'oponopono prayer is at work. Like a seed sprouting underground before pushing through the soil, cleansing happens in the unseen field of consciousness before the fruits appear.

Share your experience or seek community support: Although Ho'oponopono is an individual practice, many enjoy discussing or practicing it in a group. Look for workshops or online communities devoted to it — there are many worldwide. Hearing others' stories can be very motivating. You'll realize others have similar doubts or resistance, and how they overcame them. You can also share your small wins — how you stayed calmer in a stressful meeting by repeating "thank you, I love you." Such stories inspire both you and others. If you don't have someone nearby to share with, talk with your coach or therapist about your progress. I serve as an accountability partner for clients — someone they update about their practice, and I'm there to encourage them if they waver. Ultimately your greatest support will be the results you feel, but it's comforting to know there's a global community practicing Ho'oponopono and spreading the positive vibration of forgiveness.

Combine Ho'oponopono with other positive habits: You don't have to practice it in isolation. If you do yoga or tai chi, repeat the phrases during relaxation or stretches. If you like affirmations or gratitude journaling, add these phrases to your writing. If you pray within your faith tradition, you might end with: "And finally, God, I'm sorry, please forgive me, thank you, I love you." You may feel an even deeper connection to your spirituality. Blending Ho'oponopono with habits you already enjoy helps it fit naturally into your lifestyle.

Finally, I want to stress the importance of self-love throughout this process. Ho'oponopono teaches us to be gentle and powerful: gentle in forgiveness and understanding, powerful in our decision to create peace in our own lives. Every time you say "I love you," you're sending yourself the message that you are worthy, that you deserve healing, and that you are connected to something much greater that supports you. Each time you speak those words, imagine giving yourself a hug — or being held, metaphorically, by the universe.

Ho'oponopono is not just a technique; it's a path of love — love for yourself, for others, and for life itself. Like any path of love, it asks for practice, patience, and an open heart. From experience I can tell you that beautiful things happen on this path: you make peace with the past, lay down your burdens, attract positive change, and feel more connected to the people around you. Walk it step by step, a little each day, and you'll notice a new world of inner peace and joy opening before you.

I love you (as readers, as souls reaching for a brighter tomorrow), and I truly believe in your capacity to heal whatever hurts. I'm sorry for the moments you suffered thinking you were alone — you weren't; we all travel through these lessons. Please forgive yourself for not knowing this sooner — now that you do, a whole new tool is in your hands.

NOTES

VISION AND LIFE PURPOSE

"Healing doesn't begin when you change the world — it begins when you cleanse the room within yourself through which you perceive it."
Aleksandra Božović

From ancient philosophers to modern seekers, people have asked the same question: "Why are we here?" In every culture and across the ages there's a universal thirst for meaning. Even in the XXI century we feel a special hunger for purpose and want to believe our lives amount to more than the sum of daily chores and routines. That deep search for purpose isn't a weakness — it's proof of our humanity: the need to experience life as whole, significant, and oriented toward something larger than ourselves.

Like a traveler who glimpses the first light of dawn on the horizon, you too can feel the call of your inner North Star — a personal vision that gives meaning to every step.

You may already have noticed that when you hold a clear, inspiring goal or vision, you rise in the morning with more enthusiasm and energy. By contrast, seasons of drifting without direction bring emptiness and a loss of motivation. Vision and life purpose reach into the very core of who we are and why we exist. In this chapter we'll explore that universal longing for meaning — from a scientific standpoint, a spiritual perspective, and through real life examples — and we'll look at how a clear purpose benefits our mental, emotional, and physical health. We'll also consider the consequences of lacking purpose, and offer practical exercises to help you discover your personal vision and calling.

A Scientific Perspective on Life Purpose

Modern psychology and medicine have paid great attention to how life purpose affects well-being. The results are striking: having a sense of purpose positively influences almost every aspect of health.

For example, a 2019 study of nearly 7,000 people published in JAMA Network Open found that life meaning and purpose were strongly associated with lower mortality risk and better overall health. The same paper showed that people who feel they have purpose are less likely to suffer from depression and chronic illness, have higher-quality relationships (including lower divorce rates), and are more likely to adopt healthy habits like exercise and balanced nutrition. In other words, science confirms what we may have known intuitively — when we have a "why" to live for, we live healthier and better.

Psychologists today view meaning and purpose as core components of a good life. Leaders of positive psychology emphasize that a sense of life meaning is one of the foundations of true happiness and human "flourishing." **Martin Seligman**, founder of positive psychology, includes "Meaning" as one of the five elements of his PERMA model of well-being, alongside Positive emotion, Engagement, Relationships, and Accomplishment. Empirical studies back this up — showing positive links between purpose and physical health, vitality, and even longevity. People with purpose cope better with stress and recover more quickly from hardship, demonstrating greater psychological resilience. Notably, a recent meta-analysis confirmed that a stronger sense of life purpose is associated with significantly lower levels of depressive and anxiety symptoms.

These findings send a clear message: seeking purpose isn't a mere philosophical pastime — it's a factor that measurably improves quality of life. Science encourages us to find our personal "why," because doing so strengthens not only our spirit but our body and mind. When psychological assessments, medical studies, and statistics converge to say that purpose brings benefits, it becomes evident that discovering your life vision is an investment in your health and happiness — a path toward a more fulfilling and longer life.

The Spiritual Dimension of Vision and Purpose

From the spiritual side, we're offered a broader — and often more intimate — view of purpose. Many wisdom traditions teach that we are not here by accident — that each of us has a unique mission or calling. **Fyodor Dostoevsky** observed**, "The secret of the human being is not just in living, but in knowing why one lives."** That "why" is the focus of spiritual seeking: to know the reason for our existence is to touch the mystery that makes life sacred.

Across religions and philosophies we find similar concepts: in Hindu thought it is dharma (one's life duty and purpose); in Christianity, a "vocation" or "calling"; in Japanese culture, ikigai—"the reason you get up in the morning." Finding one's ikigai is said to foster joy and longevity; when a person lives in alignment with purpose, they feel in harmony with themselves and the world. At heart, spiritual teachings emphasize that purpose isn't imposed from outside (like social roles or material goals) but discovered within — by listening to conscience, the heart, the "inner voice." Life purpose has a transcendent dimension — it connects us with something greater than everyday life, whether you call that God, the universe, or the wider community of humanity.

It's also important to name the role of vision in a spiritual sense. Vision isn't the same as a mere goal or plan; it arises from the deepest layers of our being and is tied to our authentic essence. A true vision is flexible, creative, and deeply personal — it serves as a guiding star on the path of life, especially in times of crisis and trial. When we face obstacles or pass through a "dark night of the soul," vision offers the light of hope and direction. Spiritual teachers often say that in such moments we should look into our hearts and remember our vision — because a vision rooted in the soul helps us weather the fiercest storms while staying true to what we feel is our purpose.

In other words, the spiritual aspect of purpose reminds us that life is not just survival or meeting others' expectations. It's a call to discover what our soul longs to express in this world. Whether we answer that call through prayer, meditation, art, or service to others, the result is the same—we feel fulfilled, connected to ourselves and to the universe. Such purpose makes each day precious and our existence rich with deeper meaning and value.

Real-Life Examples

Theory and research are convincing, but nothing illustrates the power of purpose as clearly as real lives. One of the best-known examples is **Viktor Frankl**, the Austrian psychiatrist who survived the horrors of Auschwitz during World War II. In the inhuman conditions of the camp, Frankl noticed something striking: prisoners who managed to find a sense of purpose or meaning in their suffering showed greater resilience and had a better chance of survival. Some lived for the day they would embrace their loved ones again, some found solace in caring for others, and some — like Frankl himself — in the vision of one day telling their story to the world. He later wrote that **"life is never made unbearable by circumstances, but only by lack of meaning and purpose."** That insight sums up his experience: the harshest external conditions can be endured if we carry a "why" in our hearts, while without meaning even a seemingly easy life can become an unbearable burden.

After the war, Frankl developed **logotherapy**, a therapeutic approach based on the idea that the search for meaning is the primary motivating force in humans. His classic Man's Search for Meaning continues to inspire readers to seek their inner purpose and vision regardless of circumstances. Frankl's example shows how a clear purpose can literally be a matter of life and death — it was the spark that kept life's flame alive in the darkest of times.

Other examples, perhaps less dramatic yet just as instructive, are all around us. **Nelson Mandela** spent 27 years in prison, and what sustained him wasn't mere stubbornness — it was his vision of a free and equal South Africa. That vision gave him the strength to endure injustice and emerge without hatred, ready to realize his goal.

Similarly, **Malala Yousafzai** survived an assassination attempt as a teenager; her clear purpose — advocating for girls' right to education — lifted her to the global stage as a symbol of courage. What unites such figures isn't only persistence but a powerful sense of mission. They held a picture of a better world — and of their place in it. That inner picture — a personal vision — became the engine that pulled them forward when most would have given up.

Purpose and vision aren't reserved for world-famous heroes. We all know everyday examples: a teacher who devotes decades to educating children because she believes knowledge changes lives; a physician who, despite exhaustion, finds meaning in saving each patient; a parent who works tirelessly inspired by a vision of a better future for their kids. In stories great and small, the common thread is the passion and perseverance that spring from a clear sense of "this is my path." These stories remind us that finding purpose isn't a luxury — it's a fundamental need of the soul. When the vision is clear, obstacles become temporary difficulties, not immovable walls. Every challenge is seen in the light of a larger goal, gaining meaning as a lesson on the way rather than a punishment of fate.

WHEN PURPOSE IS MISSING

What happens when a person lacks vision or purpose? Most of us have lived through seasons of wandering and asked ourselves, **"What's the point of all this?"** These are the moments we wake without motivation, move through routines like automatons, or feel a hollowness despite an outwardly "normal" life. The psychological consequences of losing purpose can be serious. A person without a clear "why" often slips into what Viktor Frankl called an existential vacuum — an inner emptiness and hopelessness. It can show up as chronic boredom, apathy, a sense of aimlessness, and even depression. It's not uncommon for prolonged meaninglessness to lead to anxiety and depressive disorders, as if life were standing still or had lost its value. The lack of purpose hits young people especially hard: a recent survey of U.S. young adults (18 25) found that 58% reported lacking meaning or direction in life, and more than half said this "not knowing what to do with my life" worsened their mental health. These troubling numbers suggest that a crisis of meaning underlies many modern mental-health challenges.

Emotionally, a person who can't see a purpose often feels a heavy weight on the heart. Frustration arises ("I'm living in a loop"), cynicism ("nothing matters"), and even envy toward those who seem fulfilled. In the extreme, prolonged loss of purpose can tip into deep despair — the place where people wonder whether life is worth continuing. It isn't the world around us that breaks us; it's the inner feeling of meaninglessness.

Physically, lacking vision and motivation also leaves a mark. When we don't see the value in our efforts, self-care falters. Someone who doesn't know why they should get out of bed will struggle to find a reason to eat well, move their body, or care for their health. It's easy then to enter a vicious cycle: apathy can lead to unhealthy habits (oversleeping or sleeplessness, poor nutrition, substance use as a temporary escape), and that lifestyle further drags down mood and energy. Stress also hits harder when we don't have the protective buffer of meaning — life's problems feel bigger than they are because we can't see the bigger picture. Over time, chronic stress and listlessness can weaken immunity and raise the risk of various illnesses. In short, without the "fuel" of purpose, our psycho-physical system idles in neutral — more prone to breakdowns.

On the social level, lack of purpose can lead to withdrawal and loneliness. People who feel lost often think "no one understands," which deepens isolation. Interest in hobbies and socializing fades, and just when we need it most, our support network thins. Relationships are affected too: partners, friends, and family may struggle to understand why their loved one has lost their spark, which can create conflict or distance.

And yet, it's important to know that the loss of meaning is usually temporary — and surmountable. Many people lose their bearings at some point — after a trauma, a big life change (retirement, a breakup, migration), or burnout at work. That doesn't mean meaning is gone forever, only that it's time to rediscover it — perhaps in a new form. In the next section, we'll look at the transformations that occur when we reconnect with purpose and the practical steps you can take to walk out of the dark tunnel of aimlessness into the light of a clear vision.

THE BENEFITS OF A CLEAR PURPOSE

When you live with clarity about your purpose, your whole being shifts in a positive way.

Mentally, you focus and decide more easily because you have a criterion — does this serve my vision or not? Your thoughts orient toward solutions rather than obstacles. Many people describe a rise in self-confidence: the awareness that you're walking a meaningful path gives you courage to face challenges. Resilience grows too: setbacks feel less like catastrophes and more like detours on a road you're still determined to travel. Psychological research confirms that a sense of purpose boosts overall well-being and life satisfaction; people with purpose report lower psychological distress and better mental health.

Emotionally, when you have your "why," every morning takes on a different hue. Waking brings a sense of anticipation — you look forward to the day because your actions bring your vision closer. Even if your goal is distant or demanding, the journey itself is fulfilling. Life regains that precious element of passion. You'll notice more energy and resistance to negative emotions: frustrations and stresses soften in the glow of your enthusiasm. When you know why you're doing what you're doing, even ordinary tasks acquire meaning and value. On the emotional level, a deep peace emerges — a kind of coherence between heart and mind. You're no longer torn by doubts about whether something is worth the effort; you feel inwardly that you're living authentically, in alignment with yourself. That peace and self-contentment often translate into a kinder stance toward others — fulfilled people radiate hope, kindness, and inspiration.

Physically, the benefits show up in better health and longevity. As noted earlier, studies find links between a clear sense of meaning and lower risk for many diseases — and even lower mortality. People who have a "what to live for" naturally take care of themselves — purpose becomes a source of motivation to stay healthy and vital longer so you can realize your aims. Measurably, chronic stress tends to be lower: purpose helps us contextualize stressful events as challenges on the path, which blunts their negative impact on the body. A striking example comes from Japan, home to many centenarians, where the concept of ikigai (life purpose) plays a big role. Many residents of Okinawa, known for longevity, cite having a clear reason to rise each morning — gardening, caring for family, passing on knowledge to grandchildren — as one secret to their long, healthy lives. Purpose energizes us — almost like an inner elixir of youth.

Socially, clear vision brings its own rewards. When you know where you're headed, you more easily find people who share your values and ideals. Friendships run deeper; relationships become more authentic. Family and partnerships often improve too — rather than getting lost in minor disagreements, you work together toward a bigger picture of life. People with a strong sense of purpose often become natural community leaders: their commitment and passion inspire others to move. The environment recognizes purposeful people as pillars you can lean on — which, in turn, strengthens that person's sense of belonging and usefulness.

In short, having a clear "why" strengthens the whole of who you are. Purpose is like an inner flame — it warms you from within and lights the way ahead. Storms can be met with a smile, knowing that above the clouds your North Star still shines, faithfully pointing the way. To live with purpose is to live fully — every day, good or hard, finds its place in the grand story of your life, a story you write with meaning.

Exercises to Discover Your Personal Vision and Purpose

Finding your personal vision and purpose is an inner journey that takes time, honesty, and a willingness to explore your own being. The good news: there are concrete practices and steps that can help. Below are practical techniques and reflection prompts designed to awaken your intuition and clarify what you truly want from life:

Map your strengths and passions: Make a list of your natural talents, skills, and the activities you love. For extra insight, ask a few close people where they see you shine. Are you creative, empathetic, enterprising? These reflections reveal your unique resources. Consider how you could apply those gifts in ways that serve both you and others — purpose often sprouts right there.

Recall the obstacles you've overcome: Scan your life for hard challenges you faced and mastered — illness, loss, failure, crisis. What did you learn? Now ask: is there a way to use those experiences to support others going through something similar? Often our wounds hold our mission — **"where your pain was, there your purpose may be."** Helping others through what you've lived can bring profound meaning.

Draw a "life timeline:" On paper, mark the main periods of your life (childhood, adolescence, adulthood, etc.). Under each stage, write what mattered most then — what value or goal. Perhaps in your twenties it was freedom and learning; in your thirties, creativity or family. This exercise shows how your purpose evolves. You may spot a thread that runs through it all — a value that's always been there (helping others, a drive to learn). That thread is often a clue to your core vision. You'll also see that purpose isn't static — it changes and grows with you, freeing you to redefine it now.

Look for role models and inspiration: Who do you admire — public figures, historical icons, or people around you? What exactly do you value in them — courage, creativity, altruism, spirituality? This highlights your values and ideals. Study their lives — not to copy their path, but to notice what pulls you. If you're drawn to someone fighting for human rights, your purpose might include advancing justice in your own way. Role models mirror our own aspirations.

Practice mentorship or volunteering: One of the fastest ways to feel meaning is to contribute beyond yourself. Share your knowledge — is there someone younger or less experienced you could mentor? Teaching and encouraging others delivers an immediate sense of purpose because your effort tangibly helps a life. And/or volunteer in a cause close to your heart — humanitarian work, animal care, environmental projects, mutual aid. Service connects you with community and shows the real-world value of your efforts. Many people find their vision crystallizes through serving — what truly fulfills you becomes obvious, as does the legacy you want to leave.

Imagine your ideal future: Get comfortable, close your eyes, and let your imagination roam. Visualization is a powerful way to surface what you may be suppressing. Ask yourself: "What would I do if money were covered and every door were open?" Would you travel and learn from different cultures, open a shelter for animals, make art, write a book, start a business or a nonprofit? Write down everything you see in this no-limits vision. Hidden in those images are key elements of your purpose. You may not realize them all at once, but you can weave pieces of them into life now, in small ways. This helps you notice what lights you up — signposts of your life vision.

Write your own eulogy (a life reflection): Unusual, but incredibly revealing. Imagine you've lived a long life and someone is giving a speech about you — what would you want to be said? How would you like to be remembered by family, friends, community? What deeds, qualities, and contributions would you hope to hear? This places you at the end of life so you can see what truly matters while you're living. You may realize titles and awards matter less than the impact you had on people or the legacy you leave. Whatever you'd want in that imagined eulogy — begin creating it now. Those are likely ingredients of your purpose.

Through all of this, be patient and gentle with yourself. Discovering a life vision isn't a one-afternoon task or a linear process. It's an ongoing conversation with yourself. You may not get all the answers at once, but each step illuminates another piece of the puzzle. Listen to your emotions as you reflect — notice where you feel excitement, a lump in your throat, happy tears, or that intuitive "click." Somewhere there, your soul is answering.

At the end of this chapter, perhaps the most important message is this: **your vision and purpose already live within you**. Like a seed waiting for the right conditions, the meaning of your life is there — nourish it with attention and honesty. The search for purpose is also a path of growing emotional intelligence: you meet yourself at depth, listen to your emotions, values, and dreams, and learn to align them into a clear direction. It's an inner hero's journey worth taking.

A life filled with vision won't always be easy — but it will always be worth it. When you know why, you'll find the how, even when obstacles loom large. Every difficulty becomes a step, not a wall. In fact, by seeking your purpose, you are already living meaningfully, showing yourself love and respect by honoring your deepest longings.

I invite you to take the first step — ask yourself the questions, try the exercises, and in the quiet of your own being, look for your path. Be patient: the answer may arrive as a soft whisper or a small spark of an idea. Life may surprise you with synchronicities — the right books, people, or opportunities — once you clearly set the intention to find your purpose. Stay open and curious.

On this journey of self-discovery, grow your vision step by step. Let it evolve with you. Each clearer glimpse will bring fresh energy and joy. You'll notice the change: a different light in your eyes, a straighter posture, a calmer heart. Others will sense it too — someone who knows why they live radiates authentic strength and warmth.

In the end, the most beautiful gift you can give yourself and the world is to live your purpose. When you do what you were born to do, the whole world becomes richer for your unique note in the grand symphony of life. So step boldly onto that inner path. As the old saying goes, **"A journey of a thousand miles begins with a single step."** Take that step — toward yourself, toward your vision. Discoveries that fill your soul and reveal unsuspected strength are waiting for you. Your XXI century trinity — mind, heart, and spirit unified by purpose — wants to be realized through you. Safe travels home to yourself!

My Path to Purpose

As a child, in the midst of the war in Kosovo, I carried a vision in my heart: I wanted to change the world. While sirens wailed and the ground trembled with explosions, a spark of defiance and hope was born deep in my soul. Huddled in a shelter among tearful faces, I promised myself that one day — when the madness ended — I would dedicate my life to creating something good. The war took a piece of my childhood, but in return it gave me an early understanding of how precious peace is and how strong my desire was to help make the world a better place.

After the war, life led me through three different countries and several cities, each time asking me to rebuild from the ground up. Every new place meant saying goodbye to friends, adapting to unfamiliar streets and foreign languages, and often feeling like a perpetual outsider. Yet I kept the same inner flame the vision of a better world I had set as a child. That quiet inner compass gave me strength to find meaning in each new setting and to keep going despite the sense of impermanence and uncertainty.

In one of those cities, I met both others' expectations and my own by enrolling at university — I studied law and criminology. I believed that through law and justice I could stand against wrongdoing and contribute to the kind of world I wanted to live in. Years of study taught me discipline and analytical thinking and gave me a sense of pride in what I'd achieved. Still, deep down I knew that even all those law books hadn't filled the emptiness in my heart. Near the end of my studies I realized my calling might not be only in the courtroom or law-enforcement institutions, but somewhere I could touch people's lives more directly.

After graduating, life took me down a different path — into the world of music. I had always loved writing songs and lyrics, and I created an opportunity to do it professionally. In the studio, surrounded by notes and rhymes, I felt alive; through melodies I expressed what is hard to say with words. When I heard that someone's heart stirred at my verses, a quiet joy rose in me and I felt I was reaching people in a special way. And yet, after every round of applause and praise, a question still echoed in the quiet of my soul: Is this my final purpose, or is something else — something greater — still waiting for me?

I was never afraid of hard work, so over the years I did a variety of jobs to make ends meet and keep pursuing my dreams. I cleaned apartments and offices, worked housekeeping and service in hotels and restaurants, stood behind counters in shops and boutiques, and even helped in family businesses. Each of those jobs, however "small" they might look from the outside, taught me something important: as I scrubbed floors and served coffee and meals, I learned that no honest work is beneath a person and how vital it is to remain humble.

Talking with customers taught me the power of a smile and patience; working with family taught me the value of togetherness and responsibility. Those "small" jobs built resilience and deep empathy in me; I realized that the greatness of spirit often shows in how we carry out the simplest tasks.

At one point I bravely stepped into entrepreneurship — I started my own company, determined to bring my ideas to life. It felt like climbing a steep mountain without a safety rope. I faced countless challenges, from financial strain to sleepless nights spent second-guessing every move. Every struggle in business was personal, too — when the company hurt, I hurt, wondering at times whether I had the strength for it. There were setbacks and failures that struck me to the core, but every time I thought of giving up, I remembered that little girl in the shelter and her promise. That memory lifted me and pushed me forward — to learn from defeat and rebuild from the ashes, stronger than before.

After all that wandering, the path finally led me to a classroom where I first heard about NLP (neuro-linguistic programming). I enrolled to help myself — to better understand my thoughts and emotions and tend to the invisible wounds of the past. Each new insight filled me with excitement, and soon I recognized that here — empowering myself and others — lay the answer to the question that had followed me for years. After devoted study and practice, I became an NLP Master Coach and Trainer, certified to pass this work on to others. I remember the first time I looked into the eyes of someone I had helped break through an inner wall of fear. I saw a spark of freedom and joy and cried with her, realizing I had finally found what I had always sought.

Today, as an NLP Trainer and Coach, I can say with confidence — I have found my purpose. I now see every storm I weathered as a necessary part of the road that brought me here. My life's mission is to help people realize their dreams and most ambitious goals, just as I learned to realize the visions I've carried since childhood. When I watch someone I'm guiding move beyond self-imposed limits, change their life, and achieve what they once doubted was possible, my heart fills with the same strength and hope I felt as a child — even in a dark shelter. Then I know every step of my journey — from wartime tears to business setbacks — was worth it, because it prepared me to be a beacon for others on their path to making their dreams real.

NOTES

CLOSING WORDS OF THIS VOLUME

This book has opened the doors of your heart — to the world of emotional intelligence, sensory landscapes, inner impulses, feelings, and the messages your soul sends you every day. You may already have become aware of how emotions shape your perception, behavior, and relationships, but our journey does not end here.

On the contrary — I now invite you to go even deeper.

In the next volume — I will guide you through bodily intelligence — we will step into the realm of the body, into the quiet wisdom of cells, breath, movement, and sensation. We will explore how the body remembers what the mind forgets and the heart suppresses. Our deepest truth is hidden there — for the body never lies.

Because emotion feels — but the body bears witness. And where the two meet — presence is born.

Thank you for walking with me through this second part of the trilogy. See you in the continuation — where the soul makes its home in the body.

BIBLIOGRAPHY

1. American Psychiatric Association Blog (2023). "Purpose in Life: Less Stress, Better Mental Health".

2. Capra, F. (1975). The Tao of Physics. Shambhala Publications.

3. Dalai Lama & Cutler, H. C. (1998). The Art of Happiness: A Handbook for Living. Riverhead Books.

4. Dispenza, J. (2012). Breaking the Habit of Being Yourself: How to Lose Your Mind and Create a New One. Carlsbad, CA: Hay House.

5. Dispenza, J. (2014). You Are the Placebo: Making Your Mind Matter. Hay House.

6. Dyer, W. W. (2004). The Power of Intention: Learning to Co-create Your World Your Way. Hay House.

7. Emoto, M. (2004). The Hidden Messages in Water. Beyond Words Publishing.

8. Fehmi, L., & Robbins, J. (2007). The Open-Focus Brain: Harnessing the Power of Attention to Heal Mind and Body. Boston, MA: Trumpeter.

9. Frankl, V. (2001). Čovekova potraga za smislom. Novi Sad: Futura publikacije.

10. Goleman, D. (1995). Emotional Intelligence: Why It Can Matter More Than IQ. New York, NY: Bantam Books.

11. Hanson, R. (2013). Hardwiring Happiness: The New Brain Science of Contentment, Calm, and Confidence. New York, NY: Harmony Books.

12. Harvard Health Letter (2023). "10 ways to find purpose in life".

13. JAMA Network Open (2019). Istraživanje psihološke dobrobiti i smrtnosti.

14. Kabat-Zinn, J. (2005). Wherever You Go, There You Are: Mindfulness Meditation in Everyday Life. Hyperion.

15. Lipton, B. H. (2005). The Biology of Belief: Unleashing the Power of Consciousness, Matter & Miracles. Hay House.

16. Masaru, E. (2001). Messages from Water. Hado Publishing.

17. Salzberg, S. (2011). Real Happiness: The Power of Meditation. New York, NY: Workman Publishing.

18. Seligman, M. (2011). Istinsko zadovoljstvo: Pozitivna psihologija u praksi. Beograd: Mono & Manjana.

19. Silva, J. (1991). The Silva Mind Control Method. Simon & Schuster.

20. Stibal, V. (2006). ThetaHealing: Introducing an Extraordinary Energy Healing Modality. Hay House.

21. Tart, C. T. (2001). States of Consciousness. iUniverse.

22. Tolle, E. (2004). The Power of Now: A Guide to Spiritual Enlightenment. New World Library.

23. Wallace, B. A. (2006). The Attention Revolution: Unlocking the Power of the Focused Mind. Wisdom Publications.

ABOUT THE AUTHOR

Photo by: Christoph Ris

Aleksandra Božović is a woman of transformation and inner strength. Born in Kosovo, she lived through war, countless moves, and life in three countries — changing cities, languages, and roles, but never herself. She now lives and creates in Switzerland, where she helps others find what she found within: the keys to freedom, personal fulfillment, and authenticity.

A lawyer–criminologist by education and an NLP Master Coach and Trainer by calling, Aleksandra is the founder of the Infinity Key Coaching method — a deeply transformative approach that integrates mental, emotional, and bodily intelligence. She leads her own coaching center dedicated to personal development, awakening inner potential, and living life from the inside out.

Her book, The Holy Trinity of the XXI century, is both a personal and professional testament — a fusion of knowledge, experience, and devoted practice. She is also the creator of the self-development card deck Be Your Own Coach, designed as a tool for everyday introspective support.

She doesn't talk about transformation — she lives it. Where others see walls, she sees doors. Where others fall silent, she speaks truth. And where others look for the path — she becomes a lighthouse.

Aleksandra lives her calling through words, knowledge, unwavering persistence in catalyzing change, and the ability to reach the hearts of her clients. She believes that within every person there is a world waiting to be brought to awareness and lived freely.

"Everything is within your power, and your power is within you."

MORE BY ALEKSANDRA BOŽOVIĆ

THE HOLY TRINITY OF THE XXI CENTURY
A Guide to Mental Intelligence, Volume I

THE HOLY TRINITY OF THE XXI CENTURY
A Guide to Body Intelligence, Volume III

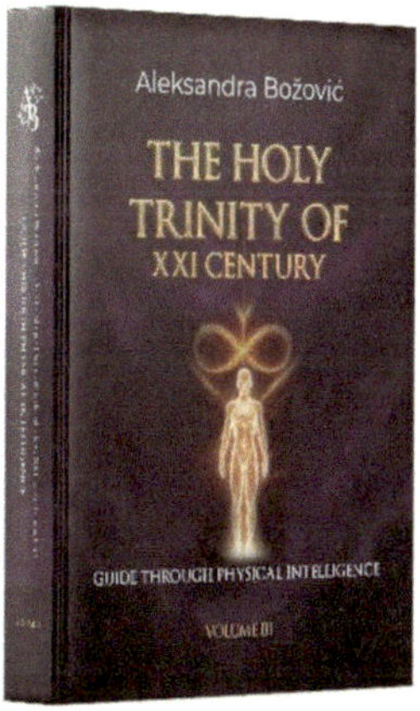

CARD SET – Be Your Own Coach
Daily impulse for spiritual growth and development
(90 educational cards)
Available in Serbian, English, and German.

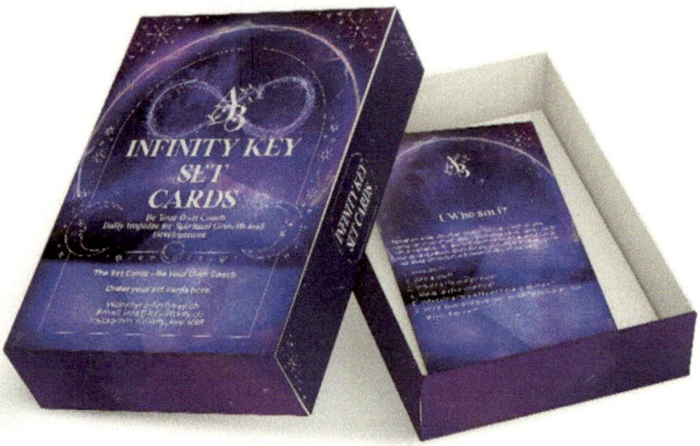

Additional Information about Aleksandra Božović
Certified NLP Master Coach & Trainer
Master of Law and Criminology

All orders:
Aleksandra Božović, Switzerland
+41 79 528 70 43 (WhatsApp)

Infinitykey.ch

info@infinitykey.ch